G000043590

ODD MAN OUT

Breaking the Vow of Male Silence

NIGE ATKINSON

with Elloa Atkinson

© 2017 Nigel Atkinson and Elloa Atkinson
All Rights Reserved.
Published by Elloa and Nige Atkinson.
Cover image: © 2017 Michelle Wildman
Image of self-pointing gun in chapter five (5): © Nige Atkinson. Art by Georgia Flowers.
Cover design and typesetting: Rochelle Mensidor
ISBN: 978-1-9997273-0-7

To men who want to know more about themselves
and women who want to know more about men.

Contents

Part Three: The New Man

Before We Begin: A Word of Warning

As you read *Odd Man Out: Breaking the Vow of Male Silence*—especially part one, which explores in details what the vow of male silence is and how it has taken hold in our world, including in my own life—you are likely going to experience some or all of the following states: judgement, shock, disgust, anger, cynicism, denial, anxiety, resistance, despair, guilt, shame and grief.

Keep in mind that I've warned you about this, and remember that the mind will usually find evidence of whatever it is looking for. Be willing to overlook your own crazy judgemental thoughts and keep reading anyway. Read until you reach a state of hopefulness—probably somewhere in part two—then keep reading some more. Stay open, pay close attention to what is going on below the surface for you, and most of all read like your life depends on it. Given the rates of suicide among men, it may be that it does.

Disclaimer

This book is not meant to be a substitute for in-person therapy. It is not an easy read and may highlight certain issues you need support with. Please get professional help if you need it. A list of resources is included in the appendix.

Preface

In 1975, when I was six years old, I got into a classroom fight with another boy. I was kicked so hard in the groin that my left testicle had to be removed. I was far too young to really understand what had happened to me. All I knew was that it really hurt. I was kept off school for six weeks and one day, after I'd had the stitches out, my grandma took me into the gent's outfitters where she worked. Two of her effeminate colleagues greeted me, looking down at me with avuncular concern. "You are such a brave boy," one of them cooed. I looked up at them and replied, "I'm not brave. I'm just the odd man out."

The adults probably found the whole odd man out declaration quite delightful—especially coming from a 6-year-old boy—but for me it was no joke. I meant every word of it. Despite being so young I already felt odd, awkward in my own skin.

I have never forgotten that moment. For a long time those three words defined me, making a massive impact on my life. Identifying with them shaped me into an off-beat rebel, a joker, and eventually, a violent and angry man. I used to think I was alone in feeling like the odd man out, in feeling different from other people, inadequate as a boy and later as a man—and most of all, alone in my differentness. Now I know better. I thought for years that I was a freak and a misfit, that I alone carried bucket loads of shame, guilt and pain, but after thousands of conversations with other men, I realise that I was speaking on behalf of boys and men everywhere when I made that matter-of-fact statement aged just six. Where once I felt isolated and alone, I now see that I have more in common with other men than I could ever comprehend.

You do too, even if you don't see it yet.

As much as the world tries to deny it, the truth is that all men are the odd man out in some shape or form. We don't talk about it but we feel it every day. We live burdened by the weight of an unspoken vow of silence that controls and imprisons us, living isolated and fearful lives, convinced that we don't belong, even if on the outside everything looks okay.

My hope is that this book will help free us—that it will help men to understand more about themselves, and women to understand more about the men in their lives.

My name is Nige Atkinson and I am here to break the vow of male silence.

PART ONE

THE FALL OF MAN

"I know you're tired but come, this is the way."

- Rumi

CHAPTER 1

THE VOW OF MALE SILENCE

"It only takes one voice, at the right pitch, to start an avalanche."
—Dianna Hardy

I was born in 1969 in Bramley Mead hospital in Whalley, a quaint town just outside Blackburn in Lancashire. According to Mum I was extremely mischievous—always up to something. One time, I pulled over the fish tank. Another time, Mum caught me sawing the legs off her favourite rocking chair. I enjoyed reading Roald Dahl books during my childhood, especially *Danny, the Champion of the World*. I was diagnosed as being colour deficient after colouring a dog bright green when I was about eight. Aged 10, I was sexually abused by the next door neighbour. In the early eighties I had a poster of Blondie's Debbie Harry on my ceiling. It fell down once in the middle of the night and I woke up thinking I was having sex with her. During my teens my best pal was a crazy black Labrador called Boss. When he died I was so upset that I shut myself in my bedroom for a week.

In 2008, aged 39, I discovered I had a heart condition called Wolff-Parkinson-White syndrome, which means that I was born with a second pathway in my heart and had been living at risk of sudden death my entire life. A white-coated doctor informed me that during the fast attacks that had plagued me for years, my heart was beating at 350 beats per minute, and that my threshold was 370. In other words, the margin between living and dying was an extra 20 beats a minute.

For years I was the Head DJ at a celebrity-owned restaurant in Central London. I met countless celebrities and hangers on. One time Brian May from the rock group Queen asked me if I'd seen his children but I couldn't help him because I didn't know what his kids looked like. Another time I got into a fight with a life-sized model of C3P0 from Star Wars and his arm fell off. Fortunately, the maintenance man was able to fix it before I lost my job.

In 2012 aged 43, I married my mighty companion Elloa. In 2014, I cycled up the hardest, steepest climb in the UK, Hardknott Pass, and left my late father's walking compass on a big rock at the top as a way of honouring him. I am a keen method actor, albeit an amateur one. I often compare myself to my wife and think she is better than me. When my father died I helped carry his coffin into the church. When I look in a mirror, I am often uncomfortable with the face I see staring back at me—especially as I edge closer to fifty years old and see the lines deepening. There's a critical, sometimes murderous voice inside my head. I often enjoy life—I love the simplicity of walking my dog in the woods or by the river—but some days the voice is so loud that I want to rip it out of my skull and bury it somewhere no one can find it.

For years I was frightened of going to sleep because I was scared that I might die in the night with my music still inside me.

My biggest fear is that I will die thinking that I am a failure as a man. Sometimes I think I should never have been born. In 2016 I won my first ever natural bodybuilding competition. I struggled to accept that I had won because I'd only ever known second place to my dad. I have been having panic attacks in my sleep since I was a little boy. One time I was literally hurled out of bed and slammed straight into the wall, tearing my rotator cuff in the process. I even had past life regression therapy a few years ago to help me get over them. They went away for a while but then they came back again.

I often feel anxious or uncomfortable in my skin. Sometimes I isolate, burying myself in organising thousands of music files or planning new bodybuilding workouts for myself. Other times I feel lonely even when I am surrounded by people who love me. I live with a chronic low level virus that often leaves me feeling physically and emotionally shit. I regularly catch myself thinking that my family and friends don't love me, that they think I'm weird and too intense. Sometimes I have guilt-ridden fantasies about having sex with women other than my wife. I have destroyed some wonderful opportunities because I listened to the part of me that was shit scared. Occasionally I feel so violent that I have to breathe really deeply to stop myself putting my fist through a wall. One of the worst things I ever did was pin my ex-partner to the floor by her throat until she could barely breathe.

Angry. Violent. Scared. Lonely.

I know that some of what I've just shared is close to the bone. I also know that what you won't want to admit right now is that you're like me, and that so are most if not all of the men that you know. Angry. Potentially violent. Scared. Lonely.

The truth is that men like me are everywhere. We make your coffee, we deliver your post, we stock your supermarket shelves and we teach your children. We wear painted smiles, slap each other on the back, and make out that everything is alright. But it's not. As you'll hear me say repeatedly in this book, we men are in pain and we need help. When this pain is driven underground, we do insane things. We react angrily. We hurt others. We hurt ourselves. We do crazy things that cause other people to call us heartless bastards, which is ironic because our hearts are bleeding and breaking every day. All our messed up behaviour conceals a despairing, warped appeal for help made by an army of men who lack the skills to be able to identify and talk about their inner struggle.

Men everywhere are quietly struggling, suffering in silence. I would go as far to say that many of us are desperate. I know we don't look it, but we are. The problem is more deeply rooted than any of us can possibly imagine. We are like flies caught in a sticky web of thoughts, expectations, beliefs, rules and assumptions about what it means to be a real man, and all of us—men, women and children—are part of it. We have been indoctrinated into a fear-driven thought system that aims to keep us isolated and alone. Symptoms of this thought system are all around us, creating a world where our inner hurt gets externalised and masquerades as external harm. For example, according to the Ministry of Justice statistics, men committed 85% of all indictable crime in the UK in 2012[1] (and again in 2015), and the same trends are repeated

---

[1] The source for this statistic, along with all the others in this book, can be found in the References section at the back of the book.

worldwide too. When it comes to fraud, theft, violence against other people, robbery, drug offences, motoring offences, burglary and sexual offences, not to mention things like terrorism, it's the fellas running amok.

Don't get me wrong—women commit crime too. But when over 90% of robbery, drug offences, motoring offences and sexual offences (a category that sits at just under 100%) are attributed to men, we have a serious global problem.

I have a theory about why men commit such a huge amount of crime: I believe it is because we are in pain, and because we are afraid—afraid that we are inadequate, afraid of other people's emotions, afraid of expressing our own feelings for fear of being judged, afraid of intimacy, afraid of being ridiculed, afraid of failing, afraid of loving other men, afraid of repeating the mistakes our fathers made before us, afraid of being seen as weak, and afraid of women and the power women wield. (Why else would we so relentlessly abuse, suppress and oppress them?) The fear we feel is all-consuming, a dark and malignant tumour that has entangled itself around our minds and hearts. We are crawling with shame. We are deeply afraid. And most of us have nowhere to turn.

For too many men, this is leading to suicide. The rate for men is substantially higher than for women—in the UK and the USA, for example, men die by suicide 3.5 times more often than women, and male suicide outstrips female suicide globally in all but two countries.

Men have not been equipped to deal with the battle scars we bear, whether those are literal, physical scars from serving in the armed forces or whether they are the more subtle but equally devastating psychological and emotional scars that any man lives with, regardless of his place in society. All around us, we hear the shame-based messages of our culture warning us not to reveal the pain we are in. Everyone joins in with keeping this message alive: our families, colleagues and friends. We suffer in silence, thinking that we are alone, bound by a vow of silence that orders us to stay mute or risk being thrown to the dogs. The name of this vow is omertà.

Omertà

Omertà (pronounced oh-MER-ta) is a cultural expression that originated from the Mafia in Southern Italy. It means both code of silence and manhood, implying that 'a real man' should be able to deal with everything without saying a word.

Anyone involved in a Mafia-type organisation lives and dies by omertà: it protects all and any criminals in the face of authority. Even when a crime has been committed by an enemy, you don't speak up. Any man suspected of being an informer is given a black mark that is punishable by death. As Sammy 'The Bull' Gravano says, "Never open your mouth, unless you're in the dentist's chair." Silence always wins.

I stumbled across the word omertà in the wake of the Lance Armstrong doping scandal. If you're not a cycling fan, bear with me because the following example will give you a powerful insight into how the vow of silence operates. During an age when entire teams of professional cyclists used and abused performance enhancing drugs to win bike races, a vow of silence was rigidly obeyed by everyone involved in order to protect the riders, trainers, teams, masseurs and the sport as a whole from the authorities—well, at least supposedly. It turns out that even the authorities were in on it. Many professional cyclists found themselves tangled in this treacherous web of corruption and lies. To be a professional cyclist essentially guaranteed that sooner or later you would become entangled in omertà, whether you liked it or not.

In the book *Racing Through the Dark*, retired pro cyclist David Millar writes, "If a rider was caught doping, then the buck stopped immediately with him. He would be fired and disowned as the management of the team expressed shock, disgust and disappointment, while his teammates would be surprised and appalled that he'd cheated them. The team held zero liability." Any rider who tested positive for drugs was expected to serve their sentence without uttering a single word to anyone, regardless of who else had been involved. The shock, disgust and disappointment emanating from the team management and other cyclists was all part of the great cover up; the truth was that everybody was in on it and everybody knew what was happening, excluding perhaps newly professional cyclists.

If a rider broke omertà, he was punished by a vendetta within the peloton. When news of a doping admission leaked out, the suspect would be snubbed. For example, when French cyclist Christophe Bassons spoke out about his team's well thought out use of doping, he was perceived as bringing unnecessary attention to the fact that there was an unruly doping problem at large within the professional cycling peloton. Instead of being recognised as a voice calling out for constructive change, he was spat at and ostracised by the other riders during races. Bassons finally reached breaking point and quit the sport when several riders attempted to run him off the road into a ditch mid-race. In *Shadows on the*

Road, author and pro-cyclist Michael Barry, who rode alongside Lance Armstrong on the US Postal Team, states that "a rider was either with the team or against it; there was little room for compromise."

Armstrong, probably the most infamous man in cycling (who incidentally also has one testicle), survived cancer against all odds and went on to win the *Tour de France* an unbelievable seven times. He was a perfect example of somebody who had secretly agreed to abide by the vow of silence, perhaps even revelling in it, expecting others to follow in his lead without question. During his reign at the top, Armstrong became extremely skilled at upholding and managing omertà, using it, as many men do, to his own advantage. According to Rogers, "Lance protected the business that he had created and the industry it fuelled with lies, threats, bullying and arrogance. But he wasn't alone in this. Few criticised his actions and most stayed silent as the juggernaut rolled on." Along the way, he succeeded in convincing an entire population of people that "they were dealing with a clean guy."

It was only when one of Armstrong's former teammates, Floyd Landis, tested positive for drugs and was stripped of his 2006 *Tour de France* title that he plucked up the courage to break omertà and share information with officials and sponsors that revealed his systematised use of performance enhancing drugs. He also exposed the names of other riders who had openly participated in doping, including Armstrong.

Armstrong, of course, fought back. During the dizzy heights of his unstoppable success, Armstrong had sued, defamed and destroyed the careers and reputations of anyone who dared to speak out against him, all the while continuing to build his army of devoted followers. But in the aftermath of Landis's confession, the cracks in Armstrong's seemingly invincible body armour finally started to show, leaving him isolated and vulnerable. In 2012, the biggest drug investigation in the history of the sport took place. As the investigation unfolded, the inspirational, cancer-surviving superstar persona disintegrated, revealing a hard-hitting, Mafioso-type front man—a man who had cheated, lied and intimidated his way to the top of the sport.

Fortunately, Landis's courageous admission moved other cyclists to step out of the shadows and break omertà too. Each man that came forward reported feeling relieved and liberated from his quiet inner torment. Armstrong's seemingly invulnerable regime came to a startling and sudden end, its dark infrastructure unable to withhold the barrage of honesty that poured forth from within the peloton as one by one his former teammates and accomplices owned up to the truth. Armstrong's legacy collapsed under a heap of threadbare yellow jerseys in a matter of days as one sponsor after another pulled out and he was ordered to pay back more money than I can conceive of making in this lifetime. Mr A was stripped of all seven *Tour de France* titles and banned from the sport for life.

Omertà however is a powerful beast, and still lives on in cycling; yet another doping scandal in early 2016 involved secret motors being hidden inside bikes that allow the cyclists to go faster without having to work as hard, which sort of defies the point of bike racing if you ask me, and in late 2016 the British antihero Bradley Wiggins came under investigation for suspect use of painkillers. The lesson is clear as day: you can take out the guy at the top, but it takes more than one wave of honesty to truly break omertà for good.

The Vow of Male Silence

I'm well aware that this is not a book about cycling. It is however a book about omertà, and the omertà of the cycling world is a snapshot of the collective vow of silence and accompanying code of so-called 'masculine' conduct that I believe men almost everywhere are initiated into when they are boys. Men then spend most of their adult lives living under this vow of silence unless they happen to stumble upon a way out. Omertà conceals the secret guilt and shame that plagues men, leaving them unable to fully connect with the people in their lives. Men are expected to act a certain way, to abide by an unspoken set of rules and above all to stay silent about it. The vow of male silence is upheld and enforced by both men *and* women, and it's killing us. It varies slightly depending on culture, geography and generation, but the basic rules for men are:

> *Don't feel. Don't cry. Don't talk about it.*
> *Compete. Conquer. Be the best.*
> *Shut up. Put up. Don't mess up.*
> *Man up.* ***Man up.*** ***<u>MAN THE FUCK UP</u>***.

This set of rules ensures the continuation and survival of society as we know it, regardless of how many injuries or fatalities it produces. We are becoming ever more aware of issues such as gender fluidity and the desire for equal rights between men and women, which is fantastic, but the underlying bullshit of a damaging patriarchal mindset still reigns. Men are instructed to live by an increasingly sophisticated yet confusing set of rules, roles and responsibilities, diligently following them day in, day out. *Be the breadwinner, but be the stay-at-home dad too. Man up, but be more sensitive (not too sensitive mind—no one likes a wimp). Be a feminist, but be a man's man too. Open up, but don't fall off your white horse.* The messages are contradictory and overwhelming.

I think we have all unconsciously agreed to some extent to uphold this twisted code of masculine conduct, keeping the collective wheels of omertà turning. We all contribute to conditioning boys and men to evade and suppress their emotions at all costs, even as we ask them to be more open, intimate and emotional. I don't think we really want men to completely break free of the rigid roles they are expected to fulfil. I often wonder if women like the idea of a man who is in touch with his emotions but struggle with the reality of what that entails: to witness a man who is in touch with his pain can be scary and overwhelming. We prefer the illusion of the strong, solid guy who has all his ducks in a row. We each do our bit to make sure that blokes can't come clean about what is happening for them by denying each other the space to talk about it. Women often tell men how those men are feeling, and men silently agree not to discuss their feelings at all. Omertà is deeply ingrained in all of us, regardless of whether you are a man, a woman or trans. It is almost never spoken about, yet its influence can be felt all around us. With every male suicide, every war hero who returns to his family in a decorated box, and every financial crisis brought about by the reckless greed of our bankers, the vow of silence hangs malignantly over us. We don't attribute these things to omertà, however—that would be too close to the bone. Instead, we look for someone to blame when it seems like the world is falling apart, and the evidence is everywhere.

On a really bad day, it can look like everything is fucked and we're all going to die: the education system is a mess, the price of everything is sky high, footballers are being paid hundreds of thousands a week while elderly people are abused in care homes, and hypocrisy is rife in our political, educational and health systems—and that's just for starters. The list of worldly problems is endless. We blame the government, genetics, the economy or, in England, the weather. Much of the time we point the finger at individuals, or at a push, entire organisations—and no prizes for guessing who's at the helm of the patriarchal ship. If it isn't men, then it's ball-breaking women playing by broken omertà-driven rules. Please don't misunderstand me here: I'm not blaming anyone specific. However, I do think it is important to take a long hard look at the connection between the state of the world we live in and the definition of manhood that has allowed us to get into this mess in the first place.

As crazy as it might sound on first reading, I want you to consider the possibility that all the problems of the world are taking place under the umbrella of this vow of silence, that at the root of everything that's a mess in our world, there is at least a trace of omertà. The many crises and seemingly insurmountable issues we are facing are often wildly different, yet I believe it is not an exaggeration to say that each issue connects back to the vow of male silence in some way. Until we break this vow of silence and find a different way to relate and to live, we will continue to breed layer after layer of crippling, malignant fear that causes generation upon generation of scared, ashamed, silenced men to become irritable at best and murderous at worst.

We have reached a point where increasing numbers of us are waking up to a critical realisation: *something has to change.* If we continue to do what we've always done, trying to cope with our pain by pointing the finger out there and making someone or something else to blame, we'll get what we've always got. Omertà is a global problem, but it's also an individual one. In reading this book, you are making change possible. The one place where you can absolutely refuse to let omertà stay alive is in *your* world.

Regardless of your age, gender, race or sexual orientation, the responsibility has landed on your shoulders to find a new definition of manhood, one that goes beyond the current ideas of what it means to be a real man. If, collectively, we don't step up to the plate, the crisis we are in will only worsen and in a hundred years, we will find ourselves asking how the hell it came to this while still futilely pointing the finger at the world.

There is another way, one that goes against the current thinking of the world. Be prepared to unlearn everything you believe about what it means to be a man today. To achieve this, we have to start by looking at who we think men are, and that means addressing the way they show up in the world. It is time to expose the masks of modern masculinity.

CHAPTER 2

THE MASKS OF MASCULINITY

"Men live under the pressure of one unrelenting
message: do not be perceived as weak."
—Brené Brown

After I had a testicle removed aged 6, my school headmaster made a well-intentioned but badly thought out decision and announced my misfortune to the entire school in order to discourage kicking. The whispers and sniggering about me started almost immediately. I felt scared and hurt, but instead of showing what I felt to my classmates, I made a decision that would change my life: I gave a smile instead—a polite, tight-lipped smile. A fake smile, one that deliberately communicated one thing to the world while concealing the truth about what was going on for me. This moment was one of the earliest experiences I can recollect of wearing a mask, my entry point into a lonely world where I constructed a pseudo-self, an artificial me, the ultimate purpose of which was to protect the real me from being hurt by others.

We all wear masks. It's human nature to do so. Sometimes they can be genuinely helpful; there are occasions, for example, when we just have to get on with the task at hand, and 'faking it to make it' can be a helpful tool. For the vast majority of us, however, the process of developing a false, masked self is deeply connected to early experiences of loss and hurt; we construct our masks in response to painful events that more often than not occurred in our childhoods when we were at our most vulnerable. Those events most likely involved at least one other human being who was important to us—a parent, caregiver, sibling or friend.

Our masks employ certain skills and characteristics from our personalities, milking them for all they're worth while discarding other less desirable qualities. For me, the loss of a testicle and the lack of understanding I had around what had happened to me, combined with the humiliation I started experiencing at primary school, provided more than enough fodder to prompt me to construct a mask that showed the world a version of myself that turned my happy-go-lucky nature up to full volume while simultaneously hiding the deep pain that I was really in. I was a boy, and boys aren't supposed to be weak.

Once I started secondary school aged 12, the teasing from other kids intensified and became full on bullying. I was made to eat grass, was kicked and called names. My days were often like a living hell. I had another decision to make: would I let myself continue to be ridiculed and bullied, or would I find a way to protect myself? I finished what I had started in primary school, constructing the perfect mask that would defend me from all forms of mockery, rejection and bullying—I became funny.

I learned from the best: Laurel and Hardy, Norman Wisdom, other actors from dodgy 1970s British sitcoms, and my dad. I looked at these men, men who didn't seem to be affected by criticism and bullying in the way I was (even if they were sometimes hapless fools), and I mimicked them all like a pro. At one point I even altered my walk so that I walked just like Stan Laurel. Being funny became my safety zone. It guaranteed me the right kind of attention and minimised the wrong kind (although I still continued to get bullied). I really believed that if I could get people to laugh on my terms, I could stop them from mocking me on theirs. With my funny boy mask firmly in place, I believed that nothing and no one could hurt me. As this mask became ever more fixed, no one could see the escalating levels of hurt and pain I carried.

Second Skin

We men fear ridicule and rejection because any singling out from the herd implies weakness. Constructing an artificial self promises that this won't happen, or that if it does, it's on your terms. Behind our masks, we learn how to be chameleons, adapting ourselves to any situation, playing by the broken rules of patriarchal masculinity, and staying confined within our safe little identities because it's easier than daring to ask ourselves who we really are and what we really think or feel, or risking the rejection or humiliation that we fear will come if we bare our real selves to the world.

Our masks help us to fit in, to adhere with societal expectations and to cope with life (or, let's face it, to cope with other people). As we become more practiced at the game of pretending, we learn to expertly modify our behaviour, language, appearance and character. The mask doesn't just cover our faces; it covers our entire being. It does a head-to-toe cover up job on who we think we are. We mould our masks to fit the archetypes that comply with accepted forms of masculinity and quietly shun the parts of ourselves that don't. This promises to guarantee us a certain outcome: acceptance, inclusion, approval, or respect, for example. Over time, fitting in becomes easier than standing out and eventually, who we really are becomes invisible even to ourselves.

Superboy

Lots of boys become the class clown or the joker like I did, covering up their pain with humour. All around the world there are classrooms full of "the joker," boys who learn how to use humour like a weapon, but there is a vast array of other roles available if this one doesn't fit or has already been taken. Many of my school friends adopted other roles, becoming known as the loud one, the clever one, the quiet one or the sporty one, among others. A lot of factors influence which particular masks we adopt, including our family history, the rules within our family system, our relationships with our parents, our birth order, the socioeconomic conditions we live in, our peers, our cultural icons and the messages we receive about masculinity from the people in our lives and the world around us.

Despite all the variables, all boys and men have one thing in common: every day, the world bombards us with messages telling us who we need to be in order to be acceptable. The messages we males receive about masculinity start young and continue throughout our whole lives. At the core of the messages we receive about how to be boys and men is a damaging, inhuman message: *do not be perceived as weak.* This message is reinforced through our exposure to various archetypes and role models. One of the first archetypes of masculinity that boys are exposed to is the highly influential superhero archetype (and to a certain extent, the supervillain).

Like millions of boys worldwide, I grew up exposed to indestructible superheroes who graced the pages of comic books. Four years after losing a testicle at the age of ten, I was circumcised for medical reasons and to help me feel better, Mum and Dad gave me a toy action figure called Maskatron who was part of the Six Million Dollar Man TV series. (How an action figure can help you feel better when you've just had skin cut off your penis is beyond me, but I will admit I was quite happy playing with the toy in a salt bath.)

Maskatron was a super-powered robot who could disguise himself with three interchangeable masks to ensure he remained incognito. He was just one of many masked characters I came to know and admire in my childhood; there was Spiderman, Superman, Batman, Iron Man, Zorro, Lone Ranger and Hulk to name just a few. There's nothing cooler to a young boy than encountering these characters. They are the stuff that 'real men' appear to be made of—and our consumerist culture feeds us more and more, plying us with an endless conveyer belt of action figures, films, comic books and branded merchandise. Since 2009, when Marvel was acquired by Disney, the various Marvel films have grossed over $10.5 billion US dollars.

Yet there is a very obvious problem with boys aspiring to be like these superheroes: while they all have admirable qualities, the masked superhero represents the kind of man who has the power to either save or destroy the world with his strength and superhuman qualities, which in itself is an unrealistic message to internalise. The masked superhero is also enigmatic, often isolated and unable or unwilling to seek support. Nobody knows who he really is, and the most human aspects of his character—his weaknesses, losses, fears and vulnerabilities—either threaten to completely destroy him (think Superman and Kryptonite), or something he suppresses and stifles. The underlying messages are clear: *Don't show weakness to anyone. Do not let anyone find out what your weak points are otherwise they will exploit them. Your weaknesses will kill you.* This is a man who can do almost anything, but who isn't fundamentally known. He carries the weight of rescuing the world on his shoulders. He has incredible superpowers, but appears to do so at the expense of the right to express his innermost feelings. He is rarely if ever allowed to just be a person.

The masked superhero provides just one example of a version of masculinity which looks edgy and cool on the surface but which, beneath the surface, leaves men isolated, burdened by a huge responsibility (to save and protect the world!), prohibiting men from experiencing or expressing the full spectrum of human emotions. It would be fine if all we did was enjoy these characters and stories as pure fiction, but unfortunately we don't; the superhero is so deeply engrained in our psyches that Father's Day and birthday cards for dads are often geared towards celebrating how invincible and powerful he is. No pressure.

The message young boys receive from these archetypes is clear: be superhuman. Do not be flawed, imperfect or weak. Do not be vulnerable. Do not ask for help. At the core of the message is a sense of shame about what it means to be simply human. Only indestructible will do. It is also worth noting that most of these superheroes and supervillains are also masked in some way, providing a double message to boys—not only should you be superhuman but you should also hide who you really are. Even Superman is masked in reverse, his everyday geeky, slightly awkward alter ego of Clark Kent disguising his true nature.

Broken Archetypes, Broken Masculinity

The breakthrough Netflix documentary about men and masculinity in the USA, *The Mask You Live In*, explores some of the main male archetypes that our society promotes: firstly there's the superhero, which we explored above. Then there is the hard man, who is violent, dangerous, hard as nails, oversexed, often tattooed, and is totally cut off from any empathy or sense of human connectedness. Next there is the thug, who in the USA is usually depicted as a man of colour. In the UK the thug is often associated with being a hard, lager-swilling, tattooed skinhead, someone you wouldn't want to upset in a dark alleyway. The thug is often seen to have immense physical strength and prowess rather than intellectual intelligence; his fists (or sometimes weapons) do the talking. Hollywood loves cashing in on this archetype; just look at the number of blockbuster movies featuring a central character that is strong but silent. The movies men love—so-called 'action' movies—tend to glorify the ideal of the hard man who is emotionally dead and who will screw over anyone who dares to disrespect him. Away from the glitz, glamour and artifice of Hollywood, everyday men who are anything but strong and hard (oh, and did I mention fictional?) are still expected to abide by the vow of male silence.

Other archetypes highlighted in the documentary include the man-child, as displayed in films such as the *Hangover* series. The man-child is fully grown but dependent on others, childish and selfish. As pathetic as this archetype is, he nevertheless still upholds two bastions of a damaging masculinity through his perpetual love affair with getting wasted and his objectification and degradation of women. In the UK, there is the lad archetype, who is often depicted as a manual labourer, a lager lout who leers over women, drives too fast, swears and eats kebabs. Throw in a bit of violence and racism, and you get the football hooligan. Then there is the strong, silent man who holds everything in. He is inscrutable, detached and never shows any weakness.

Other male archetypes that give men a sense of identity include: the successful businessman (often a workaholic), the angry man (perhaps a road rage addict), the violent drunk, the gym rat or sports fanatic, the video game addict, the arrogant sod, the intellectual superior, the cheeky chap or diamond geezer, the spiritual man and the stay-at-home dad.

I'm not implying that there is anything wrong with being successful, or being a stay-at-home dad, or loving the gym. You might be all three. Despite what I've said about how damaging the predominant male archetypes can be, I want to emphasise that in my experience, each archetype I've written about in this chapter has the potential to be helpful. They each have redeeming qualities and can teach us to appreciate more about the deeper aspects of ourselves. For example, the superhero is compassionate. He wants to help people. He is a force for good in the world, and he is incredibly focused on his mission.

The point here is that in the process of overly conforming to any single archetypal role, a man is stripped of his full humanity. As we try to mould ourselves to these rigid ideals of men and masculinity, donning whatever mask these ideals require us to wear, we sacrifice essential aspects of our characters—whatever qualities do not fit the bill. We throw out the baby with the proverbial bathwater. Despite the apparent diversity in these archetypal roles, they all help to maintain the kind of masculinity that keeps the wheels of the patriarchal mindset turning and omertà in pole position.

Real Men Aren't Weak

Brené Brown wasn't lying when she wrote that men live under the pressure of one unrelenting message, which is not to be perceived as weak. If there's one thing a man doesn't want to be called, weak (or anything associated with weakness) would be it. Tell a man to "man up" and he knows instantly what the subtext is. Even at the tender age of nine or ten, a boy understands perfectly what his dad/brother/teacher/friend means when he says, "Be a man." A young boy's initiation into a dehumanising idea of masculinity and manhood, and the vow of silence he is expected to adhere to, is sadly as predictable as learning to ride a bike. By the time he is ten years old, most boys will know the following:

> A real man is not a pussy. He is not weak, he does not cry, he does not feel.
> A real man is not a gay, a sissy or a girl. He is not weak, he does not cry, he does not feel.
> A real man is a fearless warrior. He is not weak, he does not cry, he does not feel.

*A real man is virile and sexually dominant. He is not
weak, he does not cry, he does not feel.
A real man is materially and financially successful. He
is not weak, he does not cry, he does not feel.
A real man is big and strong and muscular. He is not
weak, he does not cry, he does not feel.
Above all, a real man never, ever talks about it—whatever
'it' is. He is not weak, he does not cry, he does not feel.
A real man shuts up, puts up and mans the fuck up,
every time.*

Any man who dares to push back against this risks being
mocked, ostracised and perhaps most significantly, will lose the
respect of other men. For many men, the possible loss of respect
from other men is enough to make him play along, even though
he knows deep down that this is a load of bullshit. Herd mentality
trumps individual integrity. Under omertà respect is crucial—
even if it is only mask deep.

Men therefore will go to almost any lengths to prove that they
are not weak, no matter how risky or stupid those lengths may be.
A man can play chicken or he can push himself to his limits: he
can prove to his mates that he can drink them under the table; he
can demonstrate his sexual prowess; he can become a powerful,
high-ranking career man and make loads of money; he can be
intellectually superior (especially if he is physically weak); he can
transform his body into something massive, muscular and ripped
(an area that, being a competitive natural bodybuilder, I know a
lot about); he can excel at extreme sports; he can buy all the latest
gadgets or possess superior intellectual powers. Whatever he does,
the goal is simple: show strength (physical, mental or emotional)

over weakness every time. Men who are seen as weak by other men are cast off as damaged goods. Anything that doesn't conform to the cold, hard ideal men are taught to aspire to—any form of 'weakness' such as vulnerability, sensitivity, softness or empathy—is shunned, mocked or attacked. A man, omertà says, should be strong to the bitter end—even if it kills him. We adapt, becoming driven by pride and the near-constant threat of being emasculated.

For example, in the iconic movie *Rebel Without A Cause*, whenever James Dean's character, Jim Stark, got called chicken by anyone, he would flip out and retaliate. Behind the scenes, Jim didn't respect his father, believing him to be weak for not standing up to his overbearing mother. This weakness repulsed Jim: he couldn't stand it in his father, and he couldn't stand the accusation of it in himself. He rebelled and took unnecessary risks, putting his own and others' lives at risk. In one scene, Jim agrees to participate in a Chickie Run where he races a stolen car alongside another man towards the edge of a high seaside cliff, and whoever jumps out first is declared the chicken. As the cars race towards the edge of the cliff Jim tumbles out of the car just in the nick of time and survives, but the other driver Buzz gets his sleeve caught up on the car door handle and cannot jump out in time. The car plummets over the cliff edge and smashes down onto the rocks below with Buzz still inside, killing him.

Don't Be a Sissy

The dominant ideas of masculinity in our society also imply that men should shut down anything that is deemed remotely feminine. Forget the fact that we all have masculine and feminine traits within us; under omertà only the masculine will do. Under the vow of male silence, men repress our feminine qualities and condemn ourselves to two-dimensional lives. We make ourselves into omertà-approved models at the expense of being fully human. Men who dare to display any kind of feminine traits risk being called sissies, wimps, girls or pussies. In an article for Fusion, writer Lux Alptraum states, "Traditionally feminine traits such as emotional openness and awareness, caring about aesthetics and the arts, and domesticity are still culturally coded as frivolous, weak, and worthy of contempt. And while they may be tolerable in women—who are just naturally that way, presumably—in men they're treated as shameful, embarrassing, even downright disgusting." You only have to look at how the father treated Billy's love of ballet in the film *Billy Elliot* to see that at work.

We also associate feminine qualities with homosexuality and under omertà, we reject both. The stereotype of gay men is that they're more in touch with their feminine side (which, as I've already said, basically means that they're in touch with their full humanity), and this single quality alone makes gay men, or effeminate men, or non-macho, non-alpha men unacceptable within the realms of omertà. Our aversion to anything remotely sensitive or 'feminine' is so extreme that we now live in an age of touch-starved men. Apart from back slapping each other when drunk or while competing in or watching sport, the traditional code of conduct for men prohibits affectionate touching and even implies that any man who does so is trying to be sexual. The fear of being accused of homosexuality is so strong that in the UK, if you dare to try to say hello to another man in a public urinal, you are completely ignored at best and you risk getting your head kicked in at worst.

When I was in my late teens, I lived in a town with a homophobic and racist mentality. Some people were brave enough to come out and a small gay scene emerged. As homophobic as the general mindset was, people were also intrigued about the culture and although it was unacceptable to go to a gay bar alone if you were straight, oddly enough it was okay to go there as part of a male pack on a pub crawl (I think straight men enjoyed going there for a bit of respite from the aggression found in the typical straight hangouts). So, that's what me and my mates did. Before long I was hanging out at the main gay bar, Crackers, on my own. It took guts to go in there alone; I risked being seen as a queer and mocked for it, but I felt safe in there, I didn't have a problem with gay people, and I felt like I belonged even though I wasn't gay.

One night I watched an unusual drag act perform his final number of the evening. The artist sat at a dresser facing the audience like a mirror, and slowly started to remove all the make up from his face, little by little making the vivid switch back from woman to man. I was so deeply moved by what I saw that I started to cry. In hindsight, I think I found the act so moving because I knew deep down that I had cut off from my more feminine qualities and I missed them, as if part of me had died. Many men believe that they will lose their masculinity if they embrace their more feminine qualities. That performance proved to me otherwise.

More Than a Cardboard Cutout

The intolerance of weakness in a man's psyche or body is such a prevalent part of the dominant paradigm that we very rarely stop to question the inhumanness and insanity of it. It is insane that we ask half the population to be like this; it is literally killing us. Read chapter 10 on suicide if you don't believe me. Sadly though, we are far more vigilant when it comes to protecting the omertà-fuelled ideas of masculinity than we are about protecting our right to be fully human. We men are not here to be two-dimensional cardboard cutouts. We are here on this planet to be three-dimensional human beings.

We wear masks and play along with the masculine code of conduct in an attempt to cover up our pain. For a while, they allow us to get through the day and cope with life. They appear to protect us, saving us from being 'found out' and the potential ridicule that comes with that. Our masks allow us to get our heads down and push on through the day in a stressful world that always seems to want something from us. Behind the many masks we each wear, our insecurities and weaknesses stay hidden. It would be a perfect solution if it worked. But the tragedy is that we've got it all wrong. Our masks fail us over and over—and we know it.

The masks we learn to wear and the corresponding archetypes to which we aspire often provide dangerous, damaging and unattainable ideals for men. Slowly, over a process of months or years, as our masks become like a second skin, they begin to suffocate us, moulding to our faces and merging with us so inseparably that we become unable to distinguish who we really are from the role that we are playing. Over time, as we become more like the mask and less like our real selves, we lose sight of where our spontaneous, uncontrived self ends and the artificial, masked self begins.

Learning to pretend that we are someone different disconnects us from our raw authenticity. We turn into experts at pretending, becoming who we are told, taught or conditioned to become. As

Brené Brown writes in Daring Greatly, the fear we all share about taking off our masks is the same: "I can't take the mask off now—no one knows what I really look like. Not my partner, not my kids, not my friends. They've never met the real me. I'm not even sure who I am under here."

Power Questions

We've made it to the end of chapter two. I want to acknowledge you for that—this isn't easy reading. You should know at this point that this isn't just a book to read. Breaking the vow of male silence is going to require that you look fear and doubt in the eye. In other words, if you want to break omertà and 'man up' in the truest sense of the phrase, you will have to take action. If you just read the book, you will be impacted—no doubt about that. Answer the questions and do the exercises, however, and you will transform.

Not every chapter has Power Questions or an exercise in it, but many do. The questions are designed to challenge your current way of thinking and open you up to being the kind of man that you want to see in the world.

The Power Questions will require you to do what you're probably really uncomfortable and unfamiliar doing: looking within. I understand that this is probably out of your comfort zone. Your ego will try to convince you that it's bloody pointless. Suspend your disbelief and get on with it. Then you can assess whether it was worth it or not.

Break the Vow: Power Questions

1. What mask(s) do you wear? You can refer to the chapter or describe your own. Own up to all of them.
2. When did you first decide that you had to wear each mask?
3. What is the positive impact of wearing a mask? (e.g. *No one really knows me which means they can't hurt me.*)
4. What is the negative impact of wearing a mask? (e.g. *No one really knows me, so I feel lonely.*)
5. Finish the following sentence five times: *If you knew the real me behind the mask, you would know that…*

CHAPTER 3

BELIEFS

*"Human beings are not random creatures: all of
our actions are the result of our beliefs."*
—Tony Robbins

If there is one trait that all human beings share, it is this: we make meaning out of everything. We are, in Geneen Roth's words, "walking, talking expressions of our deepest convictions." The belief that I was the odd man out became something that eventually, my whole life revolved around. Isn't it weird that something I uttered at six years old would come to dominate and have such a negative impact on my life? Well, when you understand a bit about the power of beliefs and the mind that makes them up, you realise that this isn't actually all that weird.

Everything you think, everything you say and everything you do creates an impact. The metaphysical text *A Course in Miracles* puts it this way: "All thought creates form on some level." This is similar to what is known in chaos theory as the butterfly effect, describing how even tiny changes to something seemingly insignificant can affect large, complex systems even if they don't appear to be related. The name of this effect comes from the finding that a butterfly flapping its wings in Brazil can affect the weather in Texas. Now, at this point you might be thinking, "Yeah yeah, I've read this all before," especially if you've ever done any personal development work. However, regardless of whether you are a first-timer to this material or are a seasoned pro, I urge you to pay attention.

When we apply chaos theory to the level of the mind, the teaching is simple yet profound: there are no idle thoughts. Every thought creates a dent in the universe in some way, especially the ones that we keep repeating over and over, regardless of whether the thoughts are voiced or not. In fact, your life right now is not just the result of chance; you are where you are because of every single thought and every single choice you have ever made before this moment. This universal law applies equally to each and every one of us without exception.

The problem is that in the West, we are deeply addicted to the human condition and to the thinking that goes with that. We constantly try to figure things out. We identify so completely with the thoughts that are running through our heads that they end up running us. In other words we are shaped and driven by our thoughts and beliefs about ourselves and the world around *us*. It isn't so much the events that happen to you that really matter, but the thoughts you think and beliefs you form about those events. This process is happening for all of us, and for everyone on the planet, just as it did for me, it all starts in childhood.

Not Just Another Anonymous Kid

After the classroom brawl in 1975 which caused me to lose a testicle, and after my headteacher's badly thought out plan of telling everybody at school as a way of discouraging kicking, I started to get teased, as I mentioned in the previous chapter. It was fairly mild while I was at primary school, but nevertheless, I was a sensitive kid and it affected me. I went off to secondary school aged 11, excited about the opportunity to start over, but within a week of being there, a girl called Andi[2] kicked me in the groin. As I lay on the ground in agony, she peered over me with a smug smile on her face and said that she had heard I only had one ball and just wanted to check to see if it was true.

Any hope of being just another anonymous kid vanished. As the teasing gathered momentum and became full on taunting and bullying, my confidence became severely knocked. Like most kids that age, I wanted to fit in and be accepted by my peers, yet I was consistently told what a freak I was. Over time, as my mask became more layered, the gnawing suspicion I had about myself aged six—that I was somehow the odd man out—solidified into a toxic core belief that squirmed around inside me like a tapeworm. I became convinced that there was something fundamentally wrong with me, that I was inadequate and damaged beyond repair.

Everything sort of fell into place from then on. It all made sense in a sick kind of way. Concluding that I was some kind of freak put everything that was happening to me—the bullying, the sexual abuse I had encountered by that time (which I talk about in chapter 6), and my awkwardness around girls—into

---

[2] Not her real name. The same goes for the people who were in my life growing up: school friends, my first partner Jane (who gave her permission for me to write about our relationship provided I didn't use her name, which I hadn't planned on doing anyway), and the lady who abused me, Edna and her husband, Marty.

some kind of context. I became perpetually anxious, always worried about whether I was saying the right thing, afraid of whether someone would react with judgement or derision. Simple things made me edgy, like having to walk into a classroom full of people knowing that there was a particular person in that class who could turn on me at any second, or having to take a shower after games class, where I might get the piss taken out of me for having one ball.

Anxiety and fear tainted every day of my life so much that by the age of 13 I was taken to a psychiatrist who prescribed a round of Valium, putting me into a semi-catatonic state on the sofa for two weeks. The only way I could cope in my daily life was to put on my funny boy mask and behave like a bit of a dick. There were of course moments when the fear and worry would fade to the background, especially when I was with my misfit mates. But at school there were always people who were bigger, more powerful and more influential than me, people who could nonchalantly drop the words "one ball" into a sentence and throw me off kilter in an instant. Eventually, my whole life began to revolve around the beliefs I made up about myself. They haunted me 24/7 until I made the decision to wake up.

Children and the Power of Imagination

It's no accident that people who go to therapy talk about, deconstruct and process their childhoods. Your early years on the planet are not called your formative years for nothing. Children are remarkable meaning makers, creative little beings who want to understand the world around them and the part they play in it—and they have very powerful imaginations. A child can take anything and magically turn it into something else by the power of his imagination alone: a stick becomes a wand, a climbing frame becomes a pirate ship, and a simple box becomes a space rocket (or in my particular case, Base Camp). My dad used to bring home a huge empty cardboard box from work for me to play with. I'd put it at the top of the stairs and then starting from the bottom, would pretend I was climbing Everest in a blizzard, eventually reaching Base Camp (which for some reason was at the top of the mountain rather than at the bottom) whereupon I would climb inside and eat emergency supplies of cheese sandwiches and Monster Munch. To a child, the magical world he creates with his mind is just as real as the physical world around him. The power of a child's imagination becomes extremely relevant when we look at the impact his early experiences can have on his self-esteem and identity.

One of the primary tasks of boyhood is developing a sense of self. As a child grows, he gains an understanding of the world around him and of his place in that world, especially in relation to the most important people in it: his parents, siblings, grandparents and other close family members and mentors. The opinions, words, attitudes and behaviours of those important people in a young boy's life—whether positive or negative—leave a lasting impact on a young boy. If those relationships are abusive, dysfunctional, or lack intimacy or support, the negative impact on a young boy's sense of self will be huge.

Every experience a boy has in childhood helps shape and form his identity, from learning about gravity when he is a baby dropping toys on the floor to the first time he hears those three little words, "Be a man." His ever-developing brain is constantly connecting the dots between what's happening in his life and his sense of self.

Unfortunately, a child's imagination and inherent ability to add meaning and significance to things eventually ends up shooting him in the foot; when something 'bad' happens in boyhood, he will almost inevitably interpret it to mean something bad about himself. Without an intervention, the mistaken conclusions he comes to about himself become core beliefs that have the power to haunt him for the rest of his life. For me, for example, the belief that I was the odd man out wasn't just a passing thought. It became central to my sense of self.

There Must Be Something Wrong With Me...

Like me, you will have been physically, emotionally or psychologically wounded as a boy, albeit in different ways. (I've yet to meet a man who wasn't. If you're out there, do get in touch because I'd love to hear what it's like not to be fucked up!) No matter how much you try to brush off or rationalise the things that happened to you, the truth is that when you were wounded in boyhood, sooner or later you will have made it mean something about you.

Over the last two and a half decades, I have found that regardless of the events that shaped us, we all pretty much end up believing the same crap about ourselves. The vow of male silence makes sure that these beliefs are never revealed. Below are the most common core beliefs that I've seen countless men make up about themselves when they were young. You'll see that some of them point to the same conclusion but use different language. Notice which one(s) resonate for you—you might notice a twinge of discomfort as you read them, almost as if you've been found out.

1. I am a burden.
2. I am weak.
3. I am worthless.
4. I am unlovable.
5. I am unimportant.
6. I am not safe.
7. I am a freak.
8. I am bad. / I am no good. / I am guilty. / I am wrong.
9. I am damaged. / I am defective. / I am broken. / I am fundamentally flawed.
10. I am not enough. / I am a failure. / I am inadequate.
11. I am nothing. / I am invisible.
12. I shouldn't have been born. / The world would be better off without me in it.

At their core, all of these beliefs boil down to the same essence: *there must be something wrong with me.* These might appear to be 'just words' but make no mistake: words, like thoughts, are powerful. They have the power to become wounds. (To read a summary of some of the science behind belief formation, see Appendix I at the back of the book.) For most of us, the words that eventually became the beliefs we now live our lives by were either spoken by people who matter to us, or they were words we thought to ourselves when something traumatic or painful happened in our lives, just like I did when I declared myself to be the odd man out.

At some point in his childhood, pretty much every boy will arrive at a mistaken but powerful conclusion about himself as he interprets an upsetting event (for example his father shouting at him) to mean something about him as a person (such as "I must have done something wrong otherwise Dad wouldn't be angry. It must be my fault."). Add in the omertà-fuelled rules of masculinity, which give boys a stick to measure their manliness and worthiness against, and you have a recipe for disaster. Because these pivotal childhood events happen in relationship with someone who was important to us—a parent, mentor, friend, sibling or family member, for example (and no doubt someone who was impacted by omertà themselves)—they carry weight and significance. Without any conscious effort on our part, we give meaning to these moments, events or situations, making them mean something about ourselves. For some of us, the beliefs we form about ourselves affect every area of our lives. A pervasive sense of uselessness, worthlessness or guilt (for example) taints everything we do. For others, the beliefs will apply only in very specific circumstances, such as around work, sex or relationships.

Two Tiny Words

These core mistaken beliefs all have a couple of things in common. Firstly, they are all deeply damaging to a boy or man's sense of self and his self-esteem. To walk around believing you're invisible, damaged or inadequate, for example, is hardly conducive to feeling good about yourself. On the surface you may command respect but deep down, you'll never fully believe that you deserve it. You only have to look at the business world to see this play out; men in suits barking orders and bullying other people, 'demanding' respect while unconsciously carrying the belief that they're not actually worthy of it. Alongside this, you might start to buy into the bullshit of your mask(s), listening to society's dodgy ideas about masculinity, convincing yourself that if you could just be a bit stronger, harder or less emotional—if you could just 'man up' a bit more—then you'd feel better. Like a gambling addict who believes that he will feel better if he just gets that next win, this line of thinking is very seductive but it never, ever works.

Secondly, notice that most of the beliefs we form about ourselves start with two little words: *I am*. When used together, these are two of the most powerful words in the English language because they define who you think you are. These two tiny words are also spoken in the present simple tense, which my wife tells me is the same grammatical tense you use to describe facts. London *is* the capital of England. Mount Everest *is* 8,848 metres high. I *am* a man. I *am* the odd man out. This nifty bit of grammar makes it difficult for our brains to tell the difference between a genuine fact and a narrative that we have made up.

Basically, whatever you say after the words "I am" will determine the quality of your life. The words you choose to use after the phrase "I am" will lead to expansion or contraction, to aliveness or deadness, to possibility or impossibility. Two completely different experiences are available to you from these two tiny words. They have the potential to change everything.

For the rest of this book, we are going to refer to these beliefs as either shitty mistaken beliefs or simply SMBs. We're calling them "shitty" because they leave you feeling shitty. They are "mistaken" because they are unequivocally, 100% not true (however convinced you are of their so-called reality). Finally, they are "beliefs"—*not facts!*

Abuse and Neglect

The process forming SMBs about ourselves and the world happens for all of us (and if you don't think it applies to you, bear with me—we're getting to that), but it is even more extreme for children who have experienced abuse or neglect. The intensity of an abused child's mistaken beliefs about himself can be so acute that he will rarely if ever experience respite from the pain and shame associated with those beliefs. Unless a boy has a really good support system in place, if he has been abused or neglected, he is likely going to struggle to develop healthy coping mechanisms and resilience. He will probably grow up believing that there is something deeply and fundamentally wrong with him. I have often heard men in therapeutic circles who had tough or abusive childhoods talking about how they carry within them a pervasive sense of being defective, broken, damaged or just plain no good.

Sadly, we are not just talking about a few boys here (and the same goes for girls). Untold numbers of children are susceptible to psychological, emotional, physical and sexual abuse at some point in their childhood. Sometimes when I imagine the collective pain of what we men believe about ourselves as a result of what we concluded in childhood, combined with the compound effect of the vow of silence we live under, the weight of it feels agonising. Countless wounded boys become wounded men who go on to wound others in turn. One statistic I read said that abused or neglected children are nine times more likely to end up committing crime, perpetuating the vow of silence and everything that comes with it.

Those of us who experienced abuse or neglect when we were boys—myself included—may have to grapple with physical, psychological, behavioural and societal consequences for years to come, in addition to the loneliness that is part and parcel of living under omertà. It might take a lifetime of therapy to truly make peace with your childhood, but as hard as that can be, it's far better than living a beige, half-dead existence.

No One Gets Out of Childhood Scot-Free

Now, before you protest and say that nothing bad happened in your childhood and that you feel 'fine' (which in twelve step fellowships stands for "Fucked up, Insecure, Neurotic and Emotional"), you need to hear this next point: *no one gets out of childhood scot-free.*

Irrespective of your upbringing, keep these two vital points in mind: firstly, you're going to be wounded simply from being born human. You were born into a family that, regardless of what it looks like (including if you're adopted), will have transmitted ancestral pain, wounds, beliefs and values from one generation to the next.

Secondly, no matter how ordinary, stable or happy your childhood was, the point is that *something* will have happened. This could simply have been your entrance into the world, whether it was by C-section, forceps or even through an uncomplicated birth. It could be that time you fell and scraped your knee, discovering that your body was fallible and vulnerable to injury, or when you were left out of a game in the school yard (even Rudolph with his shiny nose made meaning out of that one). The same goes for any other seemingly harmless childhood event. Remember— kids are constantly creating meaning, and until they fully develop empathy and perspective, they are also self-centred. Add in the brain's natural bias towards noticing negativity and even a seemingly insignificant event, if it had any negative associations, will have had five times the impact of a positive experience.

Here's an example to illustrate what I mean. When I was a baby, my mum used to leave me outside in the pram while she popped into a shop. This was in the early seventies, long before the era of child kidnappings, and Mum had obviously decided that it was safe for her to leave me for a minute. Before you berate my mum, she never let me out of her sight, and in Denmark, they are still in the habit of leaving babies in their buggies outside shops.

Now, one of my earliest memories is from the aforementioned humble perambulator. I remember seeing Mum inside the shop while I was outside in my pram, and I remember panicking and crying frantically. Whilst my body was releasing cortisone (a stress hormone) and adrenaline (a fight or flight hormone), Mum was just paying for bread and milk. To any onlooker, this incident probably didn't even cause a blip, but it certainly registered inside me. I reckon it was right up there at that point in my young life, registering 8.8 on my trauma Richter Scale alongside exiting the birth canal!

Once a shitty mistaken belief has been formed, it becomes physiologically wired into your brain and body. SMBs form in childhood, solidify in adolescence and are dragged kicking and screaming into adulthood. Everything (our beliefs, our worldview, our behaviour and our choices) stems from what we believe about ourselves, and if we are to break the vow of silence, we have to uncover and expose these deeply rooted beliefs. If we don't, we will continue to be hostage to them.

It is vital therefore that you understand what your shitty mistaken beliefs are and the part they have played in shaping you into the man you are today. This probably seems like a very unmanly proposition but it is necessary if you are to experience lasting freedom from omertà. If we are to successfully break the vow of male silence, we can't just point the finger out there at the world and blame our culture for its messed up ideas of masculinity. We have to take responsibility for how we have participated in omertà, and to do that we have to address both our behaviour and our beliefs. We have work to do—hard, internal, personal work. Most men aren't comfortable touching these topics with a barge pole, but the truth is that we have to look at this stuff if we are to become free of the vow of male silence.

The process of belief formation—especially in response to pain—is a universal human experience. Everyone reading these words has wounds and SMBs. Some might be more obvious than others, but they all have an influence on the lens through which you view the world. The sooner you accept this, the sooner you will be released from their grip.

Let's recap all this info: at some point in your childhood, you are wounded, either physically, emotionally or psychologically. You interpret the inciting event and come to a conclusion about what it means about you. Unless you live in a particularly enlightened family, you probably aren't equipped with the emotional skills to process and understand that it doesn't mean what you think it means. Even in an emotionally literate family, as a child you are unable to see the full picture, and eventually, as one incident after another takes place, you develop a collection of shitty mistaken beliefs about yourself and carry them with you wherever you go.

Until you reveal and deal with them at their root, they will go on to wreak havoc in your life in one form or another, leaving a trail of heartache, guilt and shame in their wake.

Break the Vow: Power Questions

It's time to take an initial look at what your SMBs might be. Don't worry if this is all a bit like gobbledygook right now. Your understanding of this material will continue to evolve as you read the book. If on the other hand you have done some personal development work before, you might be more aware of what your core SMBs are. I encourage you to keep an open mind and answer the questions anyway.

To begin, sit quietly and reflect on your own childhood. You will almost certainly see that you experienced a number of significant and potentially traumatising events, perhaps more than you realised. It's okay if you have forgotten about them but it doesn't mean that they have forgotten about you. If you can't remember much about your childhood, start with whatever you can remember, even if it's stories that other people have told you about your childhood or simple facts such as where you lived and what the lifestyle was like. Over time, more of your childhood will reveal itself to you.

1. What events happened in your childhood that caused you emotional or physical pain? List everything you can remember.

2. Which of the following shitty mistaken beliefs (SMBs) did you make up about yourself as a result of these events? Highlight any that resonate and add any others that the

list doesn't cover. Don't worry at this point about trying to make sense of them or get rid of them. Your job is just to acknowledge them right now.

I am a burden.
I am weak.
I am worthless.
I am unlovable.
I am unimportant.
I am not safe.
I am a freak.
I am bad. / I am no good. / I am guilty. / I am wrong.
I am damaged. / I am defective. / I am broken. / I am fundamentally flawed.
I am not enough. / I am a failure. / I am inadequate.
I am nothing. / I am invisible.
I shouldn't have been born. / The world would be better off without me in it.

This work isn't easy, but it is vital. I know you can do it. Onward.

CHAPTER 4

GUILT AND SHAME

"Shame is a soul-eating emotion."
—Carl Jung

Our core shitty mistaken beliefs are like toxic seeds that take root deep in the subconscious mind, generating enormous guilt and incredible shame. Multiply that guilt and shame by the number of core SMBs you have, and you'll get a sense of the amount of guilt and shame that are within you. Now multiply that by the number of men on the planet. That's a whole lot of guilt and shame.

For lots of men, guilt and shame are intimate strangers. We feel them every day yet we don't really know what we're feeling. These dark, secretive emotions and thoughts become cloaked in ambition, pride, arrogance and competition, wrapped up in omertà and buried beneath thousands of moments of acting like the 'real men' that we feel compelled to be.

To be honest, until I started doing the research for this book, I didn't really know the difference between guilt and shame. What I did know was the horrible, all-consuming sense that I was bad that has been with me to a greater or lesser degree ever since I was a boy. Some days it has shown up as a twinge on the periphery of my awareness; other days it has eaten me up from the inside out. Half the time I don't even know what I've supposedly done wrong. All I know is that there is a nagging suspicion in the dark recesses of my mind that tells me two things: firstly that I *have* fucked up and secondly that I *am* fucked up. That, interestingly, is the difference between the two states: guilt is the shit feeling you get after you *have* fucked up, whereas shame is the shit feeling you have from believing that you *are* fucked up.[3]

We men are no strangers to guilt. It was men and not women, after all, who were responsible for most of our world's historical atrocities. My friend Duane O'Kane, co-founder of Clearmind International Institute with his wife Catherine O'Kane, says that men carry "collective guilt for the perceived sins" and acts of barbarity of all the men who came before us. If this is true, then guilt is so deeply ingrained in the caverns of the male psyche that it might as well be hard-wired into your DNA.

I don't think guilt is all bad; it can be a useful compass for men, one that shows you if you're in integrity or not. Without awareness, however, guilt can eat you up from the inside out, leading straight to hell on earth, a bit like Will Smith's character in the film *Seven Pounds*. If you want to understand how heavily guilt can weigh on a man's mind, go and watch that film.

Shame, because of its nature, is more complex. Brené Brown, the godmother of shame research, says that "shame is the intensely painful feeling or experience of believing that we are flawed and therefore unworthy of love and belonging." In *Odd Man Out*

---

[3] Some researchers says there is such a thing as "healthy shame," but for our purposes, when I talk about shame I will be referring to unhealthy or toxic shame.

terms, shame is the toxic, horrible feeling generated by your SMBs. It is the feeling that makes you wish the ground would swallow you up, the one you'd rather be dead than have to actually feel.

Shame is paradoxical: it is simultaneously a universal human experience and equally the loneliest place on earth. When you feel shame, you may experience physiological symptoms (such as sweating, flushing or feeling tense), emotional symptoms (such as feeling shy and not wanting to make eye contact), and mental symptoms (thoughts about how awkward, embarrassing or bad you are).

Brown found in her research that men in particular live under the pressure of an "unrelenting" message which tells them not to be perceived as weak. This message triggers a specific kind of shame that men know very well—the shame of not being a real man, enough of a man, or some kind of pussy or girl, all of which we explored in chapter two. Out of this shame (and the fear-driven avoidance of feeling this shame) comes all the screwed up messages that men live under on a daily basis: to man up, shut up, put up and be strong and silent. Omertà and shame feed off each other, each increasing the other's strength. Shame for men also arises from failure—or simply from the fear of failing. It arises from the fear of being seen as wrong, from taking certain risks such as daring to be emotionally vulnerable, or, as we explored in chapter two, from anything associated with weakness.

Toxic Shame

Sometimes, shame becomes toxic. This often happens to someone who has experienced trauma, abandonment or abuse, particularly in childhood. If Brené Brown is the godmother of shame research, then John Bradshaw, a psychologist and writer, has to be the godfather. Bradshaw writes in *Healing the Shame That Binds You* that "the demonic potential of shame can lead to the most destructive emotional sickness of self a person can have." Toxic shame is the worst of the worst. It is so acute and deeply internalised that the person's identity begins to form around it. A man with toxic shame will believe that he is fundamentally a mistake, that he is damaged goods or that he is beyond help and would be better off dead. Shame will become more than an occasional experience for this man; it will form the epicentre around which his whole sense of self revolves.

This of course is where the mask comes in. It has one purpose: to protect you from being known and found out. Shame says that if anyone really knew you they would recoil in terror. The mask promises never to let that happen. You become somebody else to protect yourself from ever being found out for the monster that you believe you really are. The mask is created out of pure survival instinct. Bradshaw writes, "If one feels his true self is defective and flawed, one needs a false self that is not defective and flawed," a self that will effectively hide the 'true' self. We men will go to almost any lengths to create that false self. The guilt and shame that threatens to torment your everyday life feels so potentially overwhelming and overpowering that you feel compelled to escape it.

Bradshaw talks about a process that occurs for some people during childhood, during which a "collage of shaming memories" is formed as one shaming incident after another takes place. The collage begins to form as various shame scenes get metaphorically "cut out" and glued across the surface area of the memory like a dodgy vision board. I think that's what happened to me; losing a testicle, being sexually abused, being bullied, being constantly compared to my dad and experiencing acute anxiety all got stuck together in a fucked up mental scrapbook of my life. It was only after a fair amount of personal development work and therapy that I could look back on my childhood and see the bright spots that offset the collage of shame.

When something happens in your daily life that triggers one of these memories—often something as inconsequential as someone cutting you up in traffic—shame will stir and rumble in the depths of your subconscious. Many men have suppressed shame so effectively that they can only experience anger, but I guarantee that under the anger, there is a dark, threatening pit of shame. I would go as far to say that the angrier the man, the more toxic shame he carries.

Crawling in my Skin

Let me help you understand more about how a man experiences shame by sharing what shame is like for me. When I am in shame, I feel like a zombie, the embodiment of the quote from Dawn of the Dead where it says, "When there is no more room in hell, the dead will walk the earth." Over the last 48 years, I've done a lot of walking! Seriously though, when I'm feeling ashamed, I feel numb and disconnected from myself and others. My wife always knows when I've had a shame attack because my whole demeanour changes: it's as if the lights are on but no one is home. I retreat so far into myself that no one in the outside world can reach me. The Linkin' Park song Crawling pretty much sums up what shame is like for me:

Crawling in my skin
These wounds they will not heal
Fear is how I fall
Confusing what is real.

Guilt and shame can have a devastating effect on a man's self-worth and how it impacts his ability to feel fully alive. They can suffocate and totally debilitate him, just like the hefty karmic chain Charles Dickens describes in *A Christmas Carol*. In case you don't know the story of Ebenezer Scrooge, here's the briefest account in history: Scrooge is a miserable, miserly bastard who meets three spirits—the Spirits of Christmas Past, Present and Future—whose job is to help him wake up to the error of his ways before it's too late. If he doesn't change, he faces an eternity in hell, weighed down by a colossal iron chain which he forged "link by link and yard by yard" during his time on earth with every greedy, selfish or miserly act he committed. Scrooge's story (and particularly the chain he's told he'll have to wear for all eternity) provides a powerful insight into the impact that guilt, shame and shitty mistaken beliefs can have on a man's life. The difference between Scrooge's chain and yours is that your chain isn't waiting for you in the afterlife, but is weighing you down even as you read these words.

Unfortunately, ashamed people often go on to shame others in the same way abused people can become abusers. The experience of shame is so intolerable that the psyche does anything it can to try to cope with it, and turning it outward is a strategy men are particularly comfortable with. It's obvious how men shame other men; we constantly take the piss out of each other, compete with each other and undermine each other. When a man gets a bit too close to breaking omertà, we quickly shut him down. I'm not trying to piss on anyone's parade around humour here; I love a bit of banter and mucking about with the boys when we're out on the bikes or down the gym. When it's genuine camaraderie, it has a brotherly, friendly feel to it. But when it isn't, there is a darker edge to it that feels anything but friendly. Men clearly also shame women. We are experts at objectifying, minimising, oppressing and abusing women, and the statistics of sexualised violence towards women bear this out. Much has been written about this. Collectively, we men owe a huge debt of atonement towards women. My hope is that by raising awareness of the role shame plays in men's lives, we can move beyond punitive finger-pointing, which only serves to keep reinforcing the key message of omertà—that men are bad—and instead move towards real change.

Women, Shame and Omertà

There is, however, another subdivision of omertà that I don't see anyone talking about, and it's this: as much as we men minimise and shame women, I can't count the number of times I have seen women minimising, judging and shaming men. Here's just some of my personal experience: I've been on the receiving end of a lot of sexism, put downs, shaming, emotional abuse and even violence perpetrated by women throughout my life. I've been told to man up when I've been unwell. I've been put down for not being able to multitask. I've been told that I'm inept because I'm a man. I've been told to grow a set (which is ironic given my personal history, but which is doubly ironic when you think about how sensitive a man's testicles are!). I've been called hyper-sensitive when I'm emotional. I've been told I don't have it nearly as hard as women, that because I'll never go through childbirth I don't really know what pain is.

Sometimes I wonder if women subconsciously want to lash out at men because of the inequality, violence and shaming they've been subjected to by men over the generations. This is understandable—anyone who has been on the receiving end of abuse might feel justified in lashing out and fighting back—but it's also deeply damaging. An eye for an eye, after all, and the whole world goes blind.

It is brilliant that women have started to have their voices be heard in traditionally male-dominated contexts in the last few decades, and I know that there is much further to go in terms of real equality, but I want to go out on a limb here and say that women too have a huge part to play in upholding omertà. Even the most well-intentioned person, if they're not used to seeing a man be connected to his emotions and expressing his vulnerability, might find the whole experience awkward. It may evoke feelings of judgement, discomfort or embarrassment, or memories of a time in your life when a man let you down by being 'weak' and emotional. We are all affected by omertà, and we all play a part in keeping it alive. Sadly, misandry—the dislike of, contempt for, or ingrained prejudice against men—is as real as misogyny. It's just not spoken about as much, to the point where I don't think most people have even come across the word. I think it's a bit of a taboo subject actually because of all the violence towards women that has been perpetrated by men.

Brené Brown wrote about this in *Daring Greatly*. She writes, "I was not prepared to hear over and over from men how the women in their lives—the mothers, sisters, girlfriends, wives—in their lives are constantly criticizing them for not being open and vulnerable and intimate." She goes on to describe how even though women are asking men to be more emotionally available, at the same time, another part of them doesn't actually want their men to come out from behind the "great and powerful" Oz-like image they have constructed for themselves.

I have experienced this in my relationship with Ell. In the beginning of our relationship, I was the 'strong' one; I'd been the leader in a therapeutic community she'd been part of a few years earlier, and despite the break we'd both taken from that community before getting together, the old power imbalance was still in place. About seven months into our fledgling relationship, I lost my job and felt scared and helpless. I asked for Ell's help to build me a website, and the power dynamics started to shift between us. As much as Ell had been saying that she wanted to see more of my vulnerability, when I showed it to her she freaked out and lucky for her, conveniently had a one month holiday to California coming up—which turned into a three month break in our relationship. We eventually worked through it, but it took Ell a while to come to terms with the realisation that like her, I was completely human!

I've seen this same dynamic over and over again: many women want their men to be emotionally available, but it's scary. It means changing your ideas around what it means to be "a strong man." The uncomfortable truth that I have heard a number of women share is that secretly, they don't want their men off the proverbial white horse. Reflecting on this in *Daring Greatly*, Brown acknowledged while driving home one evening, *"Holy shit. I am the patriarchy."* And yes, the italics were hers.

This leaves men in a double bind. On the one hand, we are asked by our partners to be emotionally open and available, which would mean baring our shame, guilt and fear to them; on the other, we are also asked not to fall apart, to continue to uphold the old ideals about what it means to be a man. It's an impossible conundrum in which something has to give—and much of the time, the stronger message seems to be, "Don't be weak."

The way women contribute towards keeping omertà alive is often socially acceptable, and I wonder whether because of the awful way women have been treated, we're all silently in agreement that women have the right to get their own back, regardless of the damage it's doing. It's not uncommon for women to joke about men being useless, lazy or stupid and no one bats an eyelid. For example, I've seen major supermarkets selling t-shirts and birthday cards with derogatory statements on them about how useless men are, pigeonholing us as tit-ogling, beer-swilling, lazy idiots when the truth is that these behaviours are escape routes, mechanisms men use for coping with their own anxiety, shame and pain. Some extreme third wave feminists have gone so far as to call men obsolete. Imagine if men said the same about women; there would be uproar.

We don't always want to admit that if something is sexist towards one gender, it's also sexist towards the other. For example, in the iconic comedy show *Laurel and Hardy*, the two protagonists' wives were almost always depicted as battle axes—stern, strict and controlling—while the men sat on the receiving end of their verbal and sometimes even physical abuse. We chuckle at the beating these loveable, comedic heroes receive because the scenes are amusing and entertaining, yet a part of us feels a twinge of discomfort while watching too because on some level we relate, and we know it's not actually justified (all attack is ultimately self-attack, a principle I'll be exploring in much more depth in chapter five). While these female characters reflect one of the pervasive, damaging stereotypes of women—the controlling nag—the men are shown to be under the thumb, either complying with what the women want for fear of criticism or responding with outbursts of anger.

Behind these two dimensional clichéd stereotypes is a world of pain, for men and women alike. The point I really want to emphasise here is that women's critical attitudes towards and dismissal of men might sound like a bit of harmless fun but believe me, it isn't. As a man who has experienced sexist piss taking and shaming firsthand, I'm telling you that it's soul destroying. There's no such thing as just a bit of harmless shaming of men in the same way there is no such thing as just a bit of harmless objectification of a woman's body.

It's obvious that on the surface we live in a world that favours men, especially white men. There is still a glass ceiling for women when it comes to earnings and equality in many arenas. I'm not denying any of that, and I'm not trying to assert men as the more superior sex, unlike some of the reactive "Men Going It Alone" websites I came across during my research, which seem to be defending themselves against women rather than attempting to heal the rift between us and experience true connection.

I want to ask women reading this to be mindful of how you communicate to the men in your life. Pay attention to the language you use and be mindful about the subtext, and to the way you interact with and talk about men. Take ownership for the part of you that wants to put men down and shame us. I'm not asking you to stop having a sense of humour. If it's based on love, a bit of teasing can be a sign of affection. But if it's rooted in attack, that message will be communicated. If you have issues with men, I urge you to do your work. In the same vein, if you're a man reading this and you have issues with women, you have work to do, too. And to all genders, including people who are gender fluid and do not identify with the term man or woman, I am pretty convinced that we *all* have work to do in this area.

The bottom line is this: if you have ever told a man to 'man up,' if you have ever joked that a man who is sensitive or in touch with his emotions is a sissy, queer or a pussy, or if you've ever called a man weak—even jokily—because he is physically unwell or in touch with some emotion other than anger, then you have contributed to upholding omertà. We all have a responsibility to stand for something bigger than the tit-for-tat, Mars versus Venus mentality. As it says in *A Course in Miracles*, forgiveness is the release from *all* illusions. What I hope I have done here is challenge the status quo and address the subtle ways that women also contribute to keeping the vow of male silence alive. This is hard to write about and I imagine it's been hard to read, but it's an important part of breaking the vow.

Therefore, your task, should you choose to accept it, is this: to get radically curious about how the men in your life are experiencing shame. Remember that all men are wounded, and however convincing his mask might be, if you look closely enough you'll see tiny hairline cracks in a man's armour. Once you catch a glimpse of the wounded man behind the mask, you can either give him a soft place to land, or you can condemn him to a bed of nails. The choice is yours. In closing on this issue, I want all the women reading this to know that your part in this work is critical. We can't break the vow of male silence without you.

Dare to Talk

It takes very little to trigger a man's collection of shameful memories and associations, and the instant these are triggered he will feel awkward. His conditioning will shut him down as quickly as possible, often making him incapable of feeling his deeper feelings for fear of the metaphorical death penalty. Therefore, instead of expanding and healthily expressing the emotion, he will contract, disregard and hide his feelings. Over time, a man's shame becomes so severely internalised that he starts to identify with it, believing it to be who and what he is. John Bradshaw says that "once toxically shamed, a person loses contact with his authentic self. What follows is a chronic mourning for the lost self—low grade chronic depression." The last thing our society needs is more covertly depressed men. There are already too many of us.

As uncomfortable as the conversation about guilt and shame is for men to have, it is a vital one. We men must become emotionally literate. So much of the crazy shit that's happening in the world is happening thanks to unacknowledged guilt and shame with lashings of omertà to top it off. If we are to heal the wounds of the past and stop wreaking devastating havoc in the present, we must first muster up the courage to feel the individual and collective guilt and shame that dwells in our very bones. Each and every time we do this we smash through the walls of societal and familial conditioning and take another step to becoming emotionally responsible. Breaking the vow of male silence doesn't happen once. It is a choice that must be made over and over again. We have to dare to go against the grain and do the one thing we don't want to do: talk about it. Until we do, only two options remain: offence or defence.

Break the Vow: Power Questions

1. How does shame show up in your life?
2. What do you feel you guilty for?

CHAPTER 5

ATTACK

"All attack is self-attack."
—A Course in Miracles

When it comes to the ego I have been told that I have X-ray vision. Perhaps this is because I've spent over two decades studying its dynamics in my own mind in such depth that I can pinpoint its underhanded tactics and see through its bullshit from a mile off. If you truly want to break free of omertà, it is critical that you have a good understanding of the dynamics of the ego, which is slippery, insidious and destructive. Given an inch, the ego will always take a mile.

When people think of the term ego, what usually comes to mind is somebody with a big head—a narcissistic pop star, celebrity or politician, for example. In other words, the ego is often equated with being egotistical: arrogant, excessively conceited or absorbed in oneself. In *Odd Man Out* terms, arrogance, conceit and self-centredness are characteristics of the ego, but they don't accurately describe the ego itself.

Think of the ego as the director of Project Omertà. It is the mastermind of every fearful thought and SMB you've ever had about yourself. It upholds every messed up idea about what it means to be a real man and makes sure that you conform, threatening you with horrifying outcomes if you even contemplate breaking the rules. The ego's only goal is separation. It doesn't know anything else. It deifies the idea of the rugged individual, convinced that going it alone is the only way to get what you want and win at life—usually at the expense of somebody else.

Your Inner Tyler Durden

The ego promises to get rid of the fear, guilt and shame that your SMBs generate, but what it doesn't tell you is that its real mission is to reinforce the fear that at your core, you are broken, defective or inadequate. The reason for this is that the ego has to keep generating more fear, guilt and shame in you because without them it would be out of a job. Its survival is dependent on your belief in it in much the same way as Tyler Durden's survival was dependent on Jack's belief in him in the cult novel and movie *Fight Club*.

Fight Club is narrated from the perspective of Ed Norton's awkward character (who is nameless but who is thought to be named Jack). Jack is a colourless, neurotic, one-dimensional slave of the capitalist system. He becomes entangled with the suave, disorderly anarchist Tyler Durden and together they form an underground bare knuckle fight club.

Tyler is everything Jack isn't: smooth, sexy, charismatic and masculine. As it turns out, Tyler is a creation of Jack's mind, a separate personality but not a separate person. In the closing scenes of the film we see that what appeared to be Tyler's reality is actually a projection of Jack's mind. Near the end of the film,

Jack starts to realise that something about Tyler isn't quite right. A brutal fight breaks out between the two men, and it is only when we see the fight though the CCTV screens that we, the viewers, discover that Tyler doesn't actually exist at all; Jack has been interacting with himself the whole time. The twist is compelling, a Hollywood classic. When you re-watch *Fight Club* for the second time, you see all the evidence that Tyler is a creation of Jack's mind right from the word go. Good old confirmation bias in action there.

In the final showdown between Jack and Tyler, as Jack becomes willing to do whatever is necessary to get rid of his twisted alter ego, Tyler uses every strategy in the book to try to convince Jack that Jack cannot survive without him. As Jack detaches himself from his belief that "in Tyler we trust," Tyler switches and becomes outright violent. Jack's determination to overthrow Tyler threatens Tyler far too seriously for him to bother to pretend anymore that he is Jack's friend.

Jack eventually becomes willing to go to any lengths to be free of Tyler Durden. He will even take his own life if it gets rid of Tyler once and for all. As Jack turns a gun on himself, Tyler switches strategies in a last ditch attempt to dissuade him from pulling the trigger and killing both of them. Tyler just about keeps his suave edge but there's a tangible air of panic about him as he frantically switches from pulling out the 'friends for life' card quickly followed by the 'Who would you be without me?' plea. Jack doesn't know, but he risks finding out... and he pulls the trigger.

Fight Club depicts exactly what the ego will do to you any time you get close to breaking omertà and unhooking your allegiance from it. When you make any attempt to stop relying on your ego, it will do everything it can to keep your allegiance, vacillating between threatening you one minute to flattering you the next. For most people, the ego is so cleverly disguised that we actually think it is you. You are oblivious to the moment you switch into Tyler mode and think that someone else is the cause of the mayhem in your life. You don't consciously remember the moment that you hired the ego and before long, its voice has become so familiar to you that you forget that there was ever a 'you' before it came along. You embody its teachings so well and hear its thoughts in the first person so fluently and effortlessly that over time, you become it.

Your inner Tyler Durden drip feeds you a comprehensive template about the type of man you need to be. Everything in its world operates on the shaky foundation of the fear of being found out, rejected and thrown to the dogs. When you fall under the ego's guidance, you become a shadow of your true self. This is the dilemma that most men face every single day. You walk like a ghost through the world, living, in the words of Nine Inch Nails, as "an echo of an echo" of who you really are. Eventually, as Barbara Stanny says, "the coping mechanisms that saved you as a child will suffocate you as an adult."

World War Me

Like Jack, there is a war happening right now as you read these words—and it's happening against yourself. There's also a war happening inside everyone around you. Everyone is fighting a hard internal battle. In a world where we are drowning in the relentless need to portray our picture perfect lives on social media, very few of us are disclosing this battle, but that doesn't mean it's not happening. The ego doesn't want you to acknowledge that the war is against yourself because if you did, the only peace talks that would need to take place would be with and within yourself. This would mean the end of the ego. To prevent this from happening, the ego projects your inner war outside of you and onto the world, ensuring that you never address the real problem which is always inside yourself. In a moment we'll explore attack in more detail but first, let's explore what the concept of projection means.

Projection Makes Perception

The ego keeps your personal collection of SMBs running in the background of your mind every day, like an unseen piece of software running silently on your laptop. You don't even have to think about them; they're not in your conscious awareness most of the time. The ego's job is to gather evidence to prove over and over again that your SMBs are true. In my case, for example, I have a shitty mistaken belief that I am inadequate, and the most trivial thing can push the SMB button and bring that belief to the surface. It could be something as banal and everyday as Ell checking her phone. My mind will instantly jump into attack mode, secretly thinking that she is rude and ignorant for ignoring me. Beneath the surface, what's really going on isn't about Ell at all; what's really happening is that I am projecting my own sense of inadequacy out onto the world, using this situation as evidence to prove that I am inadequate.

A Course in Miracles states that projection makes perception. This means that as your mind projects your shitty mistaken beliefs out onto the world, your perception of what is happening becomes warped as a result. In other words you do not really understand what is happening in front of you, even though you're convinced that you do. Instead, you see a shadowy image from your past—a distant, painful memory from long ago being replayed like a looping movie reel.

While you believe the problem is out there in the world, you never have to have that sober moment with yourself where you acknowledge, "I'm hurting. This situation hasn't caused my pain; it has only brought the pain within me to the surface."

To avoid having to really face yourself, the ego is constantly on the lookout for the next conflict, clash or struggle, and round the crazy loop we go. This whole cycle guarantees that the ego stays in a job for life.

Get the Bastards

Therefore, you're almost always in a state of war against someone or something. The ego needs to keep the war alive out there, so it is on a permanent mission to find potential threats and enemies, just as Jack's alter ego Tyler did in *Fight Club*. It vacillates between two states: highly suspicious at best and downright vicious at worst. If it gets even the slightest hint that you're being threatened, disrespected or minimised in any way, the ego will lock and load. Its approach to everything is rooted in one simple precept: *get the bastards before they get you*. Defend yourself at all costs.

Steven Pressfield's book *The War of Art* contains one of the best descriptions of the ego and its strategies that I've ever come across. Pressfield states that the ego "is like the Alien or like the Terminator or the shark in Jaws. It cannot be reasoned with. It understands nothing but power. It is an engine of destruction, programmed from the factory with one object only: to prevent us from doing our work. It is implacable, intractable, and indefatigable. Reduce it to a single cell and that cell will continue to attack. This is its nature. It's all it knows."

Sometimes the way we attack others is blatantly obvious: think the Twin Towers, politicians insulting each other in Parliament, road rage and domestic violence, pub brawls, rape, football hooliganism, child abuse and murder. Sometimes however attack is less obvious but just as lethal, often leaving a bitter aftertaste in the mouth: internet trolling, for example, or a government launching a 'defensive' military campaign to supposedly end the war on terror for which there is no credible evidence.

Often, attack takes a more insidious form as the ego takes refuge in the underground sewers of the mind, leaking out sideways in everyday interactions: a nasty throwaway comment, a loaded joke about a co-worker, a heavily disguised criticism, veiled in politeness yet laced with venom, or even just a look that says far more than words ever could. Make no mistake: regardless of the form it takes, the ego's sole intent is, in the words of Steven Pressfield, "not to wound or disable. It aims to kill." This is how men operate under omertà; we turn to attack as one of our primary strategies to navigate a world in which we rely heavily on the ego, perceiving threats and challenges to our masculinity everywhere we turn. Yet all attack is self-attack, and it only generates one result: to multiply the guilt and shame inside you like a virus.

A Short-Lived Victory

The ego is the part of the mind that is utterly convinced that attack leads to freedom—from shame, guilt and psychological or emotional discomfort. It claims that you have the right to do or say whatever the hell you want to, declaring that your anger is always fully justified. When someone or something has supposedly harmed you, the ego declares that this warrants criticism at best and vengeance at worst. When you get your revenge, the ego advises, you will feel vindicated. Sound familiar?

Let's face it: you *do* feel powerful for a moment when you verbally or physically attack another person, as the body experiences a rush of adrenaline like an intense pump you would get from performing a heavy bench press in the gym. You stand taller and prouder, like a silverback gorilla guarding your territory, but there is a severe flaw in the ego's plan—the victory is always short-lived.

Think about it: once you step away from the situation and your adrenaline levels drop, you're left feeling worse than you did in the first place. Your conscience kicks in and your mind becomes flooded with guilt. No matter how thoroughly you delude yourself into believing that by attacking someone else you can alleviate your own guilt and shame, the truth is that you can't.

This cycle is like the one you get caught up in if you borrow money from those awful payday loan companies. They seduce you into borrowing cash when you run out so that you continue to buy all the things you think you need, and then when the time comes to make your repayment, they whack so much interest on it that you end up in a worse situation than you were before!

The bottom line is this: the malicious thoughts you have about others never leave your own mind. **All attack is self-attack**. Try as you might to direct it elsewhere, the barrel of the gun is always pointing back at your own head.

Break the Vow: Power Questions

1. How do you indulge in attack?
2. How do you feel about attack after reading this chapter?

CHAPTER 6

HULK

"Don't make me angry. You won't like me when I'm angry."
—Dr Banner

Every Saturday night during the late seventies and early eighties, I watched *The Hulk*, a TV series which starred Bill Bixby as Dr David Banner and Lou Ferrigno as the Hulk, a fictional superhero invented by Stan Lee and Jack Kirby of Marvel Comics in 1962.

While working in his lab, Dr Banner is exposed to a gamma blast. Whenever he finds himself extremely angry or stressed, he transforms into the Hulk, a huge green monster with unrestrained human strength and power. Dr Banner is thought to be dead and spends his days on the run from Jack McGee, a newspaper reporter who is trying to further his own career by outing the Hulk. This means that until David is able to find a cure he must always stay one step ahead of his pursuer. At the end of each episode a solitary piano would play in the background, as Banner, complete with a stuff sack bursting with spare shirts, moved on to a new destination.

It would be easy to see the Hulk as a violent caricature with no depth or substance, but I actually think he is much more than a two-dimensional character. Inside the Hulk is a person, a man who as a result of his work has gone through a process that has changed him, possibly an irreversible one. Unlike other superheroes who transform from their everyday male identities into the caped crusaders ready to save the world, Hulk spends his days as a man trying to keep the monster within at arm's length, and yet the monster always eventually overpowers him. He has to constantly move from place to place, concealing his identity, unable to settle anywhere, unable to build any relationships and unable to risk letting anyone get to know him. God knows how much guilt or shame he has to contend with after the Hulk has gone on the rampage. Is it any wonder the theme music at the end of the show was called The Lonely Man?

Every single Saturday night as the episode came to an end and the solitary piano kicked in, I would feel incredibly sad. I didn't really know why the show moved me to tears, but it did. Looking back, I think I was so moved because of this man's ongoing struggle to restrain the beast within himself. In some way, even though I was very young, I wonder if I recognised in the Hulk a monster that in later years I would come to know in myself.

Just as Banner transformed into The Hulk when he found himself under extreme emotional stress, I too started to experience flashes of overpowering rage inside me during my childhood. I was a mere boy of around nine or ten years old, but I already knew the utter significance of Banner's words, "Don't make me angry. You won't like me when I'm angry."

The first time I was overcome with rage happened in the school playground after a petty argument with a boy called Cliff. All of a sudden, I lost control and started punching him in the face over and over again. Later that year a second fight broke out after school between me and another boy my age. I lost control again and battered him senseless. During those two fights, I experienced for the first time what it must have been like for Dr Banner when he mutated into the Hulk. Rage ran through my veins and I didn't know how to control it.

If losing a testicle was one of the most traumatic moments on my personal collage of shaming memories, then what happened at the age of ten has to be a very close second. I was caught up in a confusing, terrifying situation involving one of our neighbours, who started out as a family friend but turned into a monster overnight. As a trusted family friend, she had sexually abused me, something I didn't speak to anyone about for thirteen years. I speak more about this in chapter fifteen. Suffice to say for now that when she switched, becoming like Kathy Bates's character in the movie *Misery*, I was terrified. Going to bed at night scared me to death. Walking down my driveway frightened me. She absolutely terrified me. What the gamma blast was to Dr Banner, this woman was to me.

This was the moment in my childhood when things started compounding as one thing after another took place. For a while, the Hulk lay dormant underground. When I was being taunted at secondary school, most of the time I gave that same pained smile that I had given at six years old, keeping the Hulk within me at arm's length. But once in a while throughout my teenage years, the Hulk would resurface as attack began to leak out of me. I would argue with my parents about how I looked or my unconventional hair and tatty clothes; I'd throw a little insult here and there at a fellow pupil; occasionally I picked on someone weedier than me.

I felt angry about my life, angry about what I was becoming as a result of the insults I experienced on an almost daily basis, and angry that I couldn't tell anyone what had happened with my neighbour. I succumbed to omertà, turning my anger inwards. By the age of 15, like many teenagers, I had discovered alcohol and often got drunk as a way of numbing out the pain and isolation that I was feeling inside. For the biggest part though, the Hulk remained subdued during my adolescence.

Luckless Fool

Meanwhile, I was having a huge struggle when it came to being in any kind of relationship with girls. I was extremely shy and scared shitless of getting it wrong, whatever that meant, and when it came to sex, I was terrified. The first girl I ever dated was called Lorna[4]. She was so cute. I would throw stones at her bedroom window to catch her attention while I was delivering the morning papers. It was like the balcony scene in Shakespeare's *Romeo and Juliet* only the scenery was a bit different because it took place somewhere on a beat up council estate in Lancashire—and our families weren't warring. But you get the point. Finally, we went out on a first date that turned out to be our last because I was too scared to kiss her. She dumped me, told all her friends what hadn't happened, and the word quickly spread around school that I was the boy who was too afraid to kiss a girl, resulting in further mockery. When it came to relationships I was like Norman Wisdom, the luckless fool who couldn't seem to stand up for falling down.

---

[4] Again, not her real name.

In the meantime, my mate Adam who sat next to me in art class frequently spent the span of time it took to sketch a still life of a Cox apple explicitly describing his daring sexual antics with his girlfriend. For this reason, I looked forward to art more than any other lesson. I was so turned on by the thought of shagging Adam's girlfriend that I would dash home and rampantly hump the androgynous corduroy bean bag in the bedroom. Luckily, Mum was so naïve that she was baffled by the stains and my little secret remained in one piece—that is until now. Sorry Mum.

All through school, I had a bizarre tendency to fancy the big mouthed unavailable girls, the ones who could reduce me to nothing in a second by calling me "one ball." I would gawp at the backs of their bare legs in class and fantasise about hitching their skirts up and shagging them face down over the classroom desk. But, what I struggled to make sense of was how I could fantasise over them while secretly hating them.

When I left school, my mixed up feelings towards women followed me and the only way I could find any sense of relief was by downing profuse amounts of alcohol. Throughout this time, I habitually visited planet oblivion.

Hulk Smash

Fast forward to the early nineties, when I met my first partner Jane.[5] By this point, I was in my early twenties and a competitive natural bodybuilder. Jane was a good looking girl with a face similar to the screen icon Audrey Hepburn. We started to date each other. Jane was my first real relationship and I was intent on

---

[5] As mentioned earlier, this isn't her real name, and I do have her permission to share about the relationship.

getting it right. I over-functioned by pretending I was the happy fella who had it all together, a good man like my dad, but in reality my life was nothing more than a sham. My vision of what it meant to be a man was severely impaired by the trauma and abuse I had encountered as a boy.

Meanwhile, Jane had her own history and her own understanding of what being in a relationship was supposed to be like. Let's just say it wasn't long before thing started to fall to pieces. Everything I had lived through—the abuse, the teasing, the panic attacks, the undiagnosed heart condition, trying to be like my dad, and the suppressing of my anger—when fused with my warped ideology of what it meant to be a man, inherited by a society as fucked up as I was, brought me to breaking point. Sadly, Jane became the catalytic agent that would finally tip me over the edge. The Hulk emerged with a vengeance.

What followed were 13 erratic years of two-way psychological and physical abuse. Some days I was the offender, and others the offended. We clashed, fought, and struggled day after day with little or no long-term relief.

In my moments of insanity, I unconsciously projected every single person who had ever hurt me onto Jane. The only way I knew how to deal with the torrent of shame that consumed me was to attack her. My Hulk-like outbursts grew in size and force. A push turned into a shove which evolved into pinning her down to the floor by her throat. One of my craziest moments occurred while I was driving; yet another meaningless argument had broken out between us, one of hundreds we had had over the years. In a moment of utter madness, I smashed my fist through the car windscreen, pressed my foot hard to the floor, and hurtled down a dark coastal lane at 100mph on the wrong side of the road before slamming on the breaks and skidding to a halt. In the next breath I found myself running hard in the darkness, confused, overwhelmed and ashamed by what I had just done, trying frantically to get away from myself. To add to the shame, it was a hired car. I had some explaining to do when I returned it.

During the last violent outburst I ever had, I picked up a bedside cabinet and threw it at her, just missing her head. The sight of her cowering childlike in the corner of the room was the last straw. Something in me snapped back to reality. What the hell had I been doing? We told our relationship counsellor what had happened. She said that if we came back with any more of these violent stories, she would have to notify the police. She saw the insanity of what we were doing to each other and told us that we didn't need help in staying together—we needed help breaking up, and shortly after that, we did. After that last incident, which was over a decade ago, I made a solemn promise to myself that I wouldn't be violent anymore. I still feel the Hulk within me and sometimes he feels dangerously close to the surface but I have never laid a finger on anyone since.

Looking back, of course there were some genuine moments of connection between Jane and myself. We moved from one continent to another and back again. We shared a love of nature and discovered *A Course in Miracles* together. We laughed and cried and made a lot of memories. Sadly though, for the biggest part I think we lost sight of each other. I will take full responsibility here and say that I lost sight of her. I wasn't really in relationship with her at all because I was constantly projecting people from my past onto her, blaming her for the hurt and pain I'd endured years before she ever came into my life. All the good stuff that happened eventually faded into the background as each thought, word and action became directed by a sickening shadow from our pasts, a veil of fear that covered the love between us. Even now after all these years, I find it difficult and shameful to talk about what happened. It seems surreal to admit that I could transform from being a sensitive kid into a violent man, but I did, and it is my responsibility to live with my mistakes and come to terms with it.

The Bigger the Rage, the Bigger the Pain

My experience of losing control and morphing into the Hulk isn't uncommon. It's happening for men everywhere, right now, men who come from all over the world and all walks of life. A bit like the members of Fight Club, these men are "the people you depend on to cook your meals, haul your trash, connect your calls and drive your ambulances." From the high flying executives to the stay-at-home dads, every man experiences anger, and every man has the potential for violence. Eventually, some men snap, like I did. We are often shocked when this happens but we shouldn't be because inside every man lurks a potential monster.

My hope is that in sharing some of my story with you, you will have a better understanding of the connection between shame and anger. We live in a world that is constantly separating the two: we talk about anger in the context of victim and perpetrator, oppressor and oppressed. But the uncomfortable truth is that they are two sides of the same coin. Guilt and shame breed attack, which breeds more guilt and shame. The bigger a man's rage, the bigger the pain he carries. It's a vicious cycle which can only produce more of itself. When enough individuals are caught up in this sick cycle, we have a war on our hands.

Break the Vow: Power Questions

1. Think back to a time when you were violent (or tempted to be) and get really honest: what was really going on for you underneath the urge to lash out?

2. If you sometimes still act out on your rage, it's time to draw a line in the sand. Write out a new code of conduct for yourself. Include your bottom line behaviour. Read it regularly until it becomes part of you, and get professional help if you need it. See Appendix II for an example you can adapt or use.

CHAPTER 7

WAR

"The male psyche is, first and foremost, a warrior psyche."
—Sam Keen

By the end of their first decade on the planet, most boys are heavily under the influence of the vow of male silence. As they become young men, they continue to be indoctrinated into a war mindset that goes on to torment them throughout their whole lives. Boys are given toy weapons (and nowadays violent computer games) to play with while girls are generally given dolls, taught to fight their way through life. "It's a dog eat dog world," we teach our children. "The competition out there is stiff," (even for primary school places) "so you'd better be the best." The war mindset attempts to make up for what omertà has taken away; we men have been stripped of our full humanity, denied the right to feel and express the bulk of our emotions, and the war mindset offers us a paltry exchange—the opportunity to become as violent as we wish. Our range of expression is restricted to the point where only overtly 'masculine' states of mind are tolerated such as being competitive, intensely focused or determined, primed to 'crush' any obstacles placed in front of us.

Sam Keen, author of *Fire In The Belly: On Being a Man* says that have been "culturally designed with conquest, killing, or dying in mind." Just look at any advertising campaign run by the armed forces and you'll see that men are the primary target for recruitment. We're not only told that real men can endure intense pain, but we're actively encouraged to do so. Keen writes that men are "conditioned to endure pain, to kill, and to die [...] specialists in the use of power and violence." We are conditioned into a war mindset that shows up everywhere we turn; there's the war against drugs, the war against cancer, the war against terrorism, the war against ageing, the war against sugar, the war against immigration and the war against fascism. We pick fights with our partners, battle with our bosses and compete with our neighbours. Our lives are often little more than a bloody battleground.

The war mindset offers men a sense of meaning and purpose in our touch-starved, lonely lives by offering us the opportunity to be elevated to warrior status, populating our lives with heroic battles and the chance to divide and conquer. However, in exchange for providing us with significance and purpose, this mindset requires that we subscribe to a fear-based ideology and live our lives at war instead of at peace. Being permanently primed for battle is hard, but it is still better than having to deal with the unbearable pain we feel inside as a result of the wounding that took place when we were young boys and the unrelenting pressure on us to be 'real men,' pain that we are ill-equipped to deal with.

For many men, the warrior's life is more than metaphorical; in 2015, 13,450 people (men and women) joined the armed forces in the UK. The US army had a goal of recruiting 62,000 new people in 2016. Joining the armed forces provides an escape route for men to swiftly exit the painful or difficult circumstances of their lives, giving them an opportunity to prove that they are strong, tough and manly while serving and protecting your country.

We are well aware by now that men in our society are expected to have the ability to resort to violence whenever necessary. Because the expression of so-called 'weak' emotions is prohibited, a man living in an omertà-bound society is only really allowed to express two emotions: pissed off or shut down, as Brené Brown called it. Men are expected to be rational thinkers instead of feeling beings. This makes us perfect candidates for war. In our society, going to war makes a sick kind of sense, so much so that in many countries, we have even given the state, in Sam Keen's words, "the power to interrupt the lives of young men, to draft them into the army, and to initiate them into the ritual of violence. The shaved head, the uniform, the abusive drill instructors, the physical and emotional ordeal of boot camp, are meant to destroy the individual's will and teach the dogface that the primary virtue of a man is not to think for himself but to obey his superiors, not to listen to his conscience but to follow orders." Joining the army deeply dissociates men from their hearts.

Of course, millions of men never go to war. However, like Major Marco and Sergeant Shaw in the movie *The Manchurian Candidate*, we have all at one time or another been exposed to, programmed with and indoctrinated in varying degrees into the war mindset, causing our minds to gravitate towards the kind of thinking that has, as Sam Keen puts it, shaped us into a "legitimate candidate for systematic slaughter—cannon fodder—culturally designed with conquest, killing, or dying in mind." Regardless of whether we ever fight for our country or not, we still live under the same destructive, aggressive thought system and live according to its operational principles. In our world, there's no getting away from it. All men are war wounded.

The Madness of the War Mindset

When researching this subject, I read that over 1.57 trillion US dollars are spent globally on military expenditure *every year*. In 2016, the US alone spent $622 billion on defence—a fraction of what was spent on education. It's horrifying to think that such a gigantic sum of money is being 'invested' in weapons, especially when people worldwide are dying of hunger. Today, there are roughly 14,900 nuclear warheads on the planet whose combined firepower could end life on earth. More than 90% of these are owned by Russia and the United States.

Politicians meanwhile are forever justifying their line of attack by insisting that offence is the best defence and that our safety and security will be compromised unless we immediately launch an aggressive military campaign against Evil Dictator X or Crazy Country Y, perpetuating the crazy cycle of offence and defence, which is essentially how most of us run our relationships, too. This is all done in the name of world peace and everybody nods blindly in agreement (or if they don't, their petitions are sent to Parliament where the paper they are written on is probably recycled to sketch out military operations). Let's face the hard facts: this whole thing has absolutely nothing to do with world peace, and everything to do with fear, power, control and personal gain for those involved—politicians, the arms industry and the mass media to name a few.

Often, we actively participate in perpetuating war, sometimes even supplying weapons to the same countries we send our boys away to fight in. In early 2017 avaaz.org published a petition that cited that Britain has sold over £3 billion of arms to Saudi Arabia which have been used to drop British made bombs from British made planes, making Britain actively complicit in a tragedy in which thousands of people starved to death. Although in this case there weren't necessarily British troops on the ground, there often are. That is the insanity of the war mindset: killing the same people it claims it is trying to protect, and then honouring the brave by draping a flag over their coffin and giving them an official military send off, complete with salutes, firing shots and drumming, all the while recruiting the next batch of men to voluntarily risk their lives.

Please don't misunderstand me here. My intention is not to attack any individual person. I'm certainly not judging anyone who is involved in any of the armed forces. I have the utmost respect for the courage, discipline and sacrifices of our service men and women. I also recognise that it would be bloody daft for a country to just abandon its military defence strategy given how deeply entrenched the whole world is in the war mindset. What I want to emphasise is how senseless the whole thing is in the first place. What is playing out on our global stage is no different to the crazy way omertà plays out in our own lives. When we fundamentally believe that unless we defend ourselves in this world, we are going to be attacked, then of course we are going to attack others, perpetuating the war mindset without taking any real responsibility for our part in it. The thought system that fuels war in the first place is sick, damaging and deluded. The surprising thing is that we do not continuously place the entire mindset under strict scrutiny.

The insanity of the war mindset is that it is completely self-destructive. It tears families, communities, cities and countries apart, all in the name of being right. Look at any war and you'll see this play out. I studied the First World War in researching this book and was devastated by what I learned.

Two Years in the Making, Ten Minutes in the Destroying

In 1914, recruitment numbers for the armed forces had started to dwindle across Britain, so the government devised a plan: the Pals Battalion. It was thought that men would be more eager to serve their country if they were able to hang out and fight the good fight with people they already knew. That's how The Pals Battalion was born. Recruitment offices all over the country were flooded with thousands of men from all walks of life eager to do their fair share for kingdom and country alongside their friends and family members (and perhaps to avoid being shunned and shamed if they didn't).

Through use of propaganda in the form of pro-war posters and dodgy tales of German atrocities against Belgium, men agreed to patriotically stand together on the front line and fight—brothers, friends, cousins and workmates all signed up. One anonymous solider reported, "We were boys, and war was seen as a kind of super sport. War was an extension of sport, manliness and bravery." It seems that men living one hundred years ago also defined masculinity in the same way as we do now.

The British government conveniently chose to turn a blind eye to the brutalities of war, censoring battle pictures in newspapers, magazines and cinema reels. They showed substitute images of smiley, upbeat soldiers hanging out in squeaky clean trenches, keen to go over the top for king and country. Signing up with your mates probably looked like a bit of a laugh.

Many of these men came from industrial towns and the army seemed like a once-in-a-lifetime opportunity, a welcome break from the hardships and boredom of everyday living. For thousands of men, life in the army meant proper meals, decent clothing, regular pay and a chance to travel the world. They were even told that the war would be over by Christmas. Unfortunately, these young men didn't have the faintest idea what they were getting themselves into. This hi-de-hi holiday camp lifestyle promised by the British government crumbled away to reveal the unbearable hardship of war. Men found themselves beaten by relentless rain and enemy shell fire, shrinking in murky shell holes, made to wear the same stinking waterlogged uniforms day after day, forced to eat fly infested rations or to starve.

As Christmas came and went with very little peace and joy and the death toll started to rise, enthusiasm to sign up began to wane. Young men had grown wise to the horrors of the Front and were unwilling to sacrifice their lives for the cause. The Government then introduced conscription in January 1916, forcing young men to be initiated into the ritual of violence. This meant that men who were initially rejected at the start of the war because they were considered unfit to fight would now be forced over the top, alongside those young men who were absolutely terrified of fighting on the frontline.

On 1st July 1916, two years after the Pals had commenced training, the anticipation of 'doing the right thing' dissipated as they found themselves transported in the dead of night across a tumultuous ocean to their fate. The reality of what they were expected to be had become inescapable: they were no longer individuals but agents of violence who were required to sacrifice themselves for the so-called greater good under the direction of pen pushers who would never leave their cosy offices to fight even five minutes on a real battlefield.

For many, the Battle of the Somme would be their first battle and their last. They were ordered by their commanders to walk in formation towards the enemy. In a single day 20,000 men were slaughtered and 40,000 injured. The men who had been falsely lured into doing the right thing very quickly learned the gut-wrenching reality of war as they watched their families and friends get blown to pieces right before their eyes. It was an unwinnable situation.

The cost of this military mishap was huge. Communities were literally torn apart. The Pals Battalions incurred massive losses: for example, from the battalion recruited from the small industrial town of Accrington in Lancashire, just up the road from where I was born, 720 Pals went to war and 585 were killed, wounded or missing in action. With a population of just 45,000 people, the impact on the town of Accrington was devastating. Percy Holmes, whose brother went to war with the Pals, recalled: "I remember when the news came through to Accrington that the Pals had been wiped out. I don't think there was a street in Accrington and district that didn't have their blinds drawn, and the bell at Christ Church tolled all the day." Few homes remained untouched. An epidemic of grief swamped the country. As another Pal said, "Two years in the making, ten minutes in the destroying. That was our history." That is the war mindset in action.

Shellshocked

Even the men who came back never really came back. Their minds were imprinted with the stomach-turning sights, sounds and smells of the battlefield, the space between the opposing trenches that was no man's land. It was the place that men feared the most: a bleak wasteland, where death pelted down from a smouldering sky, viciously ripping apart its prey like a rabid pack of hunting dogs. The few men who were left writhing in bloody agony were quickly put out of their misery, shot in the back of the head by a fellow soldier and left to rot face down in the mud.

Those who survived were left so deeply scarred by the inconceivable horror they saw on the front line that they started to lose all sense of certainty. Their brains became like scrambled eggs. Initially, the army was blinkered when it came to understanding the influence of shell shock. Men were even tried for cowardice and shot. But as the number of brain-rattled soldiers intensified, doctors started to accept shell shock as an ailment of war. However, this didn't stop people from snubbing the jangled servicemen as they arrived back home. Many onlookers hung their heads in shame, a far cry from the standing ovations the soldiers had received as they left to fight the good fight. By the end of World War I, some 80,000 men had been treated for shell shock. This number doesn't even include those men whose internal wires had become so mixed up that they committed suicide in the twenty years that followed.

In preparation to play the role of Irish Guard Michael Bowe in the play *My Boy Jack* in 2012, I interviewed a veteran who fought for the British army in the Gulf War and experienced shell shock (known by that point as combat stress) firsthand. He likened shell shock to a coiled spring as he described his agonising, unending struggle to keep it at arm's length. He went on to describe the single, harrowing image that repeatedly tipped him over the edge: a mutilated woman whose body had been dumped in a wheelie bin. As he spoke his eyes widened with panic, filling with tears as if she were right in front of him. I was overwhelmed with emotion as I saw this man's battle to come to terms with the aftermath of war, years and years after it had happened.

The veteran I interviewed was just one of thousands upon thousands of men who have been impacted by the war mindset. As I continued to do research in order to do justice to the part of Bowe, I found myself delving deep into harrowing footage of men who had suffered shell shock during the 'Great' War and felt distressed by what I saw: everything from violent fits of shaking to fear of sleeping, from very distressing facial tics and stuttering to uncontrollable emotional outbursts. I wanted to honour the experience of our war veterans by getting under Bowe's skin and depicting shell shock as realistically as I could. As ridiculous as it sometimes looked, shell shock was shameful, dehumanising, crippling and soul-destroying. During show week, I noticed myself becoming increasingly disturbed. Knowing how important it is to express rather than repress emotion, I gave myself full permission to step onstage and feel Bowe's pain—all of it. On the final night of the play I sat by the side of the stage sobbing uncontrollably, intensely moved by Bowe's lost ability to connect with another human being. The Bowe who had gone to war was gone, stripped bare and left for dead on the frontline. The man who was left was but a shadow of his former self.

Shell shock, nowadays known as combat stress, leaves men deeply scarred, psychologically damaged, incapable of feeling real love, and subsequently inaccessible to the people in their everyday lives. This hostile place is the loneliest on earth, where ghostlike men from all walks of life wander in a metaphorical and endless No Man's Land.

Missing, Traumatised or Dead: Above All, Stay Silent

Things are not that much better today than they were back in the era of the First World War. Right now, regardless of when you're reading this, wars are taking place all over the world and the underhand use of propaganda continues to impact people's attitudes towards war, desensitising us to it on the one hand and glorifying it on the other. We barely bat an eyelid at marketing campaigns that tap into men's deeply rooted beliefs that they are inadequate, encouraging them to sign up to the army, the navy or the air force with the promise that they will get the chance to prove that they can 'Be The Best' or to experience so called 'belonging.' When my wife and I recently saw the latest army advertising campaign, we literally thought it was a fundraising plea from Help the Heroes to donate to ex-soldiers suffering from PTSD. It was in fact a campaign designed to sign young men up to the army, with the slogan, "This is belonging."

Young people who sign up for the armed forces are offered a once-in-a-lifetime opportunity to experience acceptance, inclusion, belonging and significance. It's no secret that the armed forces recruitment policy targets deprived areas and low-income families, boys and young men who may never have experienced the kind of social inclusion, acceptance and sense of community that signing up supposedly offers.

In one advert, we see a young man narrate his childhood and life up to the point where he signs up, after which things go from ultra boring (pulling pints in the local old man's pub) to edgy and exciting (flying in helicopters, travelling the world, developing into a strong man). Let's just ignore the fact that many of these men put their lives at risk in order to experience this kind of life, shall we? The Chief Creative Officer at Karmarama, the company responsible for coming up with the This Is Belonging advertising campaign, stated in an interview, "We decided to highlight real and authentic army contexts and moments that clearly show the importance of being part of a strong and selfless family that accepts you for you, and gives you the chance to work together for a meaningful purpose." In one of the other adverts in the campaign, the comrades bask in the sun, hanging out jovially as they lean against the wall of a bombed building. But the belonging comes from occupying other territories, from violence and from war. The "meaningful purpose" the CCO speaks of comes from attacking and possibly killing other human beings. What's meaningful or purposeful about that? In my opinion, any advertising campaign that equates the horrors of war with being the best or with belonging is a sad and insulting misrepresentation of what being a real man (and indeed a human) is about.

The author of the article citing the Karmarama quote also stated that "the Department of Education ignores the UN's recommendations that some form of peace education should be part of the curriculum in UK state schools, and supports initiatives encouraging a military ethos. According to ForcesWatch report, the armed forces recorded 1,783 visits to 377 Scottish education institutions. 1,455 visits were to 303 Scottish state secondary schools, of which 42% were made by the Army, 31% by the Navy and 27% by the RAF during the academic years of 2010-11 and

2011-12. This equates to an average of two visits per year for every state secondary school in Scotland."

We hear stories every day of soldiers missing or killed in action, and yet we still romance with the idea of war. We decorate our men with medals for bravery but silently expect them to keep their mouths shut when they come home. We idolise and elevate our soldiers to celebrity status, but when they end up living on the streets, debilitated by PTSD or taking their own lives (22.2% of suicides in the USA in 2016 were by veterans), we walk on by and pretend they don't exist. While they battle war-induced alcoholism and drug addiction, we sign up for army-style boot camps in droves. We even actively encourage our children to join Army Cadets and get indoctrinated into this distorted way of thinking, telling ourselves it will give them the much needed discipline that will serve them well as they make the transition into manhood.

However, the differences between the romanticism of signing up for basic army training and actually going to war are enormous. Suddenly the boot camp is over and you find yourself unceremoniously dumped into a life-threatening situation where death lurks around every corner. During your time devoted to 'securing peace,' there's every chance you're going to see some 'action'—bodies being blown apart mere feet away from you. You can't complain about this, because you willingly signed up to be a killer. And yet, when the moment finally comes around, the moment when you are faced with having to kill another brother in cold blood for the first time, no amount of army training and rubber bullets can prepare you. The soldier may have been drilled to believe that the person standing in front of him is part of a separate species, but given that we all share the same planet and breathe the same air it's difficult to completely buy into. This 'enemy,' like the solider himself, is a man made of flesh and blood, with a family, a history and a heart. And when a man takes another man's life for the first time, regardless of the reason, he is forever changed.

Break the Vow: Power Questions

1. Who are you at war with in your mind?
2. Given that every man is indoctrinated into the war mindset, how have you been affected by it?

CHAPTER 8

EGO RUN RIOT

"The 'normal' state of mind of most human beings contains a strong element of what we might call dysfunction or even madness."
—Eckhart Tolle

The vow of male silence is responsible for keeping men in a huge amount of pain, disconnecting and isolating us, denying us the right to embrace the feminine within us or to the full range of human emotions and demanding that we conform to a toxic code of conduct that is ultimately self-destructive. We've explored the impact this has on a man's individual psyche in some depth so far, to the point of identifying how the vow of silence contributes to perpetuating the war mindset that is so prevalent in today's society. There are other drastic societal consequences to the vow of male silence though, and in this chapter I am calling them out. A word of warning here: of all the chapters in this book, this is likely the one that you will be most irritated by, the one you'll find the most unreasonable. It's also possibly the one that is closest to the bone. As I said at the very beginning of the book, keep reading like your life depends on it. That is the urgency with which I am delivering this message.

The Ego-lution of Man

We have reached a point in our so-called evolution (perhaps it should be called 'ego-lution') where violence, abuse, corruption, discrimination, terrorism, tyranny, fear and war are so normalised that they are seen as seemingly inevitable aspects of human society. Alongside this, despite being the wealthiest, most privileged society in human history, we in the west are without doubt also the most addicted, depressed, suicidal, numbed out, medicated, indebted and fucked up society in history, too. We spend our days eagerly doped up on caffeine, sugar, social media, fast food, alcohol, nicotine, gambling, consumerism and porn, giving our power away, numbing our pain or dumping it outside of ourselves, complaining about the very society that we play a part in continuously co-creating and expecting someone else to come along and clean it all up.

There is a growing awareness in the western world that the patriarchal mindset has screwed us over big time. Within it, we have been obsessed with progress, growth, profit, dominance, conquest and power regardless of the cost—and the cost has been huge. Under omertà, as men's pain has been driven underground, we have become the drivers of an imbalanced patriarchal system that has abused, tortured, oppressed and repressed women, children, minority groups, animals, the planet and other men. Our financial institutions and governments are awash with the 'Old Boys Club' mentality, permitting men to be the biggest perpetrators of all acts of violence against others. We are awash with contradictions: we buy clothes made in sweat shops while tutting at pictures of children working for a dollar a day and gasp in horror at the mistreatment of animals while happily tucking into steaks, hamburgers and pork chops—and we think of this as normal. You might be reading this and thinking, "This guy is so over the top," but I don't think it's an exaggeration to say that what we accept as 'normal' and even 'healthy' in our society is often a state of madness, deep disconnection and chronic self-destruction. I don't think it's an exaggeration to say that we are all contributing to keeping it going, one sick choice at a time. All except you, of course.

In his bestselling book *A New Earth*, Eckhart Tolle describes ego as "the current state of humanity." Hardly a compliment. We are collectively dysfunctional. We've given the ego permission to run our lives, our political systems, our financial systems, our relationships and our world. Tolle states that we have essentially handed the reins of our lives over to a megalomaniac that is obsessed with power, control and separateness. If we are honest, we only need to glimpse at the state of our lives and our world to see that ego is running riot and getting away with it. This has everything to do with omertà—the vow of male silence keeps the status quo in place and prevents any real revolution from happening. There is so much corruption, so many elephants in the room that no matter how many times we break the vow, there's always more, and yet to do nothing is no longer an option either.

We are in a state of major denial. We are all loyal to different degrees to the very same thought system that the psychos of this world indulge in. None of us want to acknowledge this. It's distasteful to admit that we have a part to play. Instead, you most likely do what we all do—point the finger out at the world, or turn a blind eye and carry on like everything is okay while murder, corruption and hypocrisy stare you in the face, or perhaps sign a few petitions and sigh in despair at the state of the world. To top it all off, you may even normalise the way things are by calling statements such as this melodramatic or over the top. This isn't melodramatic though. Humanity has many redeeming qualities but we have to admit that thanks to our presence on the planet, things are pretty fucked up.

Poison is Poison

Part of how we keep our collective denial in place is by condoning certain kinds of behaviour in our own lives whilst condemning the more extreme versions of the same behaviour in others'. It's one rule for us and another rule for the rest of the world. How convenient; this means we can continue to attack, blame and be violent in our own lives to whatever degree we allow ourselves to be these things, justifying our behaviour as insignificant when compared to those bastards on the news. You should know by now that there's no such thing as a little bit of attack. Poison is poison.

In the same way, there's no such thing as a little bit of dishonesty, corruption, hatred, or fear. *A Course in Miracles* states, "What is not love is murder." This is a non-negotiable universal truth. Once you fully understand this, you won't be able to get away with as much as you could before. That, bro, is the inevitable effect that comes with breaking the vow of male silence. As you wake up out of the victim consciousness that is part and parcel of omertà, you realise that no one is coming to rescue you. Like an addict, the first step if you are to stand any chance of recovery is to come clean and admit that you urgently need help. If you want to have a different kind of society, you have to be the change.

You might be outraged reading this. That is a good sign: it probably means I've touched a raw nerve. Keep in mind that only the ego can be offended. I don't write these words from a place of superiority or holier-than-thou-ness—that would be really bloody daft given my chequered past—but I do write them with a lot of willingness to take full responsibility for how the ego runs riot in my own life. That is what qualifies me to write these words.

The Socially Acceptable Forms of Murder

Let's take a closer look at some of the specific ways that we all contribute to allowing the ego to run riot. This is not to make you feel guiltier than you already do, but simply to help you wake up and become more accountable. It's easy to point the finger and say that everyone else is making you live under the vow of male silence. It's very different to fully acknowledge your own part in things.

1. Arrogance

Given that the ego is only ever interested in self-preservation, it would be fair to say that all of us who inhabit a body have the capacity for arrogance. Men in particular are very good at it. Human beings appear to have an insatiable desire to be right about everything, even when it's blatantly obvious we are wrong. It's insane to want to be right instead of being happy, and yet we do.

2. Selfishness

We all share one planet but the ego convinces us otherwise. We are so hell-bent on defining our sense of individuality that we often fail to see beyond our own selfish needs. We withhold our love, approval and generosity, speak our minds with no heart, hurt others to meet our own selfish needs, spend our way into bankruptcy and idolise people who are doing little if anything to genuinely contribute something meaningful to humanity.

It's every man for himself on car parks, in supermarket queues, in Black Friday sales and in relationships. We don't even know how to give a bloody gift without making it conditional and about our own self-worth. Add the narcissistic selfie culture into the mix and we have a "Me-me-me, that's enough about me, what do you think about me?" ticking time bomb on our hands.

3. Judgement

Let's face it: judgement is rampant in the human species. We judge everything from our parents to our spouses to our co-workers to the neighbour's cat to the weather to celebrities to politicians without ever once stopping to question our motives or the real consequences it creates. Judgment tears families apart, ruins friendships, splits nations in half and breeds war.

We are all directly or indirectly affected by judgement just as we are all affected by cancer. I lost my dad to cancer and it affected me deeply. Witnessing Dad's struggle with cancer confirmed to me that when the disease takes hold, it can obliterate a person's life. Judgement is no different. Like terminal cancer, judgement destroys the home that it has taken up residence in. Imagine moving into your ideal home and then going out of your way to trash it.

In *The Way Of The Heart*, author Jayem reminds us that judgement is not something to be taken lightly. He says, "Judgement causes the very cellular structure [of the body] to break down. If you could see this, you would never judge again. When you judge even the cells of your body go crazy. They vibrate in a completely dissonant way. There is a contraction. The fluids do not move through the cells. The nutrients do not become transported or delivered to the cells. The waste matter is not processed properly. Everything gets clogged up, and there is dis-ease." Whether this is scientifically accurate or not, you can't deny that judgement and peace are not exactly best mates. As powerful and superior as judgement makes you feel in the short term, it leaves you feeling hollow and deeply disconnected in the long run.

4. Aggression and Violence

These days violence is pretty much considered normal, especially for men. Men have a very intimate relationship with violence, one that we pass onto our boys from a young age. As I mentioned in chapter seven, we expect boys to play fight and we give them access to toy guns and violent computer games, subtly allowing them to be indoctrinated into the war mindset as we once were. We collectively endorse activities that encourage attack thoughts and allow these thoughts to be taken to the extreme. When it comes to aggression, which is really another form of attack, each of us has made a pact with the ego to permit a certain level of aggression in ourselves and our lives. For men in particular aggression is tolerated, maybe even socially acceptable, depending on an individual's frame of reference. My neighbour, for example, always works things out with his fists. In his world, aggression and violence are normal.

Just like the Daleks in the sci-fi series *Doctor Who*, we will happily exterminate anyone or anything that gets in our way.

Aggression and violence are part of the ego's munitions. Left unchecked, aggression and violence have the capacity to ruin marriages, damage friendships, destroy families, start wars, and tear entire nations apart.

The parameters are different for each of us. Most of us love indulging in being entertained by a bit of aggression and violence, and Hollywood loves to cash in on it: think *Kill Bill*, *Sin City*, *Reservoir Dogs*, *Scarface*, *Kick-Ass* and of course *Fight Club*, to name just a few movies that expose the viewer to extreme violence in a heavily normalised way.

Until recently, my personal boundaries with aggression stopped at a little bit of road rage towards inconsiderate motorists—and yes, I'm well aware that there is no such thing as a 'little bit' of rage. Given my violent past, I am very clear of where I stand in relation to violence. I won't go there. There is too much at stake. Yet I knew that the next crucial piece of the jigsaw for me was to take responsibility for my thoughts whilst out on the roads. Thankfully since writing this things have changed for me in this area. The path gets narrower as we continue to wake up.

Progressive, Incurable and Fatal

In twelve step fellowships, the force of addiction is described as being progressive, incurable and fatal. Very rarely does an addict start out on a crack pipe, and in the beginning, everyone convinces themselves they are in control. Over time (not overnight), the addict becomes unrecognisable even to themselves and unless they admit defeat, addiction will happily leave them dead in the gutter.

The ego's lunacy is also progressive. If the ego was a controlled drug, it would most definitely be Class A. Over time—often over a number of years—we get more and more entangled in its web of lies, becoming more out of integrity as we do so. For example, the porn you watch gradually gets more extreme or closer to the edge of what you think is acceptable. One pint turns into two, then before you know it, you're knocking back five a night. You find yourself gambling more and more money on the horses, or pushing the limits a bit further during an argument with your partner. There's no doubt about it—when these things are happening, the ego has you firmly in its grip. Play with the ego and you play with fire. Usually the denial is so insidious that you won't even realise how far you've fallen until you've violated your own integrity.

Allow me to elaborate. Mix sport with aggression, add in the vow of male silence, serve with a large shot of ego-infused alcohol and a dash of racism and you get something explosive. Take football hooliganism: in the beginning you might just swear jokingly a couple of times at the referee. Then one day, after a hectic and stressful week at work and a fight at home, you find yourself taunting a player on the opposing team—especially if he's foreign. It feels good. So the following week, you do it again, but this time you scream at the ref that he's a C-U-Next-Tuesday. That feels *really* good, somewhat primal. Before long, you're eagerly watching every game though the eyes of a wild animal, with a head full of aggressive thoughts. The day might even come when you go one step further, crossing the line and becoming violent. This might sound extreme and perhaps you've never pushed it that far, but many men have and many more will continue to do so. I once knew a guy who battered someone senseless at an England football match. When he discovered he had made front page news the following morning, he was full of fucked up pride. He actually beat the living daylights out of another brother over a game of football and felt like more of a man because of it, and then threatened me for challenging him about it.

The good news is that while loyalty to the ego is definitely progressive and can be fatal, it isn't incurable. In order for things to change, however, change is required from *you*. You have to become brutally honest about the ways in which you have been hypocritical and out of integrity. Integrity is vital for men. Whenever we are out of integrity, we unconsciously feed guilt and shame—and we are out of integrity anytime we do anything that offers us an easy way out.

Everyday Unconsciousness

As I wrote earlier, *ACIM* teaches that what is not love is murder. Let's take a sober moment to consider this idea; that would mean that the 'normal' behaviour listed above—arrogance, selfishness, aggression and judgement—drip feeds into the same unconsciousness that the evil dictators, serial killers and psychos function within. You may never cross the line that separates you from the homicidal maniacs, fascists or sex offenders, but you might find yourself edging dangerously close to it, in your thoughts and words if not your deeds. In *Illuminata*, Marianne Williamson states, "The source of violence is in our heads. As it would not be appropriate to ignore 'just a little' cancer in the body, so it is not appropriate for us to ignore 'just a little' violent thinking." We have collectively convinced ourselves that because we're not out there killing people, we can get away with killing them on a screen instead.

Video Games and Violence

I knew almost nothing about violent computer games until I started researching them for this book. I was shocked to learn that some of the best-selling games on the market are virtual training grounds in stabbing, shooting, decapitating, beating and maiming other people. In at least one game, you can even split your opponent open with a chainsaw by simulating the physical movements you would have do to hack someone open in the real world. Characters in these games are programmed to seek out the most sadistic methods possible for murdering their victims.

One article I read described how in the digital world, "There are no legal and ethical considerations. When things go wrong, when innocent people are killed, there are no ramifications. If anything, the games warp these real-world consequences in the minds of players." There are no consequences to the players' actions, there is no sense of connectedness to other people, no grief, no remorse, no creative self-expression, no honesty, no integrity, no depth and no sensitivity (just like the "Hard Man" archetype we looked at in chapter two)—and all over the world, millions of children and adults spend hours a day engrossed in these virtual worlds.

Just a Bit of Harmless Fun?

These games are often depicted as 'fun,' 'beneficial' and 'educational.' Researchers and gamers alike regularly cite improved cognitive functioning, hand-eye coordination, accuracy and even teamwork as just some of the positive effects of violent video games. They fail to mention the negative effects of gaming, which include social isolation, addiction and the potential for increased aggression (even in people without a predisposition to mental illness). It shocks me to think that the methods employed in violent first-person shooter games—games which have increasingly lifelike graphics—are not really that different from the methods used by real life mass murderers. It shocks me even more that this is seen as a just a bit of harmless fun.

Some studies have shown strong connections between gaming and heightened aggression in boys. A study in 2012 conducted by psychologists Brock Bastian, Jolanda Jetten and Helena R.M. Radke using brain scans demonstrated that playing violent video games "had the potential to desensitize players to real-life violence and the suffering of others." Research from Ohio State University concluded that, "People who have a steady diet of playing these violent video games may come to see the world as a hostile and violent place." Brad Bushman, who conducted the research at OSU, said, "Playing video games could be compared to smoking cigarettes. A single cigarette won't cause lung cancer, but smoking over weeks or months or years greatly increases the risk. In the same way, repeated exposure to violent video games may have a cumulative effect on aggression."

The statistics for how much violence an average boy is exposed to are equally disturbing. The average 18-year-old has seen 200,000 acts of violence depicted in the media and entertainment, including 40,000 murders. Just comprehend that for a moment: witnessing one murder is enough to trigger a trauma response in a person. What is the cumulative effect of forty *thousand*? In addition, according to researchers Gentile and Anderson, even a limited amount of time playing a violent computer game can "prime aggressive thoughts" in a player, making them less sensitive, more aggressive and more afraid. In another study conducted in 2005, violent computer game exposure was linked to reducing P300 amplitudes in the brain, which again are associated with de-sensitisation to violence and increased aggression. In addition to this, if a player wants to get on the leaderboard and stay there, he needs to practise—a lot. Practising a lot means repetition, which, as Anthony Robbins explains in his bestselling book *Awaken the Giant Within*, creates strong neural pathways, conditioning someone's brain to operate in a certain way: "With enough repetitions and emotional intensity, we can add many strands [to a neural pathway] simultaneously, increasing the tensile strength of this emotional or behavioural pattern." We can therefore guess that the more someone plays, the more aggressive they might become. Eventually the neural connections can become so strong that a person's behaviour, desires and emotional reactions become automatic. Add trauma, unresolved psychological pain, a hulk-load of anger and the predisposition to mental illness to the mix, and you have a recipe for disaster.

Despite all of the above, violent video games are perfectly legal and readily available at the click of a button, and they are extremely popular. The global games market is destined to reach $108 billion in 2017. Obviously not all of these are violent games, but it's no accident that the *Call of Duty* franchise, which is renowned for its violence, sold almost 229 million copies to date by January 2017.

Despite some fairly shocking statistics (for example, 90% of games for children aged 10+ contain violence, 99% of boys play video games, and 31% of males say they feel addicted to video games), as quickly as any concerns are raised, we dismiss those concerns as being overly conservative, prudish and irrational, justifying their place in our society. People argue that it isn't violent video games that lead to violent behaviour including the much-debated mass killings (which are often associated with violent video games), but mental illness, which is a fair point. If somebody lacks empathy, the games certainly provide an arena where that lack of empathy can play itself out.

However, imagine if there was a first-person violent video game simply called "Rape," where the player simulates raping women in a variety of settings. There would be outrage. But if what the defenders of violent video games are saying is true—that these games don't affect people's minds, merely offering them a bit of harmless escapism and fantasy; if the only people who would be affected negatively by these games are people who already have mental illnesses, then what would the big deal be about a game called "Rape"? I mean, why hasn't it hit the shelves already? Could it possibly be because it would violate our moral integrity? Could it be because we know on some level that what we expose ourselves to affects us? We know that rape is wrong, so wrong that we can't and won't justify building a video game around it, yet we don't think twice about creating games that feature extreme violence. If anything, this highlights how ingrained and normalised violence has become in our minds. Rather disturbingly, there are multiple accounts of gamers hacking the code in certain violent video games enabling them to sexually violate other players. These hacks are illegal but nevertheless the games were built to allow the code to be altered in this way, permitting gamers to indulge in the darkest, sickest parts of their mind.

In researching this topic, I also read a lot of really positive accounts of how violent video games had helped people—especially young men struggling, for example, with loneliness or depression.

But I don't think the end justifies the means. Violence is violence, regardless of the form it takes, and no amount of research can make that into something it isn't. Our society condones violence but we don't want to admit our individual part in it. When it comes to war and peace we want it both ways. On the one hand we claim that we want world peace and yet on the other we are playing violent first person shooter games that mimic killing humans.

So what is the appeal of these violent games to your average boy or man? Why would someone want to shoot, decapitate, beat, rape or murder anyone, even in a virtual (yet scarily lifelike) world? Moreover, how did we create a culture that willingly legalises people indulging in such sick, violent fantasies? How come we created these games in the first place? In a world already spilling over with violence these games can hardly be justified as being 'beneficial' or 'educational.' This desire to be mercilessly violent gives us some indication of the kind of sick mindset we're collectively functioning within. That these games are legal shows us how blind we are to this mindset (or how reluctant we are to challenge it).

From Top Shelf to Smartphone Screen

Another huge blind spot that we refuse to talk about is the impact of pornography. Unless you've been living under a rock, you will know that the porn industry generates billions of dollars of revenue every year, and that even though more women are using porn than ever before, the majority of consumers are male. It's hardly a secret that men like and use porn, yet it's still a bit of an elephant in the room; everyone knows the elephant is there, but it's often joked about or glossed over rather than openly talked about.

The internet has obviously had a huge influence on how readily available pornography is nowadays; whereas back in the 80s and even the 90s, you could only really get access to porn via a dusty top shelf in the local newsagents or in a blue movie, it's a very different story today, with many disturbing accounts of children under the age of ten being regularly exposed to pornography via smartphones in the school playground. Not only is porn easily accessible nowadays, but it is free and the volume of material is overwhelming.

Hyper-Sexualised

Our society has become increasingly sexualised in the last few decades. When I returned from Canada all the way back in the mid-nineties, I really noticed the cultural shift that was happening with the arrival of pop groups like the Spice Girls, heralding the beginning of "girl power," encouraging young girls to dress like sexually available and mature women. In 2007, two major UK retailers were condemned for selling pole dancing kits and lingerie targeted at girls as young as seven. Advertising is saturated with alluring images and our social media feeds are bursting with sexualised selfies, girls with blow job pouts and come to bed eyes who present themselves as sexually developed, mature and available but who, if you looked beyond the suggestive pose and pout, are often naive, immature young women on the cusp of adulthood. It's easy to blame the media for the sexualisation of *everything*, but we have a huge part to play in perpetuating the culture.

Nowadays, anyone can be an object of sexual desire thanks to social media and in particular Instagram and Snapchat. Post a provocative photo and you'll get dozens, hundreds or even thousands of followers, likes and comments. (In comparison, when launching *Odd Man Out*, Ell and I put daily posts out on social media drawing attention to male depression, suicide and the vow of male silence and we would consider it a victory if we got 30 likes. If we posted anything raising awareness about hardcore porn, people actively unfollowed us. I wonder why.)

It's no accident that in this hyper-sexualised culture, the porn industry is booming. Porn offers an escape after a hard day at work and a quick fix from the stresses and strains of real (and often difficult) relationships. While he's in front of a screen or a dirty magazine, a man can't get it wrong. If he climaxes quickly, it doesn't matter. If he gets bored, he can switch videos or turn the page without offending anyone. He can go after a woman who he fears wouldn't look twice at him in real life without risking rejection. There is no threat of criticism and there is nothing to prove. There's no dealing with your partner's insecurities because there are none on display; the porn actresses are self-assured and up for it. Nowhere in a porn film is there an awkward conversation about what's appropriate or inappropriate, or whether she's enjoying herself; she says "ooh" and "yes" to absolutely everything. As one young man reported in a survey on porn said, "She isn't thrown around but the man moves her around like a doll and she wordlessly complies. She seems to enjoy it a lot... or does a better job than most of pretending." Maybe the better she is at pretending, the more successful she'll be in her career as a porn actress.

In addition, there's no need to make eye contact. There are no arms and legs all over the place like a giant, clunky game of

Twister. For many men 'Real Sex' carries a fear of being seen as a disappointment or, God forbid, as weak. In front of the screen, you're safe, you're in control and you're powerful.

Consciously Unconscious

I think it's safe to say that when it comes to porn, the majority of men who use it do so unconsciously. We don't want to admit that we mostly use it as an escape route, that we often watch it in secret and that we turn to it to relieve anxiety or escape from our lives for a few minutes (or, for some men, hours). We don't want to admit that we've been out of integrity when watching porn; it's shameful to think about the times when we've found ourselves getting off on barely legal porn, or wanking to hardcore, aggressive, degrading material. But unless you are extremely aware and selective in your choices, at some point you will have encountered porn that pushed the boundaries of what you think is acceptable.

While I know there are exceptions to the rule and that there is a small but growing movement of ethical, respectful, feminist porn and erotica, I seriously doubt that the majority of the 92 billion videos watched on Pornhub in 2016 were watched responsibly or with much consideration for the people involved. When I used to watch porn, I didn't give a shit about whether what I was watching was responsible; I was concerned with getting *my* fix.

When it comes to porn, we convince ourselves that different rules apply than they do in the everyday world. We close our minds to the fact that the 'women' in the videos are often young girls, and, like Kevin Spacey's character in *American Beauty*, we turn these girls (who are often the same age as our daughters) into sex objects for our own consumption and objectification. In 2015, the most searched for term on Pornhub was the word "teen"; in 2016, it remained in the top three. The average age of a Pornhub visitor was 35—old enough to be a teenager's dad. Imagine scrolling through your preferred porn site one day and stumbling across a video of your daughter. Unpleasant, isn't it? And yet every barely legal porn actress is somebody's daughter, and the uncomfortable truth is that most of these young women are participating in the industry without fully understanding the impact it is going to have on their lives. Barely legal porn is damaging, both to your sense of integrity as a man and to the people involved. Maybe we should rename barely legal porn "straight out of paedophila."

Then there's the issue of sex trafficking. We don't want to hear that human trafficking, of which sex trafficking is a huge part, is the fastest growing criminal industry on the planet, and that 80% of the people trafficked are women or girls, many of whom are sold as slaves into the sex industry. We might tut in disapproval and horror at the stories of sex trafficking that we hear in the news, but I think most blokes would probably rather ignore information about it altogether because it's a bit too close to the bone. There's just no way of knowing what you're actually participating in when you indulge in hardcore porn.

We also want to ignore the fact that many young boys are having many of their formative sexual experiences via illicit websites that puts them out of sync with real relationships, desensitising them to sexual violence. We don't want to know that 93% of boys have been exposed to internet porn and 18% of boys have watched someone being raped online. We don't want to think about how the porn we enjoy watching is the same material that is teaching a generation of young men how to be sexual, and that the lesson they're learning from such material is largely that they should be aggressive and rough, objectifying and 'fucking' their partner, having a very two-dimensional experience that is pretty horrid for her and emotionally and psychologically empty for him. We don't want to think about the residual guilt that we carry with us from watching porn, that we can't even look at women and teenage girls in the street without imagining fucking them. We don't want to think about how imprisoned we are by our cocks and our egos.

We also don't want to admit that to the extent that we are using porn to numb out is the extent to which we are contributing to the same level of consciousness that sexually violent men, sex offenders—including child sex offenders—and serial killers inhabit. We become downright offended at the idea that we might have anything in common with 'those bastards,' and yet when you pay attention to what one of the most infamous serial killers in history, Ted Bundy, said about pornography, the extent to which the ego is running rings around you becomes apparent.

Lessons From a Psychopath

Ted Bundy is perhaps the most infamous serial killer in US history. He confessed to battering and sometimes strangling his 30-plus victims. Whilst awaiting execution on death row, Bundy confessed to beheading some of his victims with a hacksaw and even admitted that he repeatedly visited the bodies of his victims, lying with them and having sex with their decaying bodies. In his final interview given the night before he was executed, he said, "Those of us who have been so influenced by violence in the media, particularly pornographic violence, are not some kind of inherent monsters. We are your sons and husbands. We grew up in regular families."

Bundy may have had a few screws looser than you or I, but for the vast majority of men, he has something disconcertingly similar in common with us: he frequently indulged in porn. Bundy himself reported that over time, he began to need a stronger, harder fix. Of course, Ted Bundy was a unremorseful psychopath so the progressive exposure to violent pornographic material contributed to him eventually murdering the first of his many victims. Most of us aren't psychopaths so we won't end up like Bundy, but the consequences for us may be porn addiction, Porn Induced Erectile Dysfunction, a loss of interest in everyday life, increased social isolation and again, a desensitisation towards sexualised violence and misogyny. Bundy's actions were extreme to say the least, but since 98% of all sexual crime in 2011-12 in the UK was committed by men (and that was just reported incidents), we can't blindly deny that we have nothing in common with him.

Bundy himself acknowledged that pornography is damaging and potentially dangerous, and yet our society is so obsessed with freedom of speech and consumer rights that we conveniently ignore the potentially lethal consequences of what this sick part of our minds dreams up—all in the name of choice and progress. We have agreed to give our power away on the cheap in return for our little dopamine and serotonin hits, sourced from an endless list of quick fixes. I think it's so sad that we've allowed this kind of society to be created.

I'm not suggesting that every man who indulges in porn will become the next Ted Bundy, but I do think it's important to address the question of how your use of pornography feeds into the larger web of manipulation, abuse and misogyny. Many people vociferously defend porn, claiming that it's a healthy, non-destructive part of their sex life. I am not here to comment on anybody's sexual preferences as long as they only involve consensual, self-aware adults. This might involve paying to watch ethical, responsibly made pornography, in the same way that you pay more for clothes not made in sweat shops. A general rule of thumb might be that if watching porn does not generate or trigger any shame, guilt or defensiveness for you, and if the material you are using has not or does not harm anybody else, then use and enjoy it.

Only you know what effect porn is truly having on you, and I accept that for some people, it may have beneficial effects (for example, if you've been sexually traumatised, controlled porn use may be an important part of your rehabilitation; likewise, many couples enjoy using porn together), but in my personal experience, porn took more than it gave in the long run—and from my research, I have learned that I'm not alone.

Without awareness, vigilance and a firm commitment to take radical responsibility for your thoughts, your porn preferences *will* progress because that is the nature of the beast. Even if your habit doesn't worsen, for most men, when it comes to porn the ego is running riot. Personally, I decided a while back that I refuse to be part of the secretive porn culture. I write more about this in chapter 13.

A Living Death

In conclusion, we are far too permissive about allowing the ego to act out left, right and centre, and we create dire consequences when we blatantly ignore the warning signs that are smacking us in the face. I don't think we can continue pretending that we are not part of the culture that sets the stage for these events to happen. School killings, football hooliganism, terrorism, road rage, domestic and sexual violence and the countless other examples I've shared in this book, plus the horrors that grace the news every day, are all part of what happens when we refuse to admit to our pain and provide a space for men to break the vow of male silence and talk about it. The pain has to be expressed somehow, and if we don't make room for men to speak up, we are practically inviting these destructive things to happen. We don't know how to talk to each other, and we certainly don't know how to ask for help, but we have to figure it out. Things won't automatically get better unless we intervene.

I don't give a shit if you think I'm advocating a nanny state or am taking your precious choices away from you. I don't care if you think this is over-the-top or histrionic. Ultimately, I think it's inhumane, destructive and just plain wrong to support a society that actively encourages people to indulge whatever sick whims their ego mind wants, dressing it up as evolution, free will or consumer rights. That creates the kind of sick society that subtly endorses child abuse, human sex trafficking, violence, murder, suicide and war. Unless we give men a set of tools to cope with their pain, their losses and their emotions without hurting themselves or others, we consign them and others around them to a living death.

Break the Vow: Power Questions

There is just one power question in this chapter—and all it requires is an honest, bullshit-free answer.

1. How is the ego running riot in your life?

CHAPTER 9

DEPRESSION

"Like those rare conditions which causes a person's own immune system to assault itself, depression is a disorder wherein the self attacks the self."
—Terrence Real

When it comes to the topic of men and depression, the title of Terrence Real's groundbreaking book says it all: *we don't want to talk about it*. However, given that so many men don't seek help for depression but go on to commit suicide, whether we want to discuss depression or not is no longer an option; the time has come where we have to.

For all our displays of arrogance and bravado and despite all the ways we constantly strive to be the best, men don't want to admit that we are a deeply insecure and often deeply unhappy bunch. We live haunted by the constant threat of being usurped, humiliated or beaten and see no way out other than fighting fire with fire. Our SMBs sit heavy on our chests. We are plagued by anger, guilt and shame. Omertà encourages us to let the ego run riot while we quietly die inside.

I see depression as an inevitable consequence of the vow of male silence. Men are basically walking pressure cookers, stuffed full of guilt, shame, anxiety, fear and unexpressed emotion. Omertà generates intense anxiety, worry, misery, suffering, fear of loss, loneliness and even a deep sense of helplessness. As we've seen, this ends up leaking out all over the place in the form of anger and even violence and through our coping mechanisms and escape routes—but nothing resolves the problem. The suffering that men experience builds up within us, turning dark and toxic. For lots of men, sooner or later this unexpressed gunk turns into a creeping, malignant depression.

The Disease Burden of the 21st Century

When it comes to admitting that we are depressed, there are two main issues: firstly, we don't believe it's safe to show up about what's really going on for us, and secondly, we don't really know *how* to. Male communication, after all, is fuelled by hierarchy and autonomy. The underlying motivation when men communicate is to establish who is the alpha male, which results in endless posturing and competing. When men communicate, we either avoid eye contact or glare at each other confrontationally. We tend to be hopeless at reflective listening. We cut each other off and talk over each other. We minimise, poke fun at and very rarely make physical contact with each other (except when playing sport or slapping each other on the back). We give each other the message that it's unacceptable to be intimate. Unlike women, most men tend not to process their experiences with anyone. We don't seek feedback or help. We have been so conditioned to go it alone and to man up that we bury our feelings, trying to pull ourselves together and stumble on blindly with no feedback, advice or support.

This is hardly conducive to disclosing that you're really struggling and feeling low. In a 2016 survey by Opinion Leader for the Men's Health Forum, the majority of men reported that while they would take time off work in order to seek medical support for alarming physical symptoms such as blood in stools or urine, unexpected lumps or chest pain, the statistics are very different when it comes to seeking help for anxiety (19%) or feeling low (just 15%). It's disturbing but not surprising that 41% of men in the UK who contemplated suicide in 2015 felt they couldn't talk about their feelings.

However, just because it's not being talked about doesn't mean that it isn't an issue. The uncomfortable truth is that depression is far more common among men than we like to admit. It is, in Terrence Real's words, "the disease burden of the 21st century; a silent killer, which causes inconceivable suffering, and a substantial number of deaths." I have known many men from all walks of life who outwardly seem solid, like they are coping with the stresses and strains of everyday life, but who are quietly yet profoundly unhappy at home, at work and in their relationships. I have known men who have not opened up and have gone on to take their own lives.

Depression plagues us, even and perhaps especially men who appear to 'have it all together.' In the aforementioned book *I Don't Want To Talk About It: Overcoming the Secret Legacy of Male Depression*, the author says that we do not tend to recognise male depression "because the disorder itself is seen as unmanly. Depression carries, to many, a double stain—the stigma of mental illness and also the stigma of 'feminine' emotionality. Those in a relationship with a depressed man are themselves often faced with a painful dilemma. They can either confront his condition—which may further shame him—or else collude with him in minimizing it, a course that offers no hope for relief." We've already named the stigma associated with men having feelings other than anger, and depression itself is fairly stigmatised, with common responses being to 'get over it' or 'pull yourself together,' although thankfully there's a lot of great work being done to de-stigmatise depression. However, combine the two and it's hardly surprising that so few men dare to talk to a doctor and get a diagnosis.

It's important therefore to develop an understanding of what depression is like so that you can recognise it in your life and the lives of the men around you.

Is This Depression?

Depression looks and feels different for everyone, although for men there are some commonalities. When I was 17 years old, I had my first proper job working in a factory, and I was bullied by an older guy who worked there who took an instant dislike to me; he was permanently angry and picked on me all the time. Eventually it got so bad that he physically attacked me and it went to a tribunal. He got sacked, at which point other people in the factory turned on me, picking up where the bully had left off. The bullying added to a sense of general malaise that was building up in me.

I felt like my life was falling apart and I couldn't talk about it. I did try once, with my mum, but she shut me down pretty quickly, not understanding how someone could be depressed at my age. As the weeks and months rolled by, everything became bleak. The days were some of the longest of my life: dark, long, hard and monotonous, lacking meaning and depth. I was having panic attacks daily and I felt like I was losing sight of any light at the end of the tunnel.

I went through a dark obsession with death. I put compilation tapes together of really dark music and I was drinking quite a lot. I felt alone in my struggle. I was really lonely. I felt so trapped in my life that sometimes while at work, I would loosen the head of the heavy steel press, deliberately putting myself at risk of crushing my hand in it while I worked. I felt in such a dark place that I couldn't see a way out other than hurting myself.

One day, after what felt like a lifetime of working there, the factory announced that it was closing down. All of the employees were offered a choice: we could move to a different factory or take voluntary redundancy. At that time my aunt and uncle were visiting from Canada and invited me to go over there and stay with them. I jumped at the chance, taking the redundancy package without a second thought. That was one of the biggest breakthroughs of my life to date. The experience in Canada opened me up to a whole new way of life. To be honest I think it even saved my life.

Nowadays, I still have down days and I have had periods of depression but overall my life has a lot more meaning and significance which helps me make sense of the down days. After my dad died, for example, I came undone for a while. The difference now is that I know how important it is to talk about this stuff rather than numb it out and I trust that it will pass.

My experience of depression might not be like anyone else's, although there are some commonalities in terms of how depression feels, including the following:

- Feeling bad. Your confidence might be low. You may feel worthless (thanks to those SMBs). You may feel guilty, angry and unable to enjoy your life.
- Increased use of escape routes such as alcohol or other numbing behaviours. We look at these in more detail in chapter 13.
- Feeling continually anxious, perhaps even terrified.
- Being bombarded by negative, fearful and repetitive thoughts.
- Having no energy. You might find it difficult to do anything, including even just getting out of bed.
- Sleep problems. You might want to sleep all the time, or you might suffer with some form of insomnia.
- Feeling like you're living in a goldfish bowl or Perspex bubble. You know intellectually that you love your family and friends, but you might not be able to actually feel it.

In *Reasons to Stay Alive*, Matt Haig writes, "One of the key symptoms of depression is to see no hope. No future. Far from the tunnel having light at the end of it, it seems like it is blocked at both ends, and you are inside it." Haig also describes other symptoms of depression, which might as well just be symptoms of living under the vow of male silence: "An inability to contemplate the future. Separation anxiety. A continual sense of heavy dread. An infinite sadness. An urge to be someone/anyone else."

It's worth noting that in males, depression is often acted *out* rather than in. It might not look like what we think of as depression at all. It might show up as an addictive or other numbing behaviour, or Hulk-like behaviour, or behaving recklessly, or increased irritability and discontentment.

CALM, the Campaign Against Living Miserably, states that severe depression boils down to three things: firstly, hating or disliking yourself; secondly, hating the world around you and wanting to escape; and thirdly, seeing little hope for the future or yourself.

It's Not Just a Headache

Many men are too scared to name that they feel depressed, or are genuinely unaware of what's happening for them mentally or emotionally, and instead will complain about physical symptoms such as headaches or achy joints. Like I said earlier, in our obsession with compartmentalising everything, we fail to acknowledge that our burning stomachs or achy limbs could have anything to do with what's going on for us mentally or emotionally.

Yet depression isn't just mental and emotional. It bears many physical symptoms too. Haig describes the following as some of his physical symptoms of depression: a "near-aching tingling sensation in my arms, hands, chest, throat and at the back of my head. Hypochondria. Physical exhaustion. Chest tightness and occasional pain. Aching limbs. Like I was falling even while I was standing still. As though I was on the verge of a panic attack."

The Incredible Shrinking Man

Depression causes men to shrink, like Scott Carey did in the 1957 science fiction film *The Incredible Shrinking Man*. Carey is a regular bloke who is exposed to a shadowy radiation cloud whilst on a boating trip. Six months later he starts to shrink, until he is merely 36-and-a-half inches tall. He is told by specialists that unless a miracle cure is found he will continue shrinking until there is nothing left of him. Eventually, he becomes so dinky that he has to live in a doll's house. His life becomes a living death. He is pounced on by the pet cat and ends up killing a giant spider, before finally escaping through a tiny crack in the basement window.

Whenever I watched this film as a boy I bawled my eyes out, because a part of me understood Scott's dilemma. Now, as a grown man, I look around me and see that a lot of us men are like the Incredible Shrinking Man. We shrink to fit the world around us, while the Hulk within slowly but surely grows stronger.

Beyond Coping

As important as it is to open up the conversation about male depression and to get men to talk, without understanding that depression is an effect of the vow of male silence (just as violence, criminal behaviour, alcohol abuse, addictions and so on are also effects of it), you run the risk of staying hostage to the thought system that led you to be depressed in the first place. If you admit that you are depressed but stop at the diagnosis, you run the risk of becoming so identified with the label that you box yourself in. Let's face it, pharmaceutical companies thrive on people 'coping.' I doubt they really want anyone to recover.

On the contrary, when you see depression within the context of omertà, you open up a window of possibility into a whole different way of life, one in which you don't just cope with being depressed but experience genuine freedom.

I'm not denying that depression a problem, and neither am I denying that some men may need to go onto medication as a first step. But I don't think a man should have to spend his whole life on antidepressants. I'm not implying that anyone who is working towards the de-stigmatisation of mental health issues is on the wrong track. Everyone who is contributing to this conversation is doing fantastic, essential work. My stance on this might piss a few people off, which is crazy given what I'm about to say, but I truly believe that it is possible to move beyond depression once we have a framework to help make sense of it (and hopefully this book is offering you that framework). If we want to experience this freedom, we need to get really honest about the ways in which we romance with our pain—and all of us do.

It's a really big deal for men to admit that they are depressed but once they do, it's important to keep moving forward. If you identify as being depressed, I encourage you to notice if you become attached to talking about "my depression" as if it's something that belongs to you. The risk you run is that your whole identity will begin to revolve around it, which means that regardless of whether a man admits to being depressed or not, he condemns himself to living a life "of quiet desperation." as Henry David Thoreau so fittingly put it.

This has to change. Too many of us are settling. We can't keep on resigning ourselves to a life dependent on prescribed tablets and thinking that's just the way it is, walking around in semi-catatonic state, drugged up for years on end. It doesn't need to be this way.

Writing someone off as being depressed without questioning whether it's possible to truly be free of it is a polite way of avoiding the uncomfortable conversations that we might need to have and the painful but necessary work we might need to do to break omertà and learn how to start living again. If every man who was depressed was given the opportunity to unleash the build up of toxic anger, guilt, shame and pain that has resulted from upholding omertà—the endless strategising, posturing, and stuffing and denying of emotions—we would be shaken to the core by what comes out of him. I have seen and experienced it firsthand.

Irrespective of how small we have allowed ourselves to become, we must not give up hope. Like Scott in *The Incredible Shrinking Man*, we must find the courage to look for the tiny crack in the basement window. Our potential for escape and recovery from our inner hell arises from the willingness to confess our suffering and take the necessary steps to reclaim our innocence, one thought at a time. At the end of *The Incredible Shrinking Man*, Scott concluded that no matter how tiny he becomes he will still matter in the universe. Similarly, when we grasp that it is safe to express what is buried deep within our hearts and that nothing bad will ever come of it in the long run, even if it is uncomfortable in the short run, we too will realise that we matter.

Sadly though, many men don't come to this conclusion and are so convinced that they don't matter that ending their life becomes the only option that seems to make any sense. Unfortunately, when a man seeks help for depression, it's often the last straw, the final almost inaudible cry for help before he takes an irreversible step. I once read a report wherein a doctor said that half of all men who visit a physician with undiagnosed depression will commit suicide within a month.

CHAPTER 10

SUICIDE

*"I am constantly torn between killing myself
and killing everyone around me."*
—David Levithan

My first encounter with suicide was on a New Year's Day when I was about 14 years old. A local dog walker saw the silhouette of a young boy hanging in the twisting branches of an age-old tree in the local cemetery where I frequently walked my neighbour's dog. Shortly after his death the tree was chopped down and the dog walkers silently agreed never to mention it again. When a boy or man kills himself, instead of facing the issue we get rid of the tree that he was found hanging from—in this case, literally.

I would spy on the spot from afar, unnerved by the boy's death but not able to stay away, staring at the empty space where the tree once stood. Then, one day I plucked up the courage to sit on the stump that was left after the tree had been cut down. I imagined the incident in my mind's eye over and over, attempting to piece together the shrouded mystery surrounding the boy's death, and each time I did I felt an overpowering sense of confusion. Our paths had crossed at various times and when we had spoken, he just seemed like a regular teenager, yet he had deliberately ended his life. What I've come to understand in recent years is this: suicide is a gender issue, a silent epidemic, and we all contribute to keeping it that way.

Uncomfortable Statistics

The statistics around suicide paint a decidedly uncomfortable picture in reference to the vow of male silence. Globally, one million people a year kill themselves. Of these, men are over three times as likely to complete suicide as women, although in some countries the ratio is much higher than this. The World Health Organisation states that the only two countries in the world where female suicide outstrips male suicide are Hong Kong and China. That's two countries out of 196. In every other country on the planet, the rate of male suicide is higher. And yet around double the number of women experience depression—or at least, double the number report it.

According to a 2013 survey, 78% of the 6,233 suicides in the UK were committed by males. Suicide is the leading cause of death in males under the age of 35 in the UK. In the US, suicide is the tenth leading cause of death across all age ranges. One person takes their own life in the US every thirteen minutes. The ratio of male to female suicide in the US, the country of the American Dream and male white privilege, is four to one. Every day, three or more boys commit suicide.

Meanwhile, our society swerves the subject of male suicide and its causes. We turn a blind eye to the whole issue, fearing that if we faced it head on, it would be as destructive and as damaging as hitting an innocent child in a car. The truth of course is that just as an alcoholic's denial is the primary tool keeping their disease in place, it is in avoiding the issue of suicide that we do the most damage. It is time for us to truly man up and take a long, sober look at what the hell is going on here.

Why Suicide?

So what is it that drives a person to take their own life? Suicide is the only choice that leaves a person without further choices, the ultimate line in the sand. In the book *Obstacles to Peace*, Kenneth Wapnick, a renowned teacher of *A Course in Miracles*, writes that when "a person believes that the ego's is the only voice, and it is the voice of death and despair and there is no way out, then suicide becomes the answer." A person can believe this regardless of whatever their external life looks like. If their inner world is completely dominated by fear and there doesn't seem to be a way out, the person will take the only option that appears to be left to them. Suicide is a final, desperate attempt to escape from the daily experience of "profound separation, hopelessness and guilt" that Wapnick speaks of. Of course, there can be many factors that influence whether someone becomes suicidal including mental health issues, work issues, major life changes and so on. I don't claim to be an expert on suicide but I do see the connections between suicide and the vow of male silence. To me that connection is undeniable.

Every day, men experience the soul-destroying consequences of omertà yet we don't know what to do. We don't know how to talk and we don't know how to ask for help. The prospect of ending one's life, even though it is clearly insane, seems more appealing to some men than having the uncomfortable, awkward conversations that could save his life. Undiagnosed depression often manifests itself as anger, particularly for men. For some of us, the ultimate act of anger and violence occurs against the self when a man—doting father, loving husband, loyal colleague— takes his own life.

No Way Back

More women than men attempt suicide but the number of men who complete suicide compared to women is sky high. Women's attempts at suicide often fail because they use less immediate methods like self-poisoning including drug overdose. This guarantees a short period of time after the act where they can still be saved. Men in contrast use irreversible methods like firearms and hanging which are much more likely to result in death. The upshot is that when a man decides to end his life, there is no way back.

When Ian Curtis from the English post punk band Joy Division decided to hang himself from the kitchen washing line, he had up until the moment he jolted the chair away to change his mind. Similarly, when young Neil decided to take his own life in the critically acclaimed movie *Dead Poets Society*, up until the point of squeezing the trigger he still had a choice, an opportunity to choose again. As soon as the bullet entered his head, his life was finished. The coldblooded methods men select don't leave space for a change of heart, which possibly explains why the completed suicide rate is four times higher in men than women.

So, why do women tend to leave themselves a lifeline while men do not? A desperately sad picture emerges of a gender that is so unfamiliar with communicating from within the middle of their struggle that the only choice they see is to end their struggle once and for all. When a person takes their own life, they do so because they have lost all hope of anything ever changing. They have no reason left to live. It's as if they are in a reinforced prison cell with no door or window.

For some men, the only time the vow of silence that strangulates men's voices throughout their lives is broken is in the exact second the bullet is fired or the rope stiffens around their neck. In that moment, the single gunshot or the disturbing sound of his neck snapping says more than the man has ever been able to, symbolising the desperate cry for help that he could never vocalise for fear of further shaming. The tragedy is that the instrument that finally gives him a voice for just a fleeting moment also takes away his hope of ever receiving the help he so desperately needed.

Welsh football manager Gary Speed's suicide left everybody baffled. He had appeared to 'have it all': a wife, two children, a glittering career in man's favourite sport and an MBE to boot, plus all the external trappings of a supposedly successful life. So what caused this man to intentionally tie a cable around his neck, in his family home, and violently end his life? The day of his death, people said Speed was "in fine form" on national TV, though his wife, after watching his final TV appearance said that "his smile did not appear genuine... it did not reach his eyes."

People were shocked and dumbfounded because something didn't quite add up. The pieces of the puzzle were mismatched. On the one hand, here was a "wonderful," "inspirational" and extremely talented man who was loved. On the other, he deliberately ended his life. To an outsider looking in, Speed may have appeared to have had the perfect life but if you zoom in a little closer you will see the forced smile of a man who was brutally wounded by omertà, whose inner world became so bleak that the only option he felt he had available was to hang himself.

Gary Speed's death is just one example. They are happening everywhere, every day, and very few of us stop to ask why. Perhaps because we too know what it is like to live under the cruel tyranny of a voice inside us that hates us. Perhaps it's easier for all of us to wear a painted smile, one that doesn't quite reach the eyes. Perhaps we are afraid of what we will unleash on our loved ones and the world if we admit our pain.

In Closing, Open Up

Here's what I didn't—perhaps couldn't—realise as a young boy when I first encountered the suicide in the graveyard: **every man is the odd man out without exception.** Every man feels, to varying extents, the same sense of loneliness and alienation that I felt as a six-year-old boy and which has been a lifelong companion to me. Every once in a while the pain becomes so intolerable that a brother cuts his life short, drawing our attention to the very issue that we sidestep at all costs—that many, *many* men are covertly depressed and urgently in need of help.

The men who take their own lives force us to pay attention to what's really happening for men everywhere. Suicide is seen an individual act, frequently described in terms of one human's inner battle with a personal and private depression. Yet these men are not anomalous freaks of nature. Their suffering is as universal as it is personal. Their deaths are trying to communicate something critical about what it is like to be a man today.

Each death we hear about presents us with a vital opportunity to do things differently, but we must be willing to walk a road not yet taken. People are already beginning to make that leap. A men's movement is gathering momentum, born out of the same crippling sense of constriction that the feminist movement was in the 1970s. People are starting to realise the importance of creating a safe space for men to unashamedly share and express their inner turmoil.

Spaces are beginning to emerge for men to do this work. For example, websites such as The Good Men Project and The Calm Zone (the Campaign Against Living Miserably) and documentaries such as Grayson Perry's *All Man* series for Channel Four and the Netflix original *The Mask You Live In* are raising awareness and challenging the status quo. These projects and organisations not only raise awareness of what it's really like to be a man and of issues such as male depression and suicide, but crucially, they also offer men an experience of what it means to be male in a way that they may never have had before; a place above the battleground where they can feel their feelings, express their darkest thoughts and fears, share what is really going on for them, and ultimately reclaim the truth about themselves.

We don't really need more surveys to persuade us of the role gender plays in completed suicide. Instead, we need to wake up and face the cruel facts. All men are wounded. As long as we continue to discourage men from giving voice to the hurt and pain, the underlying belief that we are fundamentally flawed, inadequate, worthless and unlovable will continue to go unnoticed, often with heartbreaking yet completely unnecessary consequences.

Denying men the right to feel or express their pain creates isolation. It pushes us over the edge into an emotional abyss where we act out on the outside, taking pointless risks to prove our bravery and manliness while on the inside, desperately crying out for help. Slowly but surely our eyes are beginning to open as we challenge the tiny mad idea that a man who is strong and silent is highly desirable or that men who feel are weak. The *Mad Men* era is coming to an end, one brave man at a time.

It is vital for us as a society to realise that once a man has made a commitment to suicide as the only option left to him, there is very little we can do save being with him 24 hours a day. We have to get in there while there is still a window of hope. We men are not really afraid of dying; we are afraid of failing. We are terrified of being shamed and ridiculed by other men, women, and a society that forbids us to feel. We are violently confused. When a man kills himself I wonder if on some level he is saying, "I don't have a right to exist. My life doesn't matter."

If, however, there is hope in a man's heart, we stand half a chance. If there is hope in a man's heart, suicide would not be the only viable option left in his mind. If a man who is burdened by the weight of omerta has some semblance that he is deeply loved, if he can truly access what that means—that he, with all his failings and weaknesses and inadequacies is precious to somebody else on this planet and that he is *okay* as he is, that he *belongs* as he is, that he is *enough* as he is, that he doesn't need to figure it all out and that he is deserving of help—he would be much less likely to take his own life.

Inside of every man there is a lost boy who crouches in a corner of a dark, dank basement. He is surrounded by discarded play things, worldly toys that promised him everything but delivered nothing—mere substitutes for love. The boy speaks softly, barely audible. And from his mouth two words… **HELP ME.**

CHAPTER 11

THE DARK NIGHT OF THE SOUL

"Sometimes when you're in a dark place, you think you've been buried, but actually you've been planted."
—Christine Caine

There comes a time in every man's life when everything feels pointless, when you feel like your days are spent wandering listlessly in no man's land, where the world feels cold, a hostile, uninhabitable wilderness. The days feel endless, empty and hopeless. You don't know who you are, where you fit, or what to do. The burden you carry weighs heavy on your heart. You might find yourself paralysed with fear, unable to see through the blackness, your anxiety levels becoming so severe that you start to panic and look for a way out, turning to every escape route you've ever known for comfort—but finding that none of them work.

Hell on Earth

My dad's death in 2009 triggered a long period of grief and perhaps even depression that lasted for a few years. When Dad died from lung cancer, I was devastated. One minute he was here and 104 days later he was gone. His death hit me hard. I felt confused, and my thirst for life began to dwindle.

I felt overwhelmed with feelings of sadness and futility which tore through me like an emotional forest fire. At different times in the months following Dad's death I experienced intense surges of sadness. My dark night of the soul came in waves. Sometimes it would sneak up on me slowly like a cat stalking a mouse, catching me when I least expected it. Other times, it was a pneumatic drill in my head. Either way, it hurt like hell. During this time of introspection I decided that I wanted to find a way to honour my dad and raise money for the hospice where he passed away. I needed something that would push me to the outer limits of my comfort zone, something that would require massive quantities of blood, sweat and tears to complete, something to make sense of the dark time I was experiencing.

That's when I discovered The Fred Whitton Challenge, Britain's hardest one day organised bike ride, a 112 mile jaunt around the Lake District that takes in some of the harshest roads in England. The Fred has been described by Ironman athletes as "hell on earth," so in my eyes it was the perfect tribute to my father, who had been a prolific hill climber on the bike back in the day. My goal was to ride up the hardest climb in England, Hardknott Pass, and leave Dad's old walking compass at the summit in memory of his adventurous spirit.

In the weeks following my application to do the Fred, I trained extremely hard. It was a bitterly cold winter that year which made riding conditions rough and sometimes risky. Each ride was an uphill battle with the elements but as hard as it was, I relished going out into the cold, endless grey. When I wasn't battling it out in the snow, wind, and pelting rain, I was in the gym training like a madman.

I lay awake night after night, worrying about the Fred. In hindsight, maybe it served to distract me from my grief. I didn't see at the time that it was an escape route. I worried incessantly about whether I would be able to finish the 112 miles and wondered if I would be able to climb the most feared climb in the country without falling off my bike. I was concerned about letting down all the people who had helped raise money for the hospice where had Dad spent his final days. I wanted to do my dad proud, even though he was dead.

A couple of weeks before the event, I got a chest infection. To say it left me feeling weary is an understatement. When the day of the event came around, I was apprehensive. My wife hadn't been able to drive across the country to support me, but my mate Dave was going to meet me on different points around the course. Apart from that though, it was just me against me. The other riders receded into the background as I came head to head against myself.

From the moment I rolled over the start line things started to go wide of the mark. I found myself short of breath and down in the mouth. My legs were heavy, my chest was heaving. It wasn't long before I found myself isolated, with no other riders around at all. I dug deep and knew that every strenuous pedal revolution would take me closer to that dreaded 30% ascent of Hardknott Pass, which would take place about 90 miles into the ride. I quickly found myself at the back of the field. Every mile proved to be an uphill battle, a bit like my life. Then, after cycling through hours of gruelling terrain, I punctured.

The valve had snapped on the spare inner tube and took an eternity to fix. Once back on the road, the sky darkened and it poured with rain, the kind of rain that is relentless, hard and heartless. The kind of rain that flows into every layer, seam, nook and cranny, leaving you so wet even your bones need drying out at the end of the day. Then an eerie mist descended and the temperature plummeted to six degrees. I could barely see six feet in front of me, the water was gushing down the road towards me and there wasn't another soul in sight. I cried out for help but no help came.

But even though my legs were crushed from the cold, and the fatigue was unbearable, I somehow found the strength to keep the cranks turning, one brutally slow pedal revolution after another. One by one, dark angels came out of the fog inside my head to haunt me: the belief that I was fundamentally flawed; the belief that I would never be as good as Dad; the belief that I was a failure as a man; the belief that I might die alone, with my hopes and dreams still inside of me—all of my deepest fears. My body shook with the cold and I sobbed through the driving rain pelting down on me, "I'm sorry Dad, I'm so fucking sorry." Somewhere along the line, the significance of the ride had changed. I knew it now. This ride was no longer about the man riding to honour his father and everything about the little boy who hadn't felt accepted or loved by his dad.

Finally I reached the summit of the fell, tears still streaming down my face and after a shaky descent, I rolled around the corner into the feed station and collapsed into the arms of a marshal, exhausted. My mate Dave, who'd lost contact with me hours before, took one look at me and said, "You're done mate." He called my by-then very anxious wife who hadn't heard a peep from me for hours to let her know I was okay. I walked into the village hall where a bunch of other riders were huddled, all of whom had also had to abandon the ride, a silver blanket wrapped around my shoulders, and I cried like a little boy.

To an outsider it may have looked like I was pursuing a noble goal in doing the Fred, honouring my father's life and raising money for a good cause, but on the inside my actual motivation for doing the ride was somehow tangled up in the grief of losing my father, the dark night of the soul I was in the middle of, and the unresolved pain from my childhood. Growing up, I had sought approval from my dad and would go to any lengths to please him. The ego had convinced me that my worth as a human being was somehow at the mercy of whether I made it up Hardknott Pass (once again hounded by the pressure to not be perceived as weak). The truth was that eventually, I wound up wanting to defeat the man whose life I was supposedly riding to honour, even though I didn't recognise it at the time. It was during that lonely, weather-beaten ride over Cold Fell that I came face to face with the wounded boy inside me—not for the first time in my life—and grieved. My time on Cold Fell was like a metaphor for everything I was going through around Dad dying. In the depths of despair, my heart opened. I never even made it up Hardknott that year. My journey ended ten miles up the road.

That whole experience—the months of lonely training and the brutal ride itself—were the culmination of a long, dark night of the soul that was triggered when my father died but which really began all the way back in my childhood when I lost a testicle. I'm grateful for my slightly obsessive nature because it allowed me to externalise my inner struggle onto a hobby which is, let's face it, dominated by middle aged men going through a mid-life crisis. It wasn't a Disney film. The dark night wasn't magically over the next day. In fact, as I write about later on, it was only one year later and as part of a team that I could fully put the Fred to bed.

The Shadow Side of the Mountain

Various events or experiences can trigger a dark night of the soul. The following is not an exhaustive list, but it will give you some idea of what can initiate this period of being "on the shadow side of the mountain":

- The death of a loved one
- Doubting whether your life has purpose or meaning
- Depression and/or anxiety
- A significant life event: a birth, marriage, divorce, redundancy, retirement
- Becoming a parent, husband, partner
- Your child or children leaving home
- Being promoted or demoted
- An unexpected change in circumstances
- Trauma or PTSD
- A sense of being isolated or alone
- Coming face to face with your mortality
- Searching for the meaning of life

- A quarter- or mid-life crisis
- An identity crisis
- A period of deep introspection
- Feeling empty and devoid of joy for extended periods of time
- A mental or emotional healing crisis, where anything that isn't love surfaces for cleansing and healing.

A dark night of the soul might seem really scary at the time, almost as if you're losing your grip on reality, but I promise you won't die. It is a time of crisis, an emergency of sorts, but not one that wants us to rush in and fix it in the way we usually attempt to in western society. Instead, this often excruciating time is actually rich with possibility. It is an emergency because something wants to emerge from it. Like the mythical phoenix that rises up out of the ashes, the dark night is a period in your life that has the potential to be potent and catalytic. It holds the possibility of alchemising a permanent change in who you are and how you live.

Sometimes a dark night of the soul can go on for years, a long and listless time of subtle apathy. For others, the pain is more acute, the suffering intensely unbearable. These folks are often lucky (although they won't feel it at the time), because the more intense the pain, the closer you are to a genuine rock bottom. As JK Rowling famously stated in a speech, hitting rock bottom can be a turning point, giving you a new foundation upon which to rebuild your life.

Our society does its best to avoid, numb and escape from the dark night of the soul. We rush to fix and escape from the pain of a dark night, failing to see it as a wake up call or a time of spiritual emergency. We often fail to recognise that a dark night of the soul is alerting you to something you need to take a long hard look at. It is an opportunity in disguise.

To navigate this time and unearth the opportunity hidden in the obstacle, you'll need to muster the courage to let yourself fall apart, break omertà and discover what the true definition of "man up" is for you. The dark night of the soul isn't proof that you're weak: it's about sticking around long enough to discover the warrior within.

Leap of Faith

In the epic 2012 Batman movie *The Dark Knight Rises*, Batman receives a crippling back blow during a ferocious face-off with masked militant Bane, leaving him defenceless. When he regains consciousness, he finds that he is trapped in a remote prison that resembles a deep well, where escape is all but impossible.

The prisoners tell Bruce the tale of a child, born in the prison, who was the only prisoner to have ever escaped. The child scaled the walls of the well-like structure and made the leap to a tiny ledge that led to freedom. The child, they said, made the leap without a safety rope. Over the years many inmates had attempted to follow in the child's footsteps, clambering the walls of the well in a bid for freedom, only to fall again and again. All of them had used a rope, too afraid of falling to their deaths to let go completely.

After a lengthy period of rehabilitation, Bruce decides to make the jump using the safety rope. He fails. One of the inmates reminds Bruce "the leap to freedom is not about strength." This is a foreign language to Bruce, whose world is built around the triumph of man-made strength and stealth. He snubs the advice, stating that his body makes the jump. He doesn't think his mind needs to be involved, that he can get out on his own terms. He attempts to scale the wall once again using the rope for safety; once again, he fails. The inmate goes on to say that his reliance on the body and its finite strength is keeping him imprisoned. He hasn't found "the fear," hasn't connected with his mortality. He hasn't jumped like his life depends on it.

It is only when Bruce connects to his deepest, darkest fear—that his city, his home, will burn to the ground with no one there to save it—that he finds the resolve to make the climb up the vertical wall without the rope, this time risking death. True, he may have had a bit of a saviour complex, but the metaphor is powerful: he had to risk losing his life in order to find it. He leaps, lands on the tiny ledge, and climbs his way to freedom.

The wisdom of this scene is simple yet profound. Bruce needed to experience the fear of death in order to survive the leap. He needed to let go of thinking that he knew exactly what he needed to do. He needed to take a genuine risk, to be vulnerable and to trust. Like Bruce, before you can come out the other side of your own dark night of the soul, you need to feel the fear and let go of the rope. To the extent that you hold on is the extent to which you will stay imprisoned.

I know how hard it can be to do this. To break the vow of male silence and talk about your experience of being a man, your thoughts, fears, emotions and beliefs—especially in a world that prohibits this—is hard. But talk you must. This is the time for one of those rare but vital courageous conversations with someone you can trust—a spouse, friend or counsellor. Opening up in this way will feel threatening at first. You might feel like you are going to be annihilated, but going back is no longer a viable option. When we take a risk and reach out in true vulnerability, the ego's stranglehold on us grows weaker. Like Bruce, once you make the leap, you find yourself on a tiny little ledge, but it is the ledge that leads you to freedom.

Wake up Call

The initial phase of a dark night of the soul is usually the most difficult. When you have made a commitment be *with* your pain rather than numb it, the mess your escape routes were blocking (and don't worry, we're getting to those) will reveal itself to you. "Much of the time, we are unknowingly affected by an unconscious reservoir of disowned emotions and experiences," writes Christina Grof in *The Thirst for Wholeness*. The task at hand is simple and difficult: we need to get better at actually feeling this pain.

Many men don't get beyond the initial phase of the dark night because the pain is so intense. As the ego tries to re-establish control you may perhaps find yourself anxiously wanting to get back to what is safe, comfy and familiar. You might want to retreat into numbing behaviours rather than dealing with your pain at this point. I urge you to go all in and stay there. Hang in there long enough to let a miracle happen. You will need to dig really fucking deep and pour all of the determination that you usually funnel into obliterating yourself into saving yourself.

Have faith, my friend. The darkest hour truly is before the dawn.

The End of Days

Ancient warriors
battle
life's dusty road
battered senseless
by winds of change
time
and motion.

The end of days
are drawing near
as miracles unveil
a deeper purpose
mending
derelict hearts
resurrecting
the dead
in a single
silvery strand
we stand
unarmed.

The war against self
is finally over.

PART TWO

THE RISE OF MAN

"You've seen my descent. Now watch my rising."
- Rumi

Introduction

When you decide that you are ready to face yourself, be prepared for fireworks. I've said before that the ego is a master of disguises, a scheming chameleon that will do whatever it deems necessary to keep itself in business. In reading this material, you have begun breaking the vow of male silence. Don't be surprised if the ego now reacts by going to extreme lengths to sabotage any attempt you make to take responsibility for your thinking.

The ego is ruthless in its drive to prevent you from taking ownership for the part you play in keeping your pain alive. The last thing it will want you to do is to continue reading this book, so don't be surprised if it starts to play dirty. Over the next little while, you might become uncharacteristically angry, intolerant or impatient, throwing temper tantrums seemingly without reason. The ego, fuelled by guilt and shame and unable to live without them, needs complex problems and everyday worldly complications to divert your attention away from going anywhere near this basement. The ego barks out orders like a military drill sergeant: "Shut up. Put up. MAN THE FUCK UP." Dare to break the vow of silence and you threaten the ego's very survival; don't break it (don't even acknowledge it) and you keep the guilt and shame alive—*exactly what the ego wants*. If you notice this happening, remind yourself it is a sign you are facing the right direction. Be accountable for your mistakes, but don't mistake things *feeling* worse with things actually *being* worse. They often have to get worse before they get better.

The only thing you need to do right now is practise vigilance and honesty around your thinking. When you do, it goes against the fundamental grain of how the ego operates. Honesty opens the door to the dusty basement of your life which is crammed with trauma, guilt, shame and emotional pain that has been locked away for years, decades even. Your choices are these:

> Option A: Don't break the vow of male silence.
> Option B: Break the vow of male silence.

This is what the ego says: Option A equals life. Option B equals death. Option A is good. Option B is bad. Option A is easy. Option B is hard. Do not be fooled. The truth is: **Option B is the only real option if you want to live.**

A word of warning though: the ego is right about one thing. Option B *is* hard, as you know by now. Whenever you break the vow of male silence, everything—and I mean everything—you have repressed whilst living under the dark cloud of omertà will suddenly surface. For a while nothing will make any sense. The world you inhabit will appear distorted. Your head will crack open. Your skin will burn. Your heart will bleed. You will feel feelings that have been buried for decades—unbearable hurt, pain, guilt, shame and loneliness. You will fall to your knees more than once. If this sounds like a living hell, that's because it is. The reason you willingly submit yourself to this experience is because it's temporary. The hell the ego delivers you to, on the other hand, is admittedly more subtle, more bearable even, but make no mistake: it is malignant and fatal.

However, if you do what is hard now, life will eventually become easy. It's going to be tough fellas. No doubt about that. But as a man who has repeatedly broken the vow of male silence, I can promise you this: it's also going to be worth it. As Maureen Brady writes, "Your instincts may tell you that you can't survive if you experience feelings. But they are leftover child instincts. They're the ones that first told you to freeze your feelings. They themselves are frozen and haven't grown with the rest of you. These instincts don't know that you're far more capable of learning to cope with overwhelming emotion now than when you were a [child]." You are not a child now, but a man. You are not just a man, but since you're reading these words, you are a man who wants to break the vow of male silence and rise up from the ashes. Every man is called to rise. Now is the time.

CHAPTER 12

TAKING RESPONSIBILITY

*"The healing of a man begins the day he can begin to
be honest with himself, the day he can acknowledge
how much his life is driven by fear, when he can beat
back the shame that then threatens to engulf him.
Only then can he recover that centre which has been
obscured by the great grey fear that haunts his soul."*
—James Hollis

At some point during his lifetime, every man reaches a fundamental branch in the road. For some, it slams into your awareness like an unstoppable juggernaut: the loss of a job, the death of a loved one, your spouse telling you she wants a divorce, or a frightening cancer diagnosis. This pivotal event can drag you into darkness (as I wrote about in chapter 11) or propel you towards the light. For others, it sneaks up over many years: perhaps you finally realise as you stare at the ceiling one morning that you no longer feel anything towards the person who is lying in bed next to you—or in fact that you don't feel anything at all; maybe you recognise that you've recently spent your daily commute quietly daydreaming about stepping off the platform in front of an approaching train; perhaps you feel a consistent, nagging sense that you're quietly dying inside.

Either way, the day comes when you are no longer able to effectively numb the lethal concoction of fear, shame, guilt and isolation that has been gnawing away at you for most of your life. You're troubled night and day and no amount of work, beer, football or porn can make your discomfort go away. You look in the mirror and don't even know the man staring back at you. There's no excitement, no sadness, no escape—nothing.

This fork in the road brings you face to face with two choices: same old shit or crazy new shit. Continue to fight a battle you simply cannot win, or surrender and take the first hesitant steps down a new road. *A Course in Miracles* puts it this way. "When you come to a place where the branch in the road is quite apparent, you cannot go ahead. You must go either one way or the other. The whole purpose of coming this far was to decide which branch you will take now."

It takes enormous courage for a man to admit to himself that the old way doesn't work anymore, and that there is no other workable choice available. Many reach this crucial point but instead of holding up their hands and admitting defeat, they become anxious and controlling, then falter and take the familiar path, cautiously returning to a life of familiarity, mediocrity, imprisonment and fear. At this point you are likely so inwardly isolated, lonely and full of shame that you genuinely don't know what to do. This state of being is so alien to a man's place within a society entrenched in a patriarchal mindset that it's terrifying to admit it. Nevertheless, the day comes when you find yourself feeling utterly defeated by how you've been living your life.

Like an addict, you have to acknowledge with brutal honesty that you have reached a pivotal moment in your life, that you are standing at the most important crossroads you will ever face. The first thing you must do is admit defeat and acknowledge that the old way simply doesn't work anymore—and that it never really did. It's time to wave the white flag. Surrender. It takes enormous courage for a man to do this. However, hold onto any lingering fantasies that you are still in control and you are setting yourself up for another rock bottom further down the road.

A Deliberate, Conscious Decision

If there was one tool that I could give you, one idea or practice that I know from decades of experience that could make the biggest difference to your life, it would be this: you have to now make a firm decision to take *full responsibility* for your thinking and your actions.

Only this will stop you from believing you are a victim—and as much as you won't want to admit it, you have been living in a state of victim consciousness. In the book *Crazy Good*, Steve Chandler writes that the victim mindset is "so conditioned, so pounded in, so deeply ingrained, it's hard to call it a conscious choice to think that way. It's more like a family tradition. A tradition of the human family. A hypnotised, knee-jerk response to everything. A default setting in the mind." To overcome this requires a deliberate, conscious decision. This world is not crying out for martyrs. It is looking for leaders, men who are willing to step up when the odds are stacked against them. So on that note, I have a powerful question for you, one that could change your life.

Are you now willing to take __full__ responsibility for your thoughts and actions?

Does this sound complicated or daunting? It might seem this way, but it's not. It really comes down to two simple words: yes or no. One decision with two vastly different consequences. There's no overlap. Take responsibility for your life, or don't take responsibility for your life. You can't be in both places at the same time—you are either waking up or you're not. So:

Are you now willing to take __full__ responsibility for your thoughts and actions?

The choice is yours. If your answer is no, there's no point in you continuing to read the rest of this book because at this point, you have decided not to take full responsibility. In a weird way, this choice makes you more responsible; you've been honest and I would rather you admit that you don't want to go any further than bullshit your way through the rest of this book. Everything that follows from here on is based on the assumption that the reader has said *hell yes* to taking full responsibility for his thoughts and actions, and if you said no, it leaves you with nowhere to go right now. On a positive note, you are free to change your mind at any time and continue with this work. You're welcome back when the pain has become so unbearable that the only real choice stares you in the face.

If you said yes, turn the page and let's keep going.

The Road Less Travelled

If you're reading these words, you must have said, "Yes, I'm willing to take full responsibility for my thoughts and actions." Congratulations. You've chosen to walk the road less travelled and you're well on your way to experiencing life on the other side of omertà. At first you might not know what the hell to do or how to change, but as long as you have the willingness to change, you're facing the right direction and help is on the way. *ACIM* states "It is but the first few steps along the right way that seem hard." The good news is that the decision itself sets the wheels of change into motion.

It's important to remember that the ego is allergic to accountability—and because we're so addicted to it, so are most of us. Cause and effect thinking by default renders you a victim or a perpetrator; in this paradigm you are always either completely to blame for how someone else feels, or else you are pointing the finger and laying the blame for any and every situation outside of self. We insist that somebody or something else is always responsible for why we are the way we are. This is the fundamental delusion that you are now being asked to lay aside—the idea that somebody or something has control over your inner world. The payoff for loyalty to this idea is of course that you don't have to take responsibility, but the cost is huge: it requires that you live your life believing you are a victim of the world—and those who believe they are victims do not feel a sense of agency over their lives.

The uncomfortable truth is that it is delusional to believe that your peace of mind is solely dependent on somebody else changing their behaviour. Our entire political system is based on this premise, and it is false. It doesn't work. It never has. It never will. While external change is often called for, such change must happen from the inside out.

Let's face it: we have very few role models for how to be a man of real integrity in our world today, so in the beginning, choosing to be a responsible human being will probably feel awkward and daunting, a bit like your first day in a new job. For most of us, accountability is such a foreign concept that we don't even know what it really means. Men in particular fear that admitting we've made a mistake means taking the blame for everything. Our so-called leaders spend so much energy and time pointing the finger at others whilst ducking and diving to avoid admitting their part that when a man puts his hand up and says, "I made a mistake," we automatically think of him as weak. It's easier to launch a few missiles—literal or metaphorical—than to admit that you might be wrong.

However, being accountable is about more than admitting your mistakes. It is about taking full responsibility for your emotional state, thoughts *and* actions. It's about acknowledging that you are always 100% responsible for 100% of your part in any dynamic, relationship or situation. You are 100% responsible for the presence or absence of respect, integrity, responsibility, honesty, kindness and courage in every situation. *ACIM* spells it out in black and white: "You may believe that you are responsible for what you do, but not for what you think. The truth is that you are responsible for what you think, because it is only at this level that you can exercise choice. What you do comes from what you think." The truth is that whatever is happening, no matter how seemingly complex the situation, you are always completely responsible for your own emotional state. Nobody else has that much power over you unless you give it to them. To quote Eleanor Roosevelt, nobody can make you feel *anything* without your consent. Allow me to illustrate what that looks like in real life.

A Radical Approach to my Tarmac Tirades

One of my pet peeves is ignorant drivers, especially when I'm cycling. If a car overtakes me on a bend, a switch flips in my head and I immediately snap into Hulk mode. Visions of punching the other driver senseless, smashing their car up and throwing my bike through their windscreen flash through my mind. This becomes very difficult to maintain if it turns out the driver is a pensioner, which has happened more than once. I've ranted and yelled at drivers on leafy Sussex lanes more times than I care to admit. This is chronic bottom-end war mindset behaviour, and I have often found it easy to justify, as Ell will verify. In fact, she remembered the following words verbatim: *That bastard nearly brought me off my bike! They could have clipped me! They should have slowed down. What kind of idiot overtakes somebody on a bend? If that car had been ten feet ahead it would have been a head on collision!* Each thought builds on the next until I'm pedalling like a madman with steam pouring out of my ears and a distinct green hue to my skin.

On the bike is one area in my life where I have tried to claim that this work doesn't apply to me because I have the supposed 'justification' of feeling unsafe—maybe even that my life is at stake. The point here is surely obvious: it doesn't matter whether you're in a genuinely threatening situation or not. *Attack is never justified.* We humans like to be selective about when we apply this universal law. We like to convince ourselves that the world needs to change first. Joseph Campbell once said, "When we talk about settling the world's problems, we're barking up the wrong tree. The world is perfect. It's a mess. It has always been a mess. We are not going to change it. Our job is to straighten out our own lives."

As you're reading this, you are possibly even thinking, "Yeah, other people do try to justify their anger!" without realising that this applies first and foremost to you. Like I already said, we humans have an inbuilt mechanism that seems hell bent on pointing the finger outside of self.

So what does taking responsibility for my thoughts look like here? Do you always have to take 100% responsibility for the whole situation? No. This is not about excusing somebody else's behaviour, but it is about consciously sweeping up your side of the street. The key point here is to do your work before demanding that the rest of the world does theirs. We're pretty addicted to doing it the other way round in our society, demanding that someone or something 'out there' changes so that we can feel okay. The good news is that by changing your perception, you get the real outcome you want, which is to feel peaceful, regardless of whether anyone else changes or not. Taking responsibility also unhooks you from the seductive yet destructive cycle of attack and blame. In case you haven't got it already, *that approach never works*. Every time I have attacked a motorist, whether verbally or just mentally, I end up feeling worse about myself. I've said it before and I'll say it again: *all* attack is self-attack.

So, in the case of me the cyclist versus the motorist, I can't change how another person drives, but I can change how I perceive him. In 2014, I decided to take a radical approach to my ongoing tarmac tirades. I was in the middle of designing a bespoke dream bike, inspired by the Robert Penn book, *It's All About the Bike*. Because I'm a student of *ACIM*, I decided to get three words hand painted on the rear stay of my bike, three words that would hold me accountable when I started to morph into the Hulk: *teach only love*. Interestingly, male riders never comment on it, even when I point it out (I often wonder if they think it's 'a bit gay'), but I didn't get it done for them and I'm not ashamed or afraid of what anybody else thinks. Those three words serve to remind me that I'm 100% responsible for my own thoughts, 100% of the time—even in the one place where fear runs rampant. Or in my case, rides rampant.

Like any tattoo, however, just because I've got the words in permanent view when I'm riding, it doesn't guarantee that I'll change my thinking or behave differently. The words are there to constantly remind me of the principles I aspire to embody. But courage, intention and commitment come into play here too. Every time I get on my bike, I have the opportunity to stand for something rather than against it. And every time I do that, I break omertà and become part of the revolution.

It's Decision Time

Now, it's your turn. The exercise you will be doing in a few moments is gritty, unsettling and essential. It begins with the willingness to continue to take full responsibility for your thoughts. To the degree that you are willing to uncover the dark corners of your mind in this exercise is the degree to which you will move forward. Be ruthless in searching your mind for the insidious, sick thoughts that may be lurking in the shadows. By not uncovering the dark thoughts inside you, you do one thing and one thing only: strengthen the ego and uphold the vow of male silence. This work is vital. I am speaking to the part of you that wants to wake up, not the part of you that wants to be right. Before we dive in, a story about a Zen master and a man.

ZEN STORY OF THE MASTER, MAN AND GOD

A monk was meditating by a river when he was interrupted by a young man who said, "Master, I wish to become your disciple"

"Why?" asked the monk.

The young man thought for a moment before replying, "Because I want to wake up."

The monk stood up, grabbed the man by the scruff of his neck, dragged him into the river, and plunged his head under the water. He held the man's head under the water for a full minute, his face peaceful. The man meanwhile was frantically struggling and fighting to break free. Eventually, after what must have been the longest minute of the man's life, the monk yanked the man's head out of the water. As the man coughed and spluttered, the monk spoke: "Tell me, what did you want more than anything when you were under water?"

"To breathe!"

"And that," said the monk, "is how much you have to want to wake up."

Like the young man in the story, that is how much *you* have to want to keep breaking the vow of male silence and be free of all the societal bullshit about masculinity. It's decision time. It starts right here. No bullshit. No lying. No hiding. It is time for you to take a long, hard, sober look at yourself and your life. I am challenging you to step up. The initiation starts here—to hunt for your inner warrior like your life depends on it.

You're about to break omertà—again. You have four power questions to answer and I suggest you block out at least 30 minutes to do this exercise. Get a notebook, a pen and get offline. Turn off your phone. Don't let anything or anyone get in the way of you answering these questions. Take radical responsibility for yourself and your life. Make it happen now. A final word of warning before you begin: the closer you get to the edge, the louder the ego will shout. Keep going anyway. You're not alone. Don't stop until you reach the truth.

Break the Vow: Power Questions

1. What isn't working in my life?
2. Who have I blamed for my pain?
3. Who do I continue to blame for my pain, however secretly?
4. Choose one of the situations from question one. Now ask yourself: What part have I played in keeping my pain alive? Brutal honesty please.
5. Repeat step 1-4 until you have gone through every item on the list. Stop when the exercise feels complete.

If you have answered these questions with depth and honesty, it will have been quite an uncomfortable experience. This is good news. It's a sign that you're starting to 'man up' in the true sense of the phrase. A man on the other side of omertà is willing to be vulnerable even when it scares him. When it comes to this work, vulnerability often goes hand in hand with responsibility. It is always a sign of true strength.

If you've answered these questions, you have taken a powerful step on the path of taking responsibility for your pain. If you haven't, do it now because you can't go any further until you have. When you're ready, read on.

CHAPTER 13

ESCAPE ROUTES

"Numb the dark and you numb the light."
—Brené Brown

I've mentioned escape routes a number of times already in this book but have deliberately not introduced them properly until now. To your average bloke, an escape route is just part of everyday living. An escape route is any behaviour, strategy or thing you use or do to get away from anxiety, vulnerability or discomfort—all the things you're going to meet when you break the vow of male silence. The ego's armoury of escape routes is endless. You probably have your own personal collection of escape routes in place in your life, behaviours you turn to anytime things get a little stressful or to "help take the edge off." You almost definitely turn to them when things get emotionally tough.

If you want to see escape routes in action, simply take a plane trip; the distractions are endless. If you're not being constantly fed or watered, you're being encouraged to numb out with an endless list of movies, TV shows, or if it gets really desperate, games of Battleships against yourself. The anxiety of simply sitting with oneself for a few hours is intolerable for most of us, so if perusing the Duty Free magazine or buying a scratch card alleviates it even a tiny bit, then sign us up!

Anything to Numb the Anxiety

Brené Brown explains why we rely so heavily on escape routes: "Just the anticipation or fear of [painful or anxious] feelings can trigger intolerable vulnerability in us. We know it's coming. For many of us, our first response to vulnerability and pain is not to lean into the discomfort and feel our way through but rather to *make it go away*. We do that by numbing and taking the edge off the pain with whatever provides the quickest relief." Author Geneen Roth describes it simply as bolting. We do or use whatever means necessary to make a run for it when things get uncomfortable—especially emotionally uncomfortable. Anything to numb your anxiety.

Men have a shit load of escape routes, many of which are often just normal everyday behaviours, used for self-medication purposes. Only you can say whether you're using each behaviour as an escape route or not. Here are a few.

<u>Socially acceptable escape routes</u>
- Watching and talking about sports
- Tinkering with or washing the car
- Fixing up the house
- Watching crap TV
- Binging on Netflix
- Reading or watching the news
- Talking politics
- Training at the gym

- Training for a sporting event
- Spending money
- Doing business
- Taking the piss out of your mates
- Working long hours
- Checking your mobile phone
- Social media
- Games on your phone
- Texting
- Checking email
- Flirting
- Pigging out on junk food
- Going down the pub
- Boozing at home in the evenings
- Talking shite
- Sex—having it, thinking about it, talking about it
- Watching porn
- Masturbating
- Ogling women (or other men)
- Playing computer games
- Watching violent action films
- Fantasising about someone else whilst having sex with your partner
- Going to strip clubs
- Smoking weed
- Stag weekends
- Taking recreational drugs
- Constantly criticising your partner
- Speeding in the car

- Being controlling
- Going on a bender
- Driving aggressively
- Punch ups
- Gambling
- Certain kinds of addiction—to caffeine, sugar or gaming, for example.

Less socially acceptable escape routes include:

- Domestic violence and abuse
- Manipulation and extreme control of others
- Compulsive masturbation
- Extreme violence
- Criminal behaviour
- Having an affair
- Using prostitutes
- Hardcore porn
- Certain more taboo addictions—to drugs, gambling, sex, and so on.

Many of the above escape routes are part of everyday living and I'm certainly not suggesting that they're all 'bad,' although I do think that the less socially acceptable ones are outright harmful. (Oh, and just because something isn't on the list, doesn't mean it's not an escape route.) It's not what you're doing that is the issue; it's the intention behind it. Anytime you use one or more of these behaviours because you're experiencing discomfort, it's an escape route that prevents you from being fully present in your life. I want to be crystal clear that I'm not trying to stop you from enjoying your life, but I am encouraging you to be brutally honest with yourself about the ways you are destroying it. Anyone who numbs out in some way—using anything from the seemingly innocuous TV or junk food through to more extreme behaviours like paying for prostitutes or snorting thousands of pounds worth of coke—is using and arguably abusing an escape route. Regardless of how acceptable it is, any behaviour that anaesthetises uncomfortable feelings is in the ego's domain. As Eckhart Tolle says, "While [these activities] may offer some relief, you pay a high price: loss of consciousness."

The ego will happily waste years of your life on escape routes. In 2016, the human race spent over 5,246 *centuries* watching pornography on Pornhub. And don't even mention mobile phones: 68% of phone users check their phones within 15 minutes of waking up; 87% have their phone by their side at all times, day and night; the average user checks their phone 150 times per day. The thing to remember is that the ego will enthusiastically throw one escape route after another at your feet, promising you that this one will finally give you what you're looking for, despite all prior experience and evidence to the contrary. It would gladly see you piss your life away in an endless, futile search for a non-existent pot of gold at the end of an illusory rainbow.

You can convince yourself that you're looking for success, wealth, respect, sex or recognition. You can go one step further and delude yourself into believing that you're really making something of yourself and building a lasting legacy. But what you're actually doing is swimming around in unconsciousness. Many millions of people live most of their life in a state of unconscious pursuit of these things while a quiet sense of discomfort and dis-ease eats away at them. They seek out their next fix with the single-mindedness of a heroin addict while an ever increasing sense of panic quietly creeps up on them day after day. To cope with this, they go back round the loop, turning to the very thing that got them into the shit in the first place to attempt to get them out of it. If this isn't insanity I don't know what is.

Only when a man has exhausted countless futile avenues will he wonder if he's been looking in the wrong place all along. I see this happening for more and more men, but on balance the men who really pay attention are few and far between. Fewer still will realise that they are being called to undertake the true hero's journey to the final frontier, the last place they ever expected to find an answer: within. That is what happened to me when I started writing this book.

How and Why I Quit Porn

Some blokes might find this difficult to believe and may even accuse me of bullshitting, but as this book goes to publish I have been porn free for over four years. Yep, no porn for well over 48 months. No quick trip to Pornhub, no cheeky vid when my wife isn't looking. Nothing. Nada. I went cold turkey. I am teetotal. The reason I quit porn is simple: I was tired of giving my power away, unable to give myself fully to Ell because I was preoccupied with the fantasy women inside my head—women who weren't really women at all, but were two-dimensional caricatures with giant bouncing breasts and elongated "oohs" and "ahhhs."

I first encountered porn as a teenager but didn't start really 'watching' it until around 2005 when a friend said to me, "You know you can watch this stuff for free online?" I didn't consider myself to have any issue with it at first. Over the coming months and years, I started using it more and more. The slippery slope was subtle but undeniable. My usage was getting progressively worse. Any time I was anxious (and I get anxious a lot), a trip to a porn site quickly followed. What started out as one day a week eventually became too frequent for my liking. I was uncomfortable with what I was doing and my conscience ate away at me. I'm not one of those guys who will watch a feature length porno like it's a blockbuster movie, a bowl of popcorn in one hand and a bottle of lube in the other. Nevertheless, I decided enough was enough when I started writing this book. After all, how could I possibly write a life-changing book for men and a whole chapter on blocking escape routes whilst mindlessly engaging in porn myself?

I knew I had to face up to what I was doing. I had started to feel like porn was controlling me rather than the other way round. Off and on I had noticed myself living in a fictitious world. I would find myself playing out fantasies in my head in simple, everyday situations. On the outside, everything looked normal, but while doing the most normal of things like queuing in a shop, I would be secretly fantasising about fucking a woman I knew nothing about. All she had done was pop out for some bread and milk, the poor woman. I wasn't living in reality; everyday events had acquired a seedy, secretive edge.

This is all fairly acceptable for men in our society today. Everyone 'knows' that men think about sex once every eight seconds, or so the common joke goes. This line of thinking is pretty sinister though; it quietly condones male objectification of women and aggression and sexual violence towards them while also subtly defining us as nothing more than sex-obsessed animals.

I can't speak for all men, but I can say for myself that this isn't accurate. Sex has been difficult for me at different times in my life.

Like millions of teenage boys worldwide, I had to learn about sex from dirty magazines, porn videos and schoolboy banter with my mates and felt pressurised to automatically know what I was doing. Nowadays the expectations are artificially enhanced, with porn actresses (many of whom have had plastic surgery) portraying unrealistic images of what a female looks like, not to mention the huge penises on display by the male porn actors, leaving young boys feeling inadequate and believing they have to mimic what they see in porn videos. Young boys' heads become saturated with these homogenised images so much so that when they eventually have sex with girls, they're disappointed by the realness of their imperfect (i.e. completely acceptable, natural, feminine, human) form. Maybe the reason men sometimes approach sex with such a domineering, conquest-driven attitude is because we're actually scared shitless by it—(*what the fuck is the clitoris and how do we find it? Oh fuck it, I'll just fuck her senseless instead like that bloke in the porn film*). We don't want to feel the emotional discomfort that would come from admitting that we don't know what the hell we are doing.

One thing I know for sure is that sex isn't straightforward for men. The fact that university aged guys in the US are having to be taught about what the word 'consensual' means, the prevalence of rape at universities and the clear need to teach young men that a partner is allowed to change their mind at any point in the process, at which point it stops being consensual sex, is a sure sign that when it comes to sex, we've got a long way to go. The vow of male silence has prohibited us from voicing our fears, questions and doubts, forcing us to go along with the herd, taking unspoken cues about how to be a 'real man' in this area and often demanding that we turn other human beings into objects, deepening our sense of disconnection and ultimately, increasing our sense of guilt and shame.

All blokes masturbate in private, but there is a distinct difference between privacy and secrecy. Porn use often happens in secret, which can generate a rush of adrenaline, adding to the sense of excitement and arousal, but which can also generate guilt and shame. Privacy is a reflection of healthy boundaries. When I used porn, I noticed a subtle but definite gap open up between me and Ell because of my dishonesty. For a while, I was more interested in getting a quick fix, so I'd never tell her before I felt like using porn, but only afterwards. Even telling her was a huge win for me because if the ego had had its wicked way, I wouldn't have uttered a single word.

One of the most horrible things that sometimes happened to me when I used to watch a lot of porn would be when one of the images that I'd been watching would flash through my mind's eye while I was having sex with Ell. Luckily, Ell and I make a lot of eye contact during sex which helped me stay connected, but nevertheless the more I watched porn, the less I wanted to look or be looked at. In those moments I would think, "Whatever you do Nige, don't let yourself be seen here, because if Ell sees you, she'll know what you've been doing. And if she knows, she'll be disgusted and she'll leave."

Refuse to Be a Pornhub Statistic

I am now 100% porn free and proud. I should get a t-shirt made. It takes guts for a man to let go of porn, perhaps more so to actually talk about it. We have normalised men using porn so much that any man who *doesn't* use it is considered the abnormal one. We just don't talk about it and it's become an inherent part of the fabric of omertà. We should be talking about it though, because porn isn't just a bit of harmless fun. Men consistently report that the more they use porn, the more extreme and deviant their preferences become. The more extreme the porn, the more guilt you will feel.

When we view porn as an escape route rather than excusing it as an everyday activity for everyday blokes, we get a disturbing snapshot into the depth of guilt that men are collectively carrying. Pornhub, the largest porn site on the internet, revealed that in 2016, it had 23 billion visits, with 91.98 billion videos viewed—that's 12.5 videos viewed for every man, woman and child on earth. 74% of viewers were male, which means that men watched 68 billion porn videos that year. Incidentally, one of the most popular search terms was the word "teen." You decide what you want these numbers to mean, but I will ask one question: what impact does just this one escape route have on you?

Personally, I don't regret my decision to stop using porn, and I don't care if casinos, strip clubs or pornographic websites are legal; they are the ego's playthings and have no place in my life. Choosing to break omertà is more important to me than indulging in my hedonistic fantasies, for which I pay a high price—loss of integrity. I value myself more than that and I value women more than that. Yes, I sometimes miss the cheap thrill that comes with watching porn and occasionally I notice myself wanting to use it, especially if I'm having a bad day. But I refuse to cross that line.

I refuse to heap that guilt upon myself. I refuse to be a Pornhub statistic.

Along the way I've become much better at dealing with the anxiety that was at the root of wanting to use it in the first place. Nowadays I'm closer to Ell. Our sex life is better—more frequent, more exciting, more real. I don't fantasise as much about random women in the street, although I do still struggle with all the skin on display in summertime.

Here's the difference though: nowadays, a thought might fly into my head, but I do my best to see the thought for what it is (nothing), and to let it fly out again. I don't feel so out of control. I'm not carrying that secretive, crippling guilt around with me like a ball and chain. I've reclaimed something that I'd given away— my power, maybe. My freedom.

Dead Ends and Cul-de-Sacs

In case this hasn't been crystal clear: *escape routes will never help you permanently escape your pain.* They always lead to dead ends and cul-de-sacs. They keep you stuck in anxiety, going round in circles and feeling increasingly guilty, trapped and ultimately, alone. *ACIM* states that "All roads that lead away from what you are will lead you to confusion and despair." The ego mind is both convinced and convincing that you are guilty and worthless; the reality is that *it isn't true.* We turn to our escape routes because we don't know what else to do. We secretly hope that one day they might actually deliver us a guilt-free fix, but they never, ever do. Regardless of how seductive or benign an escape route appears to be, the truth is that any and all escape routes will sooner or later destroy your integrity as a man and your connection to yourself.

The good news is that any craving, if it isn't acted on, will eventually pass. Sometimes, it's gone in seconds, sometimes minutes; other times, it takes longer to fall away. But once you understand that the craving is really a symptom of anxiety or blocked emotion, mirroring something essential about your relationship with life, dealing with that anxiety or blocked emotional pain becomes your focus and the need for an escape route falls away.

Your first task is to become aware of which escape routes you use to bind anxiety and then to begin to explore what is really happening below the surface. Awareness precedes choice, and choice allows change. Without awareness no progress is possible. All you are being asked to do at this point is to admit the escape routes you most often use. You do not need to give anything up yet. All we are doing is raising awareness. In fact, I would urge you *not* to make any sudden changes to your behaviour without putting a strategic plan in place, because the ego, given half a chance, will happily fill the gap with a more destructive escape route.

The ego will kick up a ruckus about the following Power Questions. Don't be surprised if you get a sudden urge to wash the car, paint the house, have a wank or take up knitting. To say that the ego doesn't want you to do this work is an understatement. To the ego, the most threatening thing you can do is to look within. When you answer these Power Questions, it will defend itself with the ferocity of a rabid dog and will do whatever is necessary to stop you from waking up. Be relentless and brutally honest in searching your mind and heart for the truth.

Break the Vow: Power Questions

1. What are your top five escape routes?
2. When and how often do you use them?
3. How far back does each escape route go in your life?
4. Beyond the quick fix, where does each escape route leave you?

If you are searching and fearless in answering these questions you will see the senselessness of using escape routes. You will probably see that you continually use them day after day, deliberately feeding yourself poison. Eventually, when the pain becomes so acute that you can't cope anymore, you'll be ready to give your escape routes up. Like an addict who has attended a few twelve step fellowship recovery meetings, you will not be able to use your escape route of choice in the same way anymore. The awareness that you are on the run, that this is not just a bit of harmless fun, will eat away at you and at some point on the journey you'll probably find that your escape routes have stopped working. They don't do the job they used to do: even when you're drunk, or high, or watching porn, or smoking, or gambling, you'll have that nagging voice in the back of your mind telling you, "You don't need to do this man. This isn't right. There must be a better way."

And there is. But you're going to have to learn a new way of coping with everything that you once numbed. For many men, this means coming face to face with the Hulk within and learning how to deal with it differently.

CHAPTER 14

BEYOND ANGER

*"Just because someone stumbles and loses their
path, doesn't mean they're lost forever."*
—Charles Xavier

Anger is a male pandemic in our society. Even as I write these
words, the newspaper headlines are screaming about the violent
behaviour of shoppers gone mad, punching and kicking their
way through Black Friday, readily entering the public gladiator's
arena to do battle with each other over a coffee maker. They are
people just like you and me—angry people, everywhere. Despite
how unacceptable many of us think anger is (especially when it is
involves females or children), the truth is that anger is the ego's
knee-jerk reaction whenever we perceive that anyone has wronged
us. As you can see from the Black Friday example above, it doesn't
actually take much to get a reaction.

We live in a society dominated by a patriarchal mindset that
condemns anger on the one hand, tut-tutting in judgement and
parental disappointment, yet on the other, champions anger the
way a boxing coach champions a prize fighter. We buy into the
story that anger is always justified and is a reaction to external

circumstances: that we are somewhat powerless over whether we get angry or not. We believe that the fastest way to get peace is to get even.

We explored anger in part one of the book in some detail, looking at the dynamics of the ego and how it always resorts to attack and blame as its primary strategy for coping with life. In chapter six I revealed my personal history of anger and violence and said that inside every man lurks a potential monster. Whether that monster emerges or not depends in part on whether a man is equipped with the tools and space to explore and express his anger in a healthy, non-destructive way, as well as upon other factors such as the rules around anger in his family system and whether the confines of his identity 'allow' him to express anger or not. Ultimately, many men turn their anger inwards, which can lead to isolation, depression and even suicide.

You Don't Have a Rocket: You Have a Bomb

Everyday anger causes so-called normal men like you and me to do stupid things. We readily use alcohol and football (often at the same time), for example, to vent our deep frustration and anger at the world, getting up the next morning as if our diatribes the day before never happened. We trudge back to our monotonous jobs and our monotonous lives, eager for the following weekend to come so that we can do it all over again. We let ourselves off the hook time and time again, engaging in a distorted process of selective remembering that we pretend justifies and validates our actions.

Some of us like to blame our anger and aggression on the fact that we have ten times more testosterone than females. However, aggression researchers Archer and Lloyd found that aggression is less do to with testosterone and more to do with a man perceiving that his reputation or honour is being threatened.

Don't be fooled into thinking that you "don't do anger" or that you are exempt just because you don't express anger violently. Even the mask of Mr Nice Guy or Mr Compliant is covering up a great well of anger. In fact, it would be fair to say that these guys are the angriest of all, although their anger isn't expressed explicitly and therefore burrows its way underground, leaking out sideways like sulphuric acid. This silent but deadly anger corrodes away a man's integrity and his relationship with those around him. Outwardly, everything might seem perfectly normal, but more often than not, his witty indirect comments, jokes or observations are laced with venomous attack, leaving a bitter taste in the mouth.

A Course in Miracles puts it this way: "The anger [you carry] may take the form of any reaction ranging from mild irritation to rage. The degree of the emotion you experience does not matter. You will become increasingly aware that a slight twinge of annoyance is nothing but a veil drawn over intense fury." That intense fury is, as Gil Schwartz said in *Men's Health* in 2006, a kind of fuel, and fuel is needed if you want to launch a rocket. "But if all you have is fuel without any complex internal mechanism directing it," says Schwartz, "you don't have a rocket. You have a bomb."

The form anger takes may vary from person to person. It could be a tiny twinge; for example, the husband who secretly resents his wife and takes subtle verbal side-swipes at her. Anger might leak out in the form of a mini outburst—an argument down the pub, perhaps prompted by a bloke's favourite footy team losing a game. Or at the extreme end of the spectrum, it may be a frenzied and shocking outburst, during which for example, a man stabs another motorist for no good reason at all. This happened near my home recently and when I read about the incident, it was beyond baffling. The man who got stabbed died, and all he was doing was driving his car. In the moment, the rush of rage is so intense and visceral that it feels completely justified. It is as if something in the mind snaps and the coordinates of sanity go out the window.

The question of *how* to stop violently acting out on anger begs for an answer. That's what the rest of this chapter will aim to do: give you a new set of tools to help you contain the beast and release anger without causing harm. The first thing to remember is that anger is an effect and a symptom. If you really want to change it, you have to look below the surface. I practise these principles myself and I assure you that they require the same focus and self-discipline that it takes to train intensely in the gym.

When I hurled a bedside cabinet at my ex in a fit of rage over a decade ago, it was the straw that finally broke the camel's back. I made the decision to face anger head-on, determined to find a way to stop myself from mutating into Hulk. Luckily, the cabinet missed its mark, but the sight of my ex trembling in fear was potent enough for me to find a way to stop the insanity. I knew it was going to be tough going trying to contain and diminish this forceful energy that would seemingly arise out of nowhere, demanding instant release.

It's Not About Anger Management

Fellas, I want to make this crystal clear: this is not about anger *management*. I think that approach can be useful for preventing anger from leaking out in the moment, but it doesn't actually solve the underlying problem. Our society is obsessed with managing anger rather than investigating what it is protecting. In fact, our society is obsessed with dealing with issues at the level of symptom rather than cause, full stop. This is true in healthcare, education, politics and almost any other arena you can think of.

You are welcome to try everything under the sun to manage or control your anger, but eventually I bet you'll find it controlling you, or at the very least, you'll likely feel that it's just there on the periphery like the Hulk, waiting for an opportunity to engulf you again. You can exercise like a madman to help work off "your" anger. (Notice how we lay claim to it, declaring that it belongs to us. Interesting that we do that.) You can attempt to refocus your anger towards finding the latest solutions in how to manage it. You can attempt to think and clear your mind, before expressing your thoughts about "your" anger to the other person (preferably using only I statements if you've done some anger management work). To be brutally honest though, managing anger is just a trendy way of strengthening ego because in keeping anger at arm's length, you give anger a huge amount of power. The more you attempt to manage your anger, the more you shut down and the more dead you become.

Lay Down Your Arms

Albert Einstein reportedly said that no problem can be solved from the same level of consciousness that created it. In other words, leaning towards the very same fear-based thought system that made the problem and expecting it to help you find a way out is delusional. I really want you to understand that this is about far more than anger management. It is really about experiencing a paradigm shift.

You can't turn to the part of your mind that is interested in maintaining the status quo to help you change. That part of you, the ego, isn't interested in finding solutions. It loves the problem. Yet until you see the ego for what it is—a dysfunctional part of the mind, a doppelgänger, an imposter that believes itself to be you—you will keep chasing your tail, habitually reacting angrily to him, her, this or that. In A New Earth, Eckhart Tolle says, "Whether the other person is right or wrong is irrelevant to the ego. It is much more interested in self-preservation that in the truth." The ego will feed you more and more bullshit to keep you engaged with the problem. If you really want to go beyond anger, you need a different perspective on it—and you certainly won't find a solution within omertà.

It's important to acknowledge that there is a very real payoff for staying angry; it means you don't have to take responsibility for your thoughts and actions. As I've already said though, the cost is huge; stay angry and you're destined to keep going round the same loop, slowly but surely heading towards more disastrous consequences.

Diminishing Anger

So if the ego isn't going to help you move beyond anger, what will? The key is to access a different part of the mind—a different quality of consciousness. To do this you will first need to diminish the anger you feel, effectively disarming yourself. I want to clarify that diminishing (or containing) anger isn't about managing it, and it isn't about denying it. Denying anger is detrimental to your health. Diminishing anger however is about taking responsibility for your thoughts and actions, creating a safe space to express what lies beneath the anger and developing the ability to remember the truth about yourself and others. This is very different from trying to manage or control your anger, and it is also very different from expressing anger without boundaries. Out is not always better than in.

Diminishing anger enables you to access the fear, shame and guilt that lie beneath it so that you can experience real change, moving beyond the prison anger creates to a better life. Here are the four vital cornerstones to diminishing anger safely in the moment:

- Practising radical awareness
- Doing nothing
- Breathing
- Using a Power Mantra to help bring about a change of mind.

Let's take a closer look at each one.

1. Practise radical awareness

Awareness is the precursor to change of any kind. Rebecca Linder Hintz says that awareness is "more than half the battle." You can't change the problem until you know what you're dealing with. Radical awareness is more than just being aware; it is awareness with a powerful intent behind it. Anytime you bring radical awareness to a situation, you bust the ego, like a police raid on a speakeasy. In bringing your darkness to the light, you realign yourself with who you really are: a warrior of the heart.

Here's a simple yet powerful example of radical awareness from my own life. The ego, as we've already explored, runs rampant in our world—not only with strangers, but with those we love and of course, ourselves. We are suspicious at best, vicious at worst, and downright savage during rush hour. You've already read about how triggered I get on the road. Well, while driving through a quaint village high street in West Sussex a while back, it didn't take very long for the ego to rear its ugly head. First up, a guy nearly hit my car on the mini roundabout. That kicked things off nicely. *What a dick!* I thought. Next, a white van didn't give way to me in the narrow street, hurtling towards me at 40mph. *Bastard! You could've been more courteous.* Then there was the jogger who was running half off the pavement and half off. *Stupid cow, does she want to get herself killed?* (No concessions for the fact that she was protecting her young children who were riding their bikes alongside her from the traffic.) Then, some idiot braked too quickly behind me. Then a stupid fool stepped into the road without looking. Then there was a fat cow, followed by a thin cow, and a pensioner who'd had so much Botox that she conned me into believing she was Cheryl Thingamajig. When I realised she was old enough to be my Great Gran, I hit the horn in disgust. Then I caught myself. I decided that I'd had enough of the ego (again!) and that enough was enough—it was time to take drastic action. I set about applying radical awareness to my attack thoughts.

Instead of letting the attack thoughts continue to gush forth, I started to consciously notice each thought as it happened. To do this, I had to imagine 'watching' my thoughts instead of completely identifying with them. Many mindfulness teachers suggest imagining that your thoughts are clouds floating across the sky. Instead of getting all caught up in the shape, size and colour of each cloud, you simply see them for what they are and remember that you are not your thoughts. When I got home that day, I decided it was time to up the ante. It was time to practise the Elastic Band Technique.

The Elastic Band Technique

I have taught this technique to people from all over the world. It always generates a laugh, along with cultivating the kind of laser awareness needed to extract yourself from the ego's clutches. The technique is very simple: wear an elastic band on your wrist and take the following steps:

1. Whenever you get angry or notice an insane thought, twang the band.
2. Take a deep breath.
3. Say the words, "I could see peace instead of this."
4. Choose peace and be the change.

Wearing an elastic band helps raise awareness and can bring about a change of mind. It consciously connects you to the present moment much like a Tibetan singing bowl or Rosary bead does in meditation or prayer. Each twang sends a short sharp electrical shock to your brain, instantly scrambling fear-based thoughts and leaving an empty space in their place so that you can think something new.

Some people may refuse to use the elastic band technique calling it unspiritual or cruel, but I assure you it's perfectly harmless. In fact, I think it's usually just denial when someone objects to using this technique on the grounds of it not being kind. (A word of warning though: the ego will hijack anything given the opportunity and will try to turn this technique against you, insisting that you use the band as an instrument of self-torture rather than a tool for expanding your awareness. A gentle twang will suffice.) Taking a zero tolerance approach to the ego may sound pretty harsh, but given that we think approximately 60,000 thoughts a day and that 59,959 of them are probably fear based, I think it's fair to say this modest technique is absolutely essential.

Twanging the band throughout the day will generate heightened awareness of your thoughts. Through this heightened or radical awareness you will discover new choices. It can be intense practising radical awareness, but the goal is to expose the insanity of this thought system. As Eckhart Tolle says, "All that is required to become free of the ego is to be aware of it, since awareness and ego are incompatible. Awareness is the power that is concealed within the present moment." Initially, heightened awareness might make you feel like you've gone nuts. It seems like the ego has become even more powerful, but as soon as you remember it's just having a hissy fit because it feels threatened, you can laugh at the insanity of it all. If there is one thing we could with practising more, it is the art of not taking ourselves too seriously.

2. Do nothing

Your second technique for diminishing anger is simply to do nothing. Imagine the following scene: you feel pulsating hot anger run through your body. You're in full on fight or flight mode, ready to punch someone, ready to lash out... and you do nothing.

You don't swallow the anger down, but neither do you act out on it. The ego is outraged at the very idea of this.

When a man gets angry, he becomes consumed with fear, adrenaline and cortisol, and his thinking often becomes highly illogical and mindless. I have yet to meet a brother who has truly resolved a situation by verbally or physically attacking another brother. So fellas, in the name of sanity, if you have nothing supportive or kind to say—and I promise you that when you're triggered, you don't—SHUT THE F**K UP!

Doing nothing might *sound* easy but in the moment it is anything but. It requires you to master your own mind and emotions. You have to become like Daniel in *Karate Kid*, capable of complete focus. Despite what our preconceptions may tell us, the weak man is actually the one using his fists or vomiting out words of spite or hate; the strong man is the one who can watch his anger but not act out on it. He doesn't deny, freeze inwardly or dissociate from his anger and the physical feelings that come with it either. He is present to it, feeling it but doing nothing with it other than experiencing it. Doing nothing looks simple but is incredibly profound and brings a quiet sense of strength. I dare you to try it next time you're pissed off. If it helps, one thing you can do is name what you're feeling. Saying out loud, "I'm so fucking angry right now!" can help release anger in a safe way. The boundary you must enforce here is not to use your words as a weapon of intimidation if anyone else is in your vicinity (again, see Appendix II for the bottom line code of conduct contract), and absolutely under no circumstances to act out on your urges to be violent. It can be helpful however to hear yourself say that you feel angry. This is part of developing greater self-awareness, which is key to no longer losing control. However, there is a huge difference between saying "I'm fucking angry" and "You're making me fucking angry." One is accountable and the other reeks of victim consciousness and is laced with threat. No prizes for guessing which is the better option.

3. Breathe

When you are angry, your breathing becomes shallow and your muscles tense up. Some theories suggest that sharks attack certain divers because they are able to detect electrical impulses given off by the diver's accelerated heart rate. Sharks have the uncanny ability to sense fear, and when they do the diver is as good as dead. Similarly, when you are in a state of heightened reactivity, the heart beats rapidly and the breath is out of control. Focusing all your attention on slowing the breath down will bring you to your senses and help you make a clear-headed decision about what to say or do.

I suggest you try a technique called "Box Breathing" which Brené Brown describes in the book Rising Strong. There are five simple steps to box breathing:

1. Breathe in for a count of four.
2. Hold for a count of four.
3. Breathe out for a count of four.
4. Hold for a count of four.
5. Repeat 4-8 times.

Breathing slowly and deeply stabilises the breath, regulates your heart rate, and in turn diminishes anger. By breathing deeply you reconnect with the moment and kick your parasympathetic nervous system into play. This helps create space in your mind for you to respond rather than react.

4. Use a Power Mantra to help bring about a positive change of mind

Mantras are short sentences, traditionally repeated over and over (often in meditation) in order to reinforce the message they communicate. They are part of many ancient spiritual traditions. I know they can sound a bit wanky especially because they're very popular in the new age movement, which is nothing if not fluffy, but I promise you, if a mantra has a strong intention behind it, it can be incredibly powerful. Remember, much of our work is about 'rewiring' the brain (which isn't hardwired in the first place) by creating new neural pathways or connections, and mantras can be an excellent tool for that. By repeating the words *I am never upset for the reason I think* or *I am determined to stand for peace*, for example, you take responsibility for your own thinking. Without a target the ego doesn't really have anywhere to go, and is temporarily neutralised.

You might want to experiment with the following Power Mantras or make up your own. Keep the emphasis on accountability you can't go far wrong.

- I am determined to see this person/situation differently.
- I could see peace instead of this.
- I am not a victim here. I always have a choice.
- My strength is my defencelessness.
- It's safe to walk away. There is nothing to prove.

Containing and Diminishing Anger in the Moment

The tools of practising radical awareness, doing nothing, breathing and using Power Mantras are four cornerstones to diminishing anger safely in the moment so that you don't explode and cause emotional, mental or physical damage. When you put it all together, you get something like this:

1. As soon as you notice you are angry (irritated, annoyed, murderous and pissed off are all forms of anger), breathe slowly and deeply into your belly.
2. Don't react or defend. Do and say nothing.
3. If you still feel angry, say out loud "I feel angry." If your body is full of tension, clench and release your fists three times. Inhale as you clench, and exhale powerfully as you release.
4. Repeat a Power Mantra to yourself.
5. Walk away.

It is vital that you apply these steps or do something similarly constructive every time you find yourself getting angry—no exceptions. You are learning how to respond rather than react here. Circumstances may vary but on every occasion when you find your peace of mind disturbed, it's a sure sign that the ego has been activated. Given half a chance, it will hit back hard so it's vital to nip it in the bud.

Now I am going to show you how to deal with anger without hurting yourself or another. The following exercise will teach you how to express anger safely and cleanly so that you can get below the anger and deepen your awareness of the thoughts, feelings and beliefs that drive it.

Exercise: Expressing Anger Safely

Instead of Power Questions in this chapter, you are going to do a written exercise, the intention of which is to create a safe container for you to be able to express pent up anger cleanly without having to harm anyone else in the process. Until you uncover and express the old emotions the anger hides, you'll continue to feel angry. This exercise will take you beyond the trigger to the root of the problem.

1. Take a blank piece of paper and a pen and set a timer for five minutes.

2. Think about all the things that are pissing you off. Put the pen to paper and write out all of your attack, blame and judgemental thoughts. Empty the mind completely, leaving no stone unturned, no matter how murderous or sick or seemingly inconsequential the thoughts may appear to you. Do not censor yourself. Scribble quickly and intensely without any gaps or pauses. No one will read this, not even you. You may notice that your writing gets larger and more distorted as the exercise unfolds. You might not write in straight lines as you do this. You might even tear through the paper with your pen. This is perfectly normal. Rationality and control have no place in this exercise.

3. When the alarm goes off, notice if there is still more. If there is, go for another five minutes.

4. When you are finished take a deep breath with your eyes closed. Then tear up the paper and say out loud, "I am determined to see this differently."

5. Take another deep breath. Close your eyes. Imagine dropping through a trapdoor to what you're really feeling underneath the anger. Let yourself feel whatever is underneath the anger—but don't force it. (Most men have forgotten how to feel. If you're one of them, know that it's okay. Read chapter 14 and 15. They will help.) Take your time.

6. Notice if any SMBs have surfaced. Acknowledge that the real battleground is inside you, not 'out there' in the world.

7. Take a deep breath and reaffirm the kind of man you choose to be and the values you commit to living by.

8. Repeat this exercise anytime you are triggered and want to release the anger safely.

A Change of Heart

The anger we men bear is like an enormous rusty chain weighing us down, and with it comes the deep, niggling suspicion that we are bad and broken beyond repair. This belief has influenced and directed our decisions and actions since time began, causing us to resort to violence over and over again.

While we continue to just look through the lens of perpetrator and victim, we will not create the culture that is needed to call men into a different way of being. The thing most people don't see is the connection between a man's rage and his pain. To the extent that we deny a man the right to feel and express this pain is the extent to which we drive it underground and trigger the Hulk.

Until we make a deliberate effort to see the call for love in somebody's actions, no matter how hateful or violent, we will continue to miss what's really happening. If you have ever known violence within yourself—and I guarantee that you have, even if you've never acted it out—I want you to consider that the extent to which you attacked was the extent to which you were in pain. I'm absolutely not excusing violent behaviour here, in myself or anyone else. What I did in my previous relationship, for example, was unacceptable. However we can't just stop the conversation here.

Men need permission to talk about the Hulk that lives inside us, not to condone or excuse it in any way, but in order to get support, take responsibility and expose what drives him to such awful extremes. Without that, we'll never get the chance to experience anything different. Rage and violence are the proverbial guard dogs protecting the grievously wounded boy in hiding. There's nothing more dangerous than an angry boy in a grown man's body, yet while we continue to focus all our attention on a man's aggressive behaviour, we overlook the boy within him who needs help. We have to be brave enough to do two things: firstly, to put firm boundaries in place when it comes to issues surrounding Hulk-like behaviour, and secondly, to dare to be compassionate enough to understand what's motivating that behaviour in ourselves and any man who has become violent.

To the extent we refuse to feel our old emotional pain is the extent to which we will react violently in our day-to-day lives, often with horrible consequences. Once a man has stopped using escape routes and has allowed himself to work *with* his anger rather than try to manage it, he will naturally reconnect with what lies beneath it—usually, a shitload of pain, grief, sadness and loss. Learning how to actually feel all of this is the key to moving and living beyond anger and it is this task that next faces us on the *Odd Man Out* journey.

CHAPTER 15

GRIEVING THE LOST BOY

"The most sophisticated people I know—
inside they are all children."
—Jim Henson

I have already discussed in some depth how we are wounded as boys and how most of the difficulties we experience as men are the result of not knowing how to process the hurt we experienced in childhood. Once you have learned how to contain and express your anger safely, your next job is to reconnect to the lost boy you split off from and left behind in childhood. I know this might sound a bit touchy-feely. It probably bumps up against every single omertà-approved idea about masculinity and what being a 'real man' is all about: *Real men don't do sissy shit like this. All this therapy talk might be fine for you Nige, but I don't talk that way. Never have, never will.* The only thing I ask at this point is that you commit to reading the rest of this chapter and keep an open mind. I want to assure you that you don't need to go to an inner child workshop to do this work. No joss sticks required!

You might think that this chapter doesn't apply to you, but the truth is that most men are like wounded boys walking around in grown men's bodies denying that the wound is there. The lost boy is the wounded part of us that we've abandoned in our quest to become 'real men'. We may be men physiologically, but most of us are still boys psychologically. As Daniel Prokop says, "We live in an adolescent society, where never growing up seems more the norm than the exception. Little boys wearing expensive suits and adult bodies should not be allowed to run big corporations. They shouldn't be allowed to run governments, armies, religions, small businesses and charities either and they make pretty shabby husbands and fathers too." And yet they do run big corporations, they do run armies and governments, religions and small businesses, and they do become fathers. The vow of male silence actively encourages us to posture and pretend that we know what we're doing, locking the lost boy away in a metaphorical box and burying him deep in our subconscious minds.

We have erected an imaginary wall between who we were as kids and who we are now, and it seems as solid as granite. We go about our days, rushing from place to place with a list of Very Important Things to do, forgetting that childhood ever happened—or, when it surfaces in our memory, quickly numbing it out. But it did happen; the truth is that manhood is simply an extension of boyhood. There isn't a magical process that occurs overnight when a human being turns eighteen or twenty-one years old that erases the impact your childhood had on you. For most of us, because childhood is painful or hard to remember, we draw a veil across it and treat it as if it was another life, lived by another person, someone we used to be but no longer are.

If this worked, it wouldn't be an issue, but there is a problem with this strategy: unexamined history repeats itself. Denial of your boyhood will create a warped view of manhood. There are few things more dangerous than a wounded boy in a grown man's body with a world of weapons at his disposal. Take a look at the global political stage if in doubt.

You've Got to Feel It to Heal It

You might say that you're done with the past, but that doesn't mean the past is done with you. If you're really honest, you probably know that history seems to keep repeating itself over and over again, both in your life and in the world in general. Denial of the past only serves to make its grip on your present stronger. Deny it and your unfinished business will bang loudly on the door, trying to get your attention.

If you look back on your childhood with a sense of apathy or lack of feeling, be curious about what that might indicate. In *Healing the Shame that Binds You*, John Bradshaw writes, "When emotionally abandoned people describe their childhoods, it is always without feeling." He goes on to quote Alice Miller, who writes that emotionally abandoned people "recount their earliest memories without any sympathy for the child they once were. Very often they show disdain and irony, even derision and cynicism. In general, there is a complete absence of real emotional understanding or serious appreciation of their own childhood vicissitudes and no conception of their true need—beyond the need for achievement. The internalization of the original drama has been so complete that the illusion of a good childhood can be maintained."

In my opinion, insisting that you had a really good childhood is normally a sign of huge unresolved inner turmoil, pain and loss from said childhood. The statement "I had a good childhood" acts as a barrier blocking any inquiry into it. In other words, if you insist you had a good childhood, you're saying, "Do not enter. Back off," a bit like the scene in *Good Will Hunting* when Sean Maguire, played by Robin Williams, tells Will (Matt Damon), "It's not your fault." Will replies by saying, "I know," first in an offhand, couldn't care less way, and then getting more and more defensive as Maguire keeps repeating, "It's not your fault." For Will to reconnect with the lost boy inside himself would mean opening up the floodgates and being engulfed by the old, long-buried pain of childhood—and Will doesn't want that to happen. Eventually, he cracks wide open, sobbing into Maguire's shoulder and saying, "I'm sorry,"—even though it was *him* who had been abused. The internalised sense of guilt, shame and responsibility, which Will had carried around with him for years, finally tumbles out. I can't watch that scene without getting emotional. It's a beautiful demonstration of one man being reunited with the lost boy within.

I often think that the measure of a man is in his willingness to revisit the 'scene of the crime'—the moment in his life when he was wounded—and take another look around so that a new story can be written and a new meaning can be assigned to the things that happened. In Will's case, he had nothing to be sorry for. He had been the victim of abuse, yet as is so common with abuse survivors, he carried guilt and shame about what had happened. Reconnecting with the lost boy was the only way for him to process that grief, see what had happened from a more accurate perspective, and truly let it go.

Sometimes we *do* acknowledge that there is a child self in us. For example, at Burning Man festival in 2015, Alexandr Milov, an artist from Odessa in Ukraine, erected a sculpture of two wire framed adult bodies sitting back to back with their heads in their hands—a couple in despair after an argument. Inside the wire framed adult bodies were two children's bodies, facing each other with their hands pressed together, reaching out for contact in the middle of the conflict. The child within is desperate to reach out and connect, even as the adult turns to their dodgy survival strategies. A photo of the installation went viral on social media, proving just how much we do actually connect to the idea and perhaps the memory of the young child inside us.

If you're a dad, you might have moments where you look at your child, or a child of one of your friends, and catch a glimpse of the boy you used to be. You might also get a sense of the lost boy in you while working through this book.

At some point in your life, you need to grieve the losses and hurts from your childhood. Even the 'nicest' of childhoods contains losses, because life is change. As a baby becomes a toddler, there is the loss of permanent physical closeness to the mother. As a toddler goes to kindergarten, there is the loss of being with mother 24/7, and so on. In a 1994 article by Tom Golden, the list of losses from childhood include, "The loss of seeing the world as a safe place, or all of the unmet expectations, thwarted intentions, or unspoken communications we might have stored inside us. When looked at in this way, we begin to see that grief is an integral part of being alive, a part of our daily living. It is woven into the fabric of life." Fail to grieve, and the pain each loss triggered will build up and calcify in the mind, body and heart until eventually you become rigid, beige and two-dimensional, unable to experience joy or pain.

A Practice, Not an Event

Reconnecting to the lost boy within you isn't a one-off event. Think of it more as a practice. The goal is to repeatedly expose the SMBs anytime there is an upset in the present, then let yourself feel whatever is there and finally move to a place of correction. You might have to revisit the scene of the crime many times, perhaps in therapy, perhaps just in your everyday life. Men in particular have to get beyond the two default defences of getting pissed off or shutting down, which as Brené Brown identified are the two main ways men react to being vulnerable. On the other side of pissed off or shut down you will experience sadness, grief, fear, guilt and shame. This sounds unappealing, but as I've repeatedly explained, until you go there you cannot move through to genuine correction and will remain in the purgatory of attack and blame.

Identifying the beliefs (the SMBs) that are running the show is a vital practice to incorporate into your life. Doing this over and over again will enable you to make powerful choices about the kind of man you want to be. Resist going there, and the belief will persist, and all your efforts to conquer, succeed or strive for recognition will be hollow and pointless. When you identify what you have made a situation mean about you, remember the lost boy who made that belief up in the first place and then correct the belief, a new world opens up to you. Before you can correct any mistaken belief, however, you must first recognise it. Bringing the SMB into conscious awareness places you in a prime position to make a better choice.

How to Reconnect With the Lost Boy

The bad news is that there is no manual for doing this work. You can't just follow a neat sequence of steps and tick this work off your list. The good news is that the boy within is easily accessed if you know where to tap. From that point on, it's all about the relationship you have to that part of yourself.

The easiest and most effective way to connect with the lost boy within you is to start paying attention to your triggers—the events in your daily life, whether big or small, that cause you to react aggressively or shut down—and instead of seeing them as proof of how everyone is out to get you or how hard life is or whatever bullshit story your ego likes to weave, use the triggers as an opportunity to uncover the SMBs that you made up about yourself when you were a boy. Every current upset is an opportunity to change your mind about who you believe you are.

We've already talked at length about why it is necessary to contain the Hulk and about how the vast majority of men use anger to avoid feeling old emotional pain. We've talked about why we must be vigilant about our escape routes and hyper-vigilant about when we are turning to them. We're about to explore that really dodgy terrain for men—feelings. If you dare to let yourself feel your feelings, you're more than halfway there with uncovering the SMBs and reconnecting with the lost boy within because for most men, simply feeling upset brings up all sorts of beliefs: if you have feelings, many men believe, it makes you weak, pathetic, not a real man, a failure. As soon as you think to yourself that you've got to man up, you're close to uncovering an SMB.

For some men, the beliefs you carry about yourself will be so prominent that you face them on a daily basis in your life. You might be plagued by fear, insecurity and doubt. For others, trying to connect with the lost boy within will be more confusing than revealing. Some men might not be able to get beyond the Hulk who feels angry at the world all the time. I know that place. I spent years hanging out with the green monster, believing that I was him. If that's you, I encourage you to hang in there fella. Don't you dare quit now because that's exactly what the ego wants, for you to bin this bloody book and get back to what's comfy and familiar. Don't be fooled: what's comfortable and familiar will kill you, slowly and almost imperceptibly. To make the dash to freedom, all you are asked to do is to be willing to look back at your childhood and open your mind about what you might discover there. It could save your life.

In summary, anytime something happens in the present that causes you upset, you are gifted with a unique opportunity to use your feelings as a window to the past. You are given a second chance to go back to the scene of the crime and find something different there—something you may have missed the first time around. As we've explored, as a child you didn't understand the bigger picture. Any trigger in the present therefore becomes a timely invitation from the universe, with the potential to lead you out of darkness.

The purpose for exploring your past is to take another look at what happened back there and to uncover the story you made up about yourself, others and the world so that you can make a conscious, informed choice about whether you want to continue believing it. This is what unhooks you from the web of societal omertà. This doesn't mean negating your past. If you are to heal old wounds then you must first have reverence for them. But until you expose the SMBs that you made up about yourself back there and make a conscious effort to change your mind and reconnect with your heart, then the past will continue to haunt you in the present.

Exercise

Understanding the theory is one thing, but doing the work is another. So how do you actually reconnect with the lost boy? Use the following process. Notice when something in the present triggers or upsets you and ask yourself:

1. How do I feel? (If in doubt, choose one from the following list. Simplicity beats complexity every time. Angry. Sad. Scared. Lonely. Guilty. Ashamed.)
2. When was my earliest childhood memory of feeling like this?
3. Let yourself really remember how it felt to be that young boy. Remember your favourite hangouts, clothes, friends and activities. Notice how you feel about him and just allow it all.
4. To uncover the SMBs, ask yourself: What did I believe about myself as a boy at that moment?
5. The SMB will be staring you in the face at this point. Finish the sentence "I believe that I am…"

The Japanese Manga author Ai Yazawa once said, "Forgetting about our wounds isn't enough to make them disappear." In fact, our memories and the meanings we give them do anything but disappear. They might not be visible to the human eye, but more often than not they find their way underground, taking up residence deep in the subconscious. Trauma lives in the cells, often for many years. Stephen Levine has this to say on the matter: "It is not only the loose ends of recent traumas that are the cause of our grief, but those traumas long sequestered in our flesh and bones. The hurt burrows into the tissues of our body and the fibre of our mind and contracts around pain, turning it into suffering." Recently, I read that it isn't the events themselves that cause long-lasting trauma or pain, but the inability to express the emotion those events provoked. Repressed, unexpressed emotion is what does the damage.

In doing this work, you have revealed who you believe you are. You are now standing face to face with the lost boy who was buried alive all those years ago and has been gasping for air ever since. This boy has been yanking on your sleeve, day after day, trying to get your attention. Your job is to rebuild a relationship with him, to stop abandoning him in the way he felt abandoned as a kid. You have to learn how to talk to that part of your psyche as if he were an actual child, giving him the kind of love you thought you were denied.

If there was ever a time to say fuck it and cry this is it.

CHAPTER 16

REAL MEN CRY

"The path to a manly heart runs through a valley of tears."
—Sam Keen

A few weeks after I lost a testicle aged 6, the district nurse arrived on the doorstep clutching scissors and tweezers to remove the stitches from my scrotum. It was 1975 and for whatever reason, I wasn't given dissolvable stitches. The buggers had to come out. As she unthreaded the first stitch, I felt a sharp pain rocket through my body. I desperately wanted to cry, but something stopped me dead in my tracks. I had heard somewhere from a big person that "big boys don't cry," so I pushed out my tiny chest, gritted my teeth, clenched my fists so hard that they turned a milky white, and held my breath as a way of crushing and distorting the pain. When the ordeal was finally over the nurse smiled at me and said that I had been a very brave boy, just like the men in the gent's outfitters had, affirming me for burying my emotions. I felt anything but brave, but I looked up at her and smiled back anyway.

As far as I can recollect, this was the very first time I suppressed my feelings. I grew up in an environment that didn't really do crying except at weddings and funerals. Vulnerability—in fact, emotion of any kind—was seen as weakness, and weakness wasn't acceptable. My experience wasn't unique; we socialise boys out of crying in public starting at the tender age of five years old. A boy is expected to have perfected the art of not crying publicly by the age of ten; if at 11 or 12 he is still doing it, we feel that something must be wrong.

I remember seeing my dad cry for the first time when I was 14 or 15 years old. My parents had been squabbling in the bedroom, and Dad retreated to the bathroom. When he saw me standing in the doorway he broke down. I watched as he bit his knuckles to deaden his feelings. It was as if he was obeying an unspoken rule that forbade him from feeling. Or maybe he couldn't cope with the overwhelming feelings and had to try to shut them down. We never spoke about it, and I didn't see Dad cry again until many years later at his mother's funeral. Imagine that: I had lived 15 years on this planet without seeing my dad shed a single tear and then lived a bunch more without ever seeing it again. That is weird. What's weirder is that for so many children, this is considered normal.

Real Men Don't Cry

I'm definitely not normal because I am a man who is comfortable crying. When my dad died in 2009, my wife and I made the 300 mile trip up to see my family and attend the funeral. We arrived after driving for hours and within seconds of walking in the front door, I began to cry. The reality had suddenly hit me that I'd never see my dad in that house again.

My then 19-year-old nephew swiftly cut me off. "He's gone to a better place, so you don't need to cry," he said. He was trying to be helpful, but there was something defensive about his comment, something in it that was driven by anxiety at seeing me show even a moment of so-called weakness (otherwise known as grief, a normal and healthy response to losing a loved one). A few moments after seeing my nephew, I greeted my mum in the kitchen and broke down again as the full force of Dad's death hit me in the gut. She held me for a few seconds in total silence, after which the tension must have become unbearable because she said, "Come on, we're not having any more of that," (the word 'that' being the one syllable acknowledgement of my grief). She was trying to comfort me, and yet without even knowing it, Mum basically told me to stop feeling—or at least to stop showing it. I refused to conform. It had taken me long enough in my life to remember that it was okay to cry and I wasn't about to stop just because my mum wasn't comfortable with it.

What happened wasn't personal. In my family, as in a lot of western culture, feelings are a no-go area. People actually apologise for feeling even on the biggest days of their lives: at births, weddings and funerals; I heard about one dude who said he "almost cried" the day his child was born. Men are seen as weak or 'gay' if they cry at films (remember that under omertà, being homosexual, like being feminine, is still seen as something bad). Under certain very specific circumstances, feelings are permitted but only within strict limitations. Usually, the only time a man is allowed to really blubber is if his sports team gets relegated or promoted.

My wife told me recently about a man she knows who told his girlfriend, "The day I stopped crying, I became a man." This typical fella touched on something fairly universal in the male experience—the expectation that *real men don't cry*. Personally, I found this guy's brag pretty tragic. What exactly is our problem with crying? Why do we live in a world where 'real men' are expected to be solid as a rock in a crisis, a man of steel who can deal with the hardships of life rationally, logically and without emotion? What's so wrong with emotion, with being human?

I think that if men were more in touch with their feelings, they wouldn't be able to commit or sanction so many awful crimes— including inhuman hate crimes and acts of terrorism, paedophilia and so on. My guess is that this is why we collectively shame men into not feeling and expect them to walk around half dead. Heart-led leaders would be a serious threat to the status quo, and we can't have that now, can we?

When Did You Last Cry?

Seemingly, it all kicked off back in the Victorian era, where crying was viewed as better suited to a woman than a man. Patriarchy and omertà got a real boost in those days. According to researchers who collected a bunch of studies on crying, modern women shed tears between 30 and 64 times per year, but us blokes only cry between six and 17 times a year. I even think that for many men, those numbers are pushing it. I know lots of blokes who haven't cried for years.

Some professors say that a man's biology and physiology mean he will cry less than women and children, but I'm not entirely convinced. You might be surprised to learn that until they're teenagers, there is no difference between females and males in terms of how often or how intensely they cry. Even in adulthood, researchers Archer and Lloyd state that hormones only influence behaviour in the context of societal influences. Puberty is obviously a hugely influential process, but biology is not solely responsible for the huge discrepancy in the above statistics.

You might have convinced yourself that you don't need to cry, that it's pointless and doesn't achieve anything. Underneath that story there lurks a fear, and sadly it is all too real a fear. For many men in our world today, crying simply isn't acceptable; it is a threat to your whole identity.

We know that men have been routinely drilled to think and behave according to a code of 'masculine' conduct, and not crying is a prominent feature of that code. I don't care how much people protest that we men don't cry because it's "just the way men are," I'm convinced that the way we are is not solely influenced by biology. Along with biology, our social and cultural environments shape and influence us, right down to the long-lasting and often underestimated impact of the household we grew up in. I don't think you can segregate different influences and say that biology influences us but environment doesn't—or vice versa. I often wonder if biology plays a smaller part than we care to admit and that the vow of male silence is a highly influential force.

Using biology to justify why men appear to be the less emotional sex is, in my opinion, a convenient way of upholding the vow of male silence. It is as if we find it acceptable for very little boys to feel, but as soon as they begin edging their way towards manhood, we start to shut them down, sending out the subtle yet unmistakable message that it's no longer okay to cry.

However, there are negative ramifications for shutting down little boys' feelings. In the book The Prosperity Game, Steve

Nobel says, "Problems arise when a person feels ashamed of their vulnerability and seeks to suppress or cover it up with a hard exterior." He goes on to say, "Repressing or hiding vulnerability does not work in the long run. If we lose touch with our vulnerable side, we lose touch with our needs and our childlike spontaneity and zest for life. We become deadly serious adults." If you don't believe me, then take a long hard look in the mirror.

Catch 22

Lauren Bylsma, Ph.D., a post-doctoral scholar at the University of Pittsburgh conducted a series of studies on crying. She found in one study of over 3,000 crying incidents that one factor in particular affected whether the crier felt better or worse afterwards: whether they received social support or not. This puts us in a catch 22 situation. Collectively, we currently don't support men when they cry because we believe it's a sign of weakness; and even if we think we are supporting a man in tears, we're most likely not—we're just trying to dress the metaphorical wound as quickly as possible and get him to stop crying because *we* feel uncomfortable. And yet the paradox is that if we don't make it safe for men to cry, they'll never feel better when they do and the story that crying is weak and pathetic will continue. In addition, because men have stuffed so much emotion down, when a man finally cries, the torrent of emotion that pours forth threatens to totally consume him—or at least it feels that way. No wonder most men don't feel safe crying.

Men and women need to address their part in this. I have read more than a few articles written by caring women who are deeply concerned about the importance of men expressing their tears, which is very nice, yet when the time comes around for a man to express himself, many women can't actually handle it. On the one hand, they are ready to embrace change and welcome in a new, more equal era—yes, this is like feminism, but for men and about feelings—but on the other hand, a man crying somehow brings into question the knight in shining armour that they duly appointed to save the day. Brené Brown talked in *Daring Greatly* about how the last thing women really want is for men to get off their white horse. I'm not a woman so I can only hazard a guess, but I wonder if a man crying triggers anxiety for some women, feelings of being out of control, which are obviously uncomfortable to experience. Perhaps these women don't want to experience these feelings so the safest thing to do is to shut the man down. I know there are many women who are comfortable with men crying (fortunately I am married to one of them), but I also see many who aren't. As I've said before, we are all affected by omertà.

Expecting a man to always be strong and silent is downright unrealistic and causes pointless suffering to both men and women alike. When a man is minimised, ridiculed or shamed for simply being human, an ancient wound is opened and an SMB from that man's past is activated, stirring up deep-rooted emotional pain. We have to learn how to support and be with a man in his tears, not shut him down and wipe them away as quickly as possible.

Authentic Tears Favour the Brave

Your goal now is twofold. Firstly, you are challenged to become aware of the deeper feelings that any defences are masking; remember that your tears will usually be veiled in anger. Secondly, allow yourself to feel these feelings fully without having to disguise or apologise for them. Your task is to shine a conscious light on the grief, sadness, hurt and pain that you have been carrying inside of you and to allow yourself to express it fully. In other words, you have got to let yourself do three things: feel, grieve and cry. I know how hard it can be to break the vow of male silence and do this. Becoming reunited with your pain might be the hardest thing you ever do. If part of you is too scared to let your pain speak for fear of being rejected, please know that I understand. I know that deep pain because it is my pain too. But here's the deal fellas: crying isn't actually something that needs to be overcome or conquered. It is just something to be experienced. Crying doesn't make you weak. In fact, the mark of a real man is how deeply he lets himself feel. Regardless of what you have been taught about crying being weak, authentic tears do favour the brave.

Not only is it brave to cry, but it is also healthy. Some researchers have found that emotional tears (which are indeed in a category all of their own, distinct from onion tears for example), contain stress hormones, and the body is able to physically release these hormones through the process of crying. In the same way a good downpour can help cleanse the earth, crying is how we organically cleanse our bodies of stress. In addition, crying may release feel good endorphins, whether the tears you cry are happy or sad.

When we are emotionally naked, vulnerable, raw and open, it opens a direct pathway to the emotional heart and helps us feel more connected with ourselves and the people in our lives. We men who cry are a growing number of brave souls who have said fuck it to upholding omertà. We feel just as deeply as women; we cry freely and unapologetically.

Here are the real factoids about men and tears:

- Real men cry.
- Crying is how the body releases stress.
- It's perfectly okay for a man to cry in public.
- Crying is a radical act of self-care and love.
- The world is a better place when you let others into yours.
- There's no need for a man to repress, minimise, or apologise for his tears—ever.
- You won't die if you cry but you might die trying not to.
- Crying is not a punishable offence.
- Vulnerability is the stuff of legends. It signifies honesty, strength, courage and wholeness.
- Whenever a man cries he breaks the vow of male silence, playing a vital role in redefining masculinity.

Exercise

Unfortunately fellas, there is no magic formula when it comes to feeling your feelings, just as there's no formula for reconnecting with the lost boy within. The only thing to 'do' is to feel them. This involves radical awareness and the willingness to let go completely. You may have skilfully taught yourself to avoid feelings at all costs, but deadening your feelings is hardly heroic and often manifests in the world as violence, hatred, pain and suffering. You might believe that you are so far removed from your feelings that there is little hope of resolution, but just because you "don't do feelings" right now, it doesn't mean you can't ever do them. It also doesn't excuse you from having to take responsibility for them. Until you do, you will continue to remain cut off from the lost boy within, hurting yourself and in due course hurting others.

Firstly, we need to take a sober moment and establish where you are in relation to where you want to go. The first step might be to admit that you have forgotten how to feel. It's not your fault that you have forgotten. After all, you most likely grew up being told to "shut up, man up and stop being a sissy."

Bro, with every part of my being I want you to know: IT'S NOT YOUR FAULT! Regardless, of what you currently believe, it's not actually possible to lose your feelings completely; if you had, you wouldn't be reading this book. You may have merely lost sight of them, which is good news because it means that you can connect with them again. Think of this as developing a new skill set, or kicking a stubborn muscle into growth in the gym. If you're a beginner right now, can you be okay with that?

Here are some simple crying guidelines for you to implement:

1. Next time you are on the verge of tears, notice what happens for you physically and mentally. (For example, you might feel anxiety or an aching, burning or tingling sensation in your throat, maybe even a sudden powering down.) Whatever is happening, in the words of Corporal Jones from *Dad's Army*, "Don't panic!"
2. Take a risk and let go. Let yourself cry freely.
3. Don't repress, minimise or apologise to anyone for your tears.
4. When you have finished crying, take a deep breath and sit quietly for a moment. Notice how you feel.
5. Go about your day with your head held high. You have nothing to be ashamed of.

Fall Down Seven Times... Stay Down

Crying is very personal. If you haven't cried for years, it might take you a while for the waterworks to thaw out, and in the beginning you'll likely want to cry alone. Sooner or later you might risk being vulnerable in front of another human being. Eventually you might even make eye contact while you're in tears (which is incredibly intense but can be absolutely life changing).

I remember the day I cried in front of a group of people for the first time. It happened during a personal development workshop where I'd been using my comedic mask to avoid connecting with the rest of the group, thinking that I needed to make people laugh in order to get them to like me. The workshop facilitator, who I realised in hindsight had me well and truly sussed out, invited me to the front of the room and said, "There's your stage. Make them laugh." I took up the challenge but after a few moments the jokes started to wear a bit thin and I began to feel awkward. My mind screamed for me to get out but there was nowhere left to hide—my mask was cracking open. I knew it, the facilitator knew it and the whole room knew it. The game was up. I felt myself falling apart dangerously fast, like a spacecraft re-entering the earth's atmosphere with nothing to break the fall.

Out of the blue, an uncontrollable flash flood of emotion surged through my body. I literally fell to my knees weeping. This was the moment I had been avoiding for years. I was done with all that "fall down seven times, get up eight" macho bullshit, so I just gave up trying to look composed and stayed down there on the floor. For the first time in my life, I asked for help. Instead of mocking me, the people in the room literally stepped towards me.

They were moved by my tears. They cried with me and held me in their arms like a baby boy.

That was a life changing moment for me. It filled me with courage and hope. I had actually broken omertà and lived to tell the tale. There would be no going back after that. Today, many years later, I am no longer afraid to cry because I have that experience as an anchor. I know now that crying doesn't make me weak. Rather, it shows just how strong I really am. Most of all, crying makes me real.

My hope is that reading these words will persuade you to take off your mask and feel, and trust that it's perfectly okay for you to cry without having to minimise or apologise for your tears—ever.

Break the Vow: Power Questions

1. When did you last cry, and why?
2. When did you last feel like crying but didn't let yourself cry?
3. What kind of thoughts or feelings do you experience when you are on the verge of tears?
4. What do you normally do instead of crying? (i.e. What escape routes do you turn to?)
5. What could you do differently?

CHAPTER 17

YOUR DAD, FORGIVENESS AND YOU

"I am your father."
—Darth Vader

You have probably been wondering when we were going to get here, to the man that is 50% responsible for giving you life: your father. Whether you have a relationship with him or not, your dad is almost certainly one of the most influential people in your life and a book about men and the vow of male silence would be incomplete without this piece of the puzzle.

The job of a man breaking the vow of male silence is to do what author and psychologist Steve Biddulph describes as "fixing it with your father." This is an essential task for every man, because regardless of what you currently believe, your father—or the absence of one—is a key influence in your life. Fixing it with your father is as vital as breathing. It is extremely challenging, gut-wrenching, messy, clunky as fuck and humbling, and as Biddulph writes, "a necessary step in your own liberation."

I'm going to share some of my experience of fixing it with my dad in this chapter, before inviting you to take a courageous step towards fixing it with yours. As you'll see, the healing is like the wounding; both take place over multiple encounters, sometimes taking many years.

The Most Marvellous and Exciting Father

Recently, I had the privilege of reading *Danny, Champion of the World* by Roald Dahl to a man in his eighties as part of my job as a care worker. When I finally got round to reading the final chapter of the book entitled "My Father," I knew that it was going to stir up some emotion, especially since I had used an excerpt from the chapter in a scrapbook which I had given to my pops as a gift just before he died in 2009.

I gave myself the go-ahead to take every single line off the page, to express those words like my very life depended on it. As the words tumbled out of me and the tears flowed freely, I delivered the final line of the book with the conviction of a sprinter making the final dash for the finish line. When I had finished reading I lifted my head and looked at the frail man sat opposite me, his eyes wet with tears. He confessed to being deeply moved by what had just taken place and mentioned about how the story of Danny had reminded him of his relationship with his father. Incidentally, earlier in the visit the elderly gentleman had asked me to describe *Odd Man Out* in one sentence, but it was only after I finished reading that I was able to give him the answer, and the answer was enclosed in the emotional interaction that had taken place between us—how two men from different generations had just broken the vow of male silence across a kitchen table.

Sadly, my friend passed away recently. I saw him the day before he died and even though he was incoherent, he squeezed my hand and looked at me with tears in his eyes. It's like he was saying thank you to me for everything that we'd shared, and goodbye. I knew this would be the last time I'd see him, and it was. I am honoured to include him in this book. He was a true gentleman.

The story of Danny was very poignant for me to read because it reminded me strongly of my childhood, giving me the opportunity to reflect on my relationship with my dad and on the "father wound" that came with it. Decades ago during story time at primary school, I had encountered *Danny* for the first time as my class teacher read it to us. When I heard it, I wondered if Mr Dahl had been secretly spying on me and my dad because he seemed to have written an entire book about us.

Danny's father had a zest for magical adventure, just like my dad. My dad adored the great outdoors and from an early age taught me how to appreciate nature. While my friends were sunbathing on family holidays in Spain, our family would be camping in the English countryside, spending our days on windy coastlines exploring castles and caves. Then, when I was ten years old, Dad led me, Mum and my sister up England's highest mountain, Scafell Pike. He was also a keen cyclist and took me on big bike adventures with him and sometimes even with his cycling club. Instead of wanting to become an astronaut when I grew up, I decided that I wanted to be just like Dad. I thought, like Danny, that my dad was "the most marvellous and exciting father any boy ever had."

That I experienced such a strong bond with my father in my early childhood is something I am grateful for, despite what happened between us in later years. I am fully aware that a lot of men did not experience this with their fathers when they were boys, and I realise I was fortunate, especially when I hear stories from other men about the horrendous wounding they had to endure growing up, stories of abuse, neglect and abandonment.

When I was a little boy, I really had no idea that my dad was just a human being, a man made of flesh and blood. I had no idea he had a past, that he was part of a lineage of "bad men" and that when he met my mum, he had two choices facing him—to repeat history and be a bad man like his father and his father's father (and God knows how many men before them), or to reverse the story and become a knight in shining armour. He did the latter. I think he and Mum made an unconscious pact that he would make up for all the bad men in both their families of origin. Dad became good, and mum held up and protected his identity as a good man at all costs.

He was amazing: he had done two years in the army; he was kind and generous, fit and strong, handy and helpful, chivalrous and thoughtful. He was so amazing in fact that I was often reminded by Mum throughout my childhood and into adulthood that I would never be like him, that no one would ever be like him. He didn't really know how to support me emotionally when I lost a testicle (in fact we never spoke about it), and he was clumsy in communicating with me about subjects like death and sex, but he was made into a kind of demigod in our house. Dad was a good man and that was that.

In early childhood, I learned the message quickly. My dad might as well have had the letter 'S' emblazoned across his chest. Perhaps I gave him the attributes of a superhero because in my world he was one. He was my first experience of God, and the centre of my world. My dad meant everything to me. The transition into becoming a young man was made all the more awkward for me because I had these early experiences as a reference point.

A Trillion Miles Apart

Throughout my teens, things became tense between Dad and me. We lived under the same roof yet somehow seemed to be a trillion miles apart. We tried to communicate, but for some bizarre reason it was like we were both tuned into different radio stations. No matter how hard we tried we just couldn't seem to get along.

The main cause of friction between us was my appearance. Dad loathed my weird hairdos and dogged me about it every day. Developing a distinctive look was important to me and I was at the forefront of experimenting with radical 1980s haircuts, which started one night when my sister styled my hair for school youth club. The response was amazing; suddenly people liked me. I discovered Independent Heads, the most cutting edge hairdressers in town, and started trying out everything from undercuts to skinheads to flat tops to mohicans. My way-out pals and I would frequently have competitions as to who could get the whitest hair.

This infuriated Dad, who would say things like, "Why can't you leave a little bit more on the sides? What's so wrong with your normal colour? Your hair isn't made to stand up. Why can't you just blend in with the crowd?" I knew that one wrong move and I'd get walloped, but I still spoke up. "Why can't you just accept me for who I am? I'm not taking drugs, or smashing up somebody's house. I'm not hurting anybody."

One time, I arrived home with the latest hairstyle—a fully shaved head apart from a Tintin-style tuft at the front. Dad and I ended up at each other's throats. He lost his temper and hit me with such force that I fell backwards, pulling over the kitchen table with me. In the next moment I found myself sat on the floor, covered in food, dazed and confused. Whenever Dad hit me I would see stars. He may have been short but he was strong as an ox, and the flat of his hand was like a shovel. One sideswipe would usually be enough to reduce me to a trembling wreck.

Afterwards, he wouldn't speak to me for a week. The deafening silence throughout the house would culminate in an emergency meeting between Mum, Dad and me, where they would talk about what they thought I needed to do to toe the line. I would sit in silence while they talked at me for a while. Then they'd say, "It's good to talk things through," and we'd get on with our lives.

Dad and Mum had been brought up in a generation where being hit was normal. Children were seen as beings who could be disciplined into changing their behaviour. Perhaps more upsetting was that I didn't have a voice in the middle of it. Being a teen is bloody awkward at the best of times particularly when you are trying to carve an identity for yourself. Having my originality bashed out of me was painful, especially when it was by the one person in the world who I most admired and wanted to be like.

Regardless of the agony I would go through, I intentionally continued to wear the weirdest hairstyles and clothes. Each and every time I stepped out of line, I knew what was coming next, and in fact I started to enjoy the sensation of being clouted by my dad. I reckoned that any attention was better than nothing at all. Through those moments of madness, I felt intensely muddled, since on the one hand his love looked close by, yet on the other it was so far away, and I hated him for it. The man I had once wanted to be when I grew up became an enemy.

In the ten years that followed (and, truthfully, right up to the present day), I often felt crippled by a sense of inadequacy that echoed the words, "You'll never be like your dad." I became determined to prove to my mum and dad, and to the whole world, that I wasn't the odd man out but no matter what I did in that decade, I still felt like I didn't have a right to exist. I tried desperately to prove myself to everyone, all the time. Then, aged 17, I discovered bodybuilding. It changed everything. Dad scoffed at me, saying that you could never put muscle on a frame as scrawny as mine. I set out to prove him and all the other doubters wrong—and I determined to do it drug-free—believing that if I did, I would feel better. If I proved myself to him, I would finally feel adequate. I dedicated years to building an awesome physique, competing in amateur bodybuilding shows all over the UK, but an underlying belief plagued me: the belief that I would never be as good as Dad. Bodybuilding was the one thing my dad had never done, the one thing he could never compete with me on, yet even there I felt his shadow haunting me. (In fact, it wasn't until I was 47 years old, 23 years after my last bodybuilding competition, that I would go on to win first place in a bodybuilding show for the very first time. Before then, it was like I never really had permission to come first in my life.)

In my late teens, Mum got me a job working in the factory she'd worked in for many years. I hated it. I was bullied, I was different and I didn't fit in with the tough northern mindset. Even with my new physique, I was still the odd man out. It was an awful time in my life. After I'd been there for a couple of years, the company decided they were going to close the factory I worked in. They offered everyone the choice between a job in another factory or redundancy. I took the redundancy without a second's thought and I went to Canada for six weeks to stay with my Aunty Ivy and Uncle Bob.

Facing my Father

Canada became a place that I would run away to more than once. I went back again in 1994 to take a break from my relationship with my girlfriend. But that first winter out there, I found myself in a life-changing workshop called The Awakening. It offered me at long last a safe place to do away with the bandage that I'd been using to cover up my childhood wounds, which were slowly but surely killing me. This workshop was a matter of life and death for me. It was a tiny chink of light at the end of a long dark tunnel, which gave me a chance to express past hurts and rebuild my life, one thought at a time. Subsequently, I decided to take the organisation's Practitioner Training Course, a year-long exploration of family systems, *A Course in Miracles* and counselling skills. This was the start of a mind-blowing trip with my life at the core of the curriculum, a deeply personal journey that would take me to the remotest corners of my mind, uncovering a twisted fear-based belief system that had determined how my life looked to date.

I was hungry to find the lost boy inside me, determined to patch up my relationship with myself, my family and anyone who had wronged me or whom I had wronged. Above all else, I wanted to know how to be a man in the world who feels everything without feeling compelled to apologise, minimise who I am, or hide for fear of being judged or rejected.

I believe that every man is called to face his father at some point in his life, and my time came during that period in Canada when I was 25 years old. I was constructing and presenting a family genogram as part of the Practitioner Training programme I was doing. A genogram is a hardcore version of a family tree, where you identify not only births, marriages and deaths, but also the losses, traumas, abuse and illnesses in the family and how these were or were not dealt with and got transmitted from one generation to the next. My mission was to fly back to England from Canada and interview my family members one by one so that I could try to piece together which unresolved issues I was carrying for the rest of my family system. I was cornered. There was no escaping the task in front of me. I had to face my dad.

At that point in my life, Dad and I were getting along better than when I'd been a teenager, but we were really just going through the father-son motions, bantering about surface level meaningless stuff without ever really touching on the deeper issues that had caused our relationship to fragment and turn sour. The days of being intrepid explorers were long gone. We no longer did anything together. To be honest, we seldom left the living room when I visited him and Mum that winter. Our relationship had disintegrated into a ghostly shadow of its past. Whenever it came time for me to leave we hugged clumsily and I always got a sense that he was pulling me in and pushing me away at the same time. There was so much to talk about, so much that needed to be said but because neither of us would take the first step things came to a standstill.

Nonetheless, I felt excited about the possibility of having a candid conversation with Dad about his past because of the deep inner work I was doing on myself in Canada. I was nervous too, most likely because I didn't know how he would react to my questions. I sensed that I was standing at the edge of a family system that was desperately crying out for change.

Getting to Know Dad

One evening, after Mum had gone to bed, the conversation started. To begin with I asked him to share his earliest memories with me. He looked cheerful as I learned about how, as a young boy, he had loved to sail matches down the tram tracks on the street where he lived, and how he had got his head stuck in the railings and the local firemen had to cut him free.

I then took a risk and asked him what his relationship was like with his father. His face changed from smiling to serious. The colour drained from his cheeks. He shifted awkwardly in his chair, his sad eyes searching for a place to hide. And then he spoke. Because I recorded the interview, I was able to capture his exact words.

"I never understood what having a father was. Dad was a smart, well-groomed man, a womaniser. Mum told me how he would come and go. She said that he would often disappear for days on end, and then show up like nothing had happened. That's when the fighting started. I remember aged six returning to an empty house. Dad had told the neighbours we were moving and emptied the house. He had even taken the beds."

My dad was forced to grow up quickly and had to learn to take care of himself. He believed that he didn't have a childhood.

He said that he was never cuddled and grew up believing that he wasn't wanted, "a non-entity" and "second rate." My dad, second rate? It was so far from the superhero he'd been to me, but it also made so much sense.

Hearing him talk, I started to want to know him again. I was awed by his honesty and his humanness. The conversation opened up further, and we talked for the first time about the kicking incident where I'd lost a testicle when I was six. I needed to set the record straight and find out what really happened. When I asked Dad about what I often call "the accident," even though it wasn't really an accident, he looked sad. I had never understood why he and Mum had never, ever spoken to me about me losing a testicle. There was no acknowledgement of it, no conversation about this huge change that had taken place in my little body. Dad told me that evening that he knew how hurtful youngsters could be at that age, and admitted feeling frustrated because he'd wanted to help, but wasn't really sure how to approach the situation. Instead, he and Mum "shelved" the issue, believing that this would help things eventually settle down, giving me the opportunity for a "normal" childhood.

Unbeknownst to me, the impact of Mum and Dad's decision to shelve the situation, (even though it was certainly done with my best interests at heart) triggered a devastating tidal wave of hurt and confusion in my young mind. I grew up believing that he didn't love me, that he had abandoned me when I needed him most, and that it was my fault. Dad also said that I never brought it up so he didn't think anything was wrong. I understand that; I don't think I knew *how* to break the vow and broach the subject. That's the thing about SMBs—they're so secretive and insidious that the last thing you want to do is talk about them, lest your worst fears about yourself are confirmed. Yet in not talking about them, your worst fears are confirmed.

Having this difficult conversation with Dad helped me see things differently. For the first time in my life, I saw a situation in which I'd always thought of myself as guilty and my dad as having failed me through fresh eyes. Never before had I understood what my father's childhood had been like, what he had grown up believing about himself, and the grief and loss that he had experienced which was so similar to my own. I started to realise the error of my ways: I had criticised Dad because I thought that the inner discomfort I was feeling was because of something he had done to me. In truth, it was the complete opposite since it was my own sense of guilt that I was holding against him. I was blaming Dad for something I had done to him. After realising this, I felt connected to him in a way I never had done before, and I began to understand that I had never had the whole story, and I had filled in the blanks with my own fear-based misperceptions.

Dad and I talked into the early hours of the morning, with him answering questions about everything from his dreams and ambitions to his transition into manhood. He told me about his first love who had died of polio, about his best friend having an affair with his first wife and about his love of cycling. The following evening, we did it all again and I asked him about sex, death, money and anger, topics which are so universal but so little talked about in families. Hours and hours later, we came back around to the issue that was driving my dad's life—his misplaced childhood.

Something Missing

There was a moment that stood out more starkly than any other. I asked him if he was happy with his life. He walked over to the window and stared out as if he was checking to see if he had been followed by someone or something. When he spoke his voice broke. "It's like there is something missing in my life, like I never had a childhood." His eyes filled with tears. Maybe the closest he ever came to reclaiming his lost boy within happened during his epic cycling adventures or when he climbed a huge mountain and stood staring out at the heavenly view hand in hand with my mum. As I sat in silence and watched my father's story unfolding before me, it became apparent the child he was searching for out there in the world was right here in the room with us, inside him. I was overwhelmed. I felt my dad's grief and for the first time, I saw him. I actually saw him. I met my dad. As I watched him, he was looking out the window, and I realised that tears were running down my own face.

His pain was familiar, like it was part of me too. I realised that we were both dealing with something so much bigger than the both of us put together. We had both unconsciously agreed to play out a toxic legacy that in all probability spanned generations. However, the contaminated fuel supply that had kept it alive, handed down from father to son over and over again, had at long last been cut off. Our vow of silence was broken.

Who knows if anyone had ever had this conversation in my family before. I have a funny feeling we were the first fellas to do it. It was powerful, raw, and even heroic. It redefined the future of our relationship and made a huge imprint on my family. In an instant, things changed for good. My dad stopped being the bad guy or the superhero and became a human being instead, full of fear and love and doubt and wonder. He was my dad and I was his son.

When I finally said the words, "I love you, Dad," he fought to hold back the tears, but no matter how much he tried he couldn't stop them from falling. I had waited my whole life to hear him say those words to me and in the end, it was me who said them first. When I did, I think I gave him a piece of his life back, so much so that he was able to respond. "I love you, son."

Perhaps he had been waiting his whole life too, to say the words that his own father had never said to him—that he loved his son, that he was proud of the man he had become. In that moment I found the missing piece of a gigantic father-son puzzle. The sense of relief on hearing those three little words was huge. I started to cry and we hugged each other tight. Then we pulled apart and looked at each other.

"See you in the morning lad."

"Night Dad."

That conversation changed things. It wasn't like a Hollywood happily ever after moment. I was 25 years old and over the next two decades before he passed away, Dad and I would continue to dance with different levels of intimacy and distance. I would go on to forget that experience of being unconditionally loved and accepted just for being me, and then at different times, I would remember again. But it did change things, that conversation. Something became fundamentally different. I don't know if I would have been able to throw my dad a farewell party in the weeks leading up to his death or to make him a scrapbook all about his life if we hadn't had that series of conversations. It was a rite of passage, an initiation. It was like coming home.

Escaping the Chains that Bind Us

At some point in your lifetime, you too will be called to make the quest into your father's past. Every man is called to do this. You are free to put it off, avoid it, delay it or swerve the issue, but you can never fully escape from the task in front of you. If you do, then a part of your life will never make sense, and it will always seem like something is missing, no matter how rich or successful you become.

Like it or not, you are connected to your father and every ancestor that came before him. You are part of a great lineage going back generation upon generation, and every fuck up and triumph and loss they went through. Each generation is gifted with the opportunity (although it might come disguised in wolf's clothing) to expose and eventually heal your pain. Your pain is yours, yes; yet your pain is also intimately connected to the pain of your father and all the fathers who came before him. This is true even if you don't know anything about your family history, even if you've never met your dad. If you were to study the last three generations of your family, you would be stunned by the similarities in what they lived through and what your life has been like.

One way or another, the brave work must be done, especially if you are to make the genuine shift from boyhood to manhood. In the book *Manhood*, Steve Biddulph says, "The fact is until you reach a place where you can feel love and respect for your father and also receive the love and respect of older men, you will remain a boy." Like the great illusionist Houdini we must make a conscious choice to escape from the family chains that bind us, otherwise we will spend the rest of our worldly days choking, at war with the version of your father who lives in your head, with masculinity and ultimately with yourself.

Exercise

This next exercise is one of the hardest exercises in the book and with good reason. Whether your father is alive, dead or completely unknown to you, this piece of work is critical because until you fix it with your father, you will continue to be haunted by the ghost of who you think he is and who you fear you are.

The task in this chapter consists of making a decision, writing two letters and making a demonstration. The purpose of this exercise is to see your father's humanness, to see his innocence and to reconnect with him—to use Steven Biddulph's phrase, to fix it with your father. This might be the last thing you feel like doing right now, but let me be crystal clear: you are doing this for *you*, not just for him.

Your task is to give voice to the pain that has plagued you and let your father do the same. He could be dead, alive or living in Timbuktu. It doesn't matter; the work still has to be done. This exercise is a starting point that will set the wheels of father-son change in motion. It might be the biggest step you have ever taken in your life around your father, or if you've done lots of work on him already, it might just be the next piece of the puzzle. Either way, this is a great opportunity to give voice to all your fearful, choked up feelings and crushed dreams.

The point of this exercise is to dig up the bones of your past. This is no time for suppressing and burying what has been shut down in you for so many years. You are doing this to finally break the vow of male silence.

This exercise is not optional. If you choose to dodge it, you will continue to suffer. It is as simple as that. It depends on whether you want to live life like a zombie, walking around the planet half dead, an artificial man, which isn't really an option or you wouldn't be reading this book. Like I said above, this exercise is not optional: it's essential.

1. Firstly, find a photo of you and your dad from your childhood and place it next to you. If you don't have one, take a moment to reflect on your childhood experience of him. Notice any memories or images that flash through your mind.

2. Sit quietly with no distractions. Turn off your phone (in fact, put it somewhere you can't reach it), shut down your computer and tell the relevant people that you will be off the radar for the next little while.

3. Make a steadfast commitment to be present for this exercise and do whatever it takes to finish it.

4. Your task is to write a "no-send letter" to your father. You are going to do as Biddulph advises, emptying your heart "of all the things you might have choked back for years, telling him everything you feel till there's nothing left." This might take 10 minutes, 30 minutes, or two hours. Keep writing until you are empty, until you have said everything you have ever wanted to say to him. If you've ever done this before then tough because you're doing it again. (Remember, the ego always has more to say, and so does the heart.)

<u>How to make the most of the exercise</u>

Refuse to be interrupted.

Refuse to allow distractions.

Keep the pen moving. This is a stream-of-consciousness exercise. The more you allow the pen to run across the page, the deeper you will go.

If emotion comes up, go with it. Don't hold back. If ever there was a time to feel, this is it.

If you get stuck, write out one of the prompts from below and just see what comes out.

- *I'm angry because...*
- *I'm sad because...*
- *What I really wanted from you was...*
- *I'm thankful because...*
- *What I really want to say is...*

Decide now. When are you going to take this step? Commit to it, and do it. See you on the other side.

If you are reading this and you have yet to write your no-send letter to your father, stop reading. You are not ready to go on. Go back, take the step you need to take and come back once you've done it.

Exercise: Part II

Welcome back. Take a moment to check in with yourself. How are you feeling? You might be feeling angry, relieved, vulnerable, guilty, numb, or a combination of lots of feelings. I want to remind you that all your feelings are perfectly valid. You're in the middle of a process here, and in the middle is not the best time to judge the outcome. You're not finished yet, so let's keep moving. Neither part of this exercise is complete without the other. The two are mutually dependent on each other.

Again, this second exercise is not optional. Dodge it and you remain half dead. Do it and reclaim your true masculinity. The choice is yours.

1. Take the photo of you and your dad from your childhood that you used in the first part of the exercise and place it next to you. (Yes, again.)

2. Sit quietly with no distractions. Turn off your phone (in fact, put it somewhere you can't reach it), shut down your computer and tell the relevant people that you will be off the radar for the next little while.

3. Make a steadfast commitment to be present for this exercise and do whatever it takes to finish it.

4. Your task is to write a letter from your father to you. He is going to empty his heart *through you* of all the things he might have choked back for years, telling you everything he feels till there's nothing left. This might take 30 minutes, or it might take two hours. Keep writing until you are empty, until he has said everything he ever wanted to say. Start with the words "Dear Son."

How to make the most of the exercise

You might find it difficult to let your dad's voice come through you. You might fall into criticism and attack, or disconnection and writer's block. I want you to suspend your judgments and walk a mile in your father's shoes. Allow yourself to see life through his eyes. Sink into what it was like for your father as a boy, his relationship with his father. It doesn't have to factually accurate—just trust your instincts and keep the pen moving.

Write about his relationship with you. How he prepared for your arrival into the world, what it was like to hold you in his arms when you were a baby boy, to watch you grow, say your first word, take your first step, become a little boy, an adolescent and finally a man.

If your father was absent throughout your childhood, allow yourself to write about that. How was it for him to miss those moments, to not be there? Where did that leave him as a man? What did he feel, fear and cover up?

Refuse to be interrupted.

Refuse to allow distractions.

Keep the pen moving. This is a stream-of-consciousness exercise. The more you allow the pen to run across the page, the deeper you will go.

If emotion comes up, go with it. Don't hold back. If ever there was a time to feel, this is it.

If you get stuck, write out one of the prompts from below and see what surfaces.

- *Son, I'm angry because…*
- *I'm sad because…*
- *What I really wanted to give to you was…*
- *I'm thankful because…*

The point of this exercise is to dig up the bones of his past and make peace with him and yourself.

Exercise: Part III

Once you have completed both letters, you are ready to move on. Again, do not rush this process. Most of the time, a book that has the potential to be life-changing does not end up being so because the reader did not fully engage with the material. Do not proceed until you have completed the above exercises. When you have, you are ready to answer the following questions:

- What am I willing to let go of to have peace in my relationship with my father?
- What am I taking with me from this exercise?
- What is the truth? (For example, "My father was doing his very best and if he had known different then he would have done it differently.")

If your father is still living, pluck up the courage to make contact and have a conversation with him. Call or visit him. Remember to listen more than you speak. It might be a bit raggedy at the edges but it's still worthwhile. See Appendix III at the back of the book for a list of questions you can use to start the conversation.

If your father is long gone find a way to honour his memory. Visit his grave or somewhere significant to you both. Reaffirm your connection with him. Honour his life and the lives of all the men who came before him. Thank him for the life he gave you, take the parts of the legacy that you want, and let the rest go.

CHAPTER 18

WHAT ABOUT MUM?

"There's a story behind everything. How a picture got on a wall. How a scar got on your face. Sometimes the stories are simple, and sometimes they are hard and heartbreaking. But behind all your stories is always your mother's story, because hers is where yours begin."
—Mitch Albiom

I've written a lot about how your relationship with your dad (or the absence of one) will have impacted the man you became. But there is another glaring relationship that so far, I haven't mentioned much. As my friend Mike asked after reading the draft of the manuscript: What about Mum? Initially I replied "What about Mum?", clearly reluctant. I didn't want to look at this second crucial relationship and how it shaped me as a man. But as much as I'd love to say that there just isn't room in this book for a chapter about mothers, when I read the following in the book *Under Saturn's Shadow* by James Hollis, I had a bit of a wake up call: "The man who denies that the mother-child relationship is fundamental, that it influences everything he feels about himself, about life and about others, lives in profound ignorance." Ouch!

When Ell told me in no uncertain terms that I needed to write about my relationship with my mum, I literally exclaimed, "Oh God!"

It's hard for me to write about my relationship with my mum because it doesn't feel as clear or complete as my relationship with my dad. This makes perfect sense given that she is still alive. As earth shattering as it is to lose a parent, in some ways it's easier to make sense of than it is when you have to face the interactions with parents who are very much alive. I wonder if you can relate.

I wrote an in depth piece about my relationship with my mum, but at the eleventh hour, Ell and I decided to cut it from the book because even though we knew we'd written a very heartfelt piece, we didn't have my mum's permission to tell parts of her story, and I can't fully explain my relationship with her without including her history. After some heated debate between Ell and I, we both agreed that the kindest thing to do was to cut the piece. However, the power of the mother-son relationship is undeniable, so let's spend a few moments addressing what James Hollis calls the "mother complex."

The Power of the Mother Complex

In the book *Under Saturn's Shadow: The Wounding and Healing of Men*, author James Hollis talks extensively about the mother-child complex and how it impacts men. He states that the way men act (and act out) around women reflects a lot about their relationship with their mother. In a rather uncomfortable paragraph to read, he states that untold numbers of men "have not yet left home," remaining attached to the mother-son complex and "out of touch with their own soul." He describes men who fantastise that their wife may be having an affair, men who blame their partner for not being attentive or nourishing enough, men who accuse their partner of being "incompetent with finances" (or simply imply this is so by, for example, being controlling around money), men who are always away with work, men who are needy and unable to go a day without calling for reassurance, men who are overly distant, men who have "an incessant roving eye," or who are homophobic or misogynistic, or men who completely give up a sense of self in order to please their partner—all of these, he says, are "still compensating for the power of the mother complex." This applies whether a man feels internally driven to be "a good boy" or a bad one, or even a man who identifies as being "wild." Whether you agree with Hollis or not, he definitely stirs up some questions about our identities as men.

Maybe we men, regardless of how we present ourselves to the world, are looking for the kind of nurturing that only mother can give. Recently, Ell and I have been taking turns to hold each other as a way of deepening the intimacy between us. Ell literally holds me on the sofa, sometimes for five minutes, sometimes for longer. It's very hard for me to put into words the experience I have when I'm in her arms. It's really emotional for me; all I wanted to do the first time Ell held me in her arms was cry—not like a man, but like a little boy. In giving that young part of me space, he stops running the show.

I know this chapter isn't as comprehensive about the one I wrote about fathers and forgiveness. I hope what I have shared about the mother complex is enough to set the wheels of mother-son healing in motion. I will close by recommending that you read *Under Saturn's Shadow*, which in places is a powerful and fascinating read, and I will leave you with the following thoughts from Hollis:

"A man's relationship to himself, to others and to the life force that courses through him is profoundly channelled by his primary experience of his mother. To the extent that she is unable to meet his needs, and imposes her personal complexes on him, so he will suffer the wounds of abandonment and overwhelm. From the former he learns to distrust his own worth and the reliability of the world. Because of the latter he feels powerless to defend his fragile frontier and so evolves a generally compliant, co-dependent personality or a fearful, overcompensated, power-dominated one. In either case he is not himself, but lives in reaction to an experience so powerful that it subordinates his natural truth."

The purpose of *Odd Man Out* is to support you to face your demons so that you are no longer a shadow of your whole, authentic self, living in reaction and defending yourself against the world you made. In doing the painful, liberating work of healing your relationship with your mum, you will be stepping ever closer towards the truth of who you are and the truth of who your mum is. Maybe this is what it really means to grow up. As Tony Robbins says, when you heal the boy, the man will appear. And at some point on this journey, somewhere above the battleground, you might even meet your mum, encountering her divinity right in the middle of your messy, imperfect humanity. That single encounter will set you both free and has the power to transform your relationship with the women in your life.

God knows there is an unbearable amount of violence acted out by men towards women in our world. This insanity has got to end. I said to the women earlier in this book that they are needed if we are to truly transcend omertà. Now, I say the same to you. You have a responsibility to play your part in healing your relationship with women. Whether you are holding onto a single resentment or many, if you are reading these words, you still have work to do. It's time to stop making excuses and go and do it.

Break the Vow: Power Questions

1. Describe your relationship with your mum.
2. What's the overriding feeling you have about your relationship with your mum?
3. What are your wounds in relation to your mum and how have they impacted your life?
4. How have your mother-son wounds impacted your relationships with women?
5. You might also want to use the no-send letter exercise from chapter 16 or the questions in Appendix III for your work with your mum.

CHAPTER 19

THE DECISION TO REMEMBER

"Even if you are a minority of one, the truth is the truth."
—Mahatma Gandhi

Doing the inner work to fix your relationship with your parents is brave. Many millions of men will not dare to venture here, because these relationships are often full of old emotional pain, and daring to feel that pain hurts. If you're reading this, I hope you heard and acted on my pleas in the previous two chapters and did the work of fixing it with your father and your mother. If you have, you will likely be feeling raw. You've probably dug up memories, fears and feelings that you long thought you had left behind. Do your best to just feel whatever you're feeling, bro. It won't kill you. If you haven't done the work, I urge you to go back and complete it. Reading will only take you so far.

Now, however, it's time to talk forgiveness. I can hear you thinking, "What the... Forgiveness?! What a load of shit!" For so many Westerners, especially us blokes, the mere mention of the F-word conjures up a distorted image of some bloke sat in a

Catholic confession box and being told to go and say a few hail Marys.

Let's face it: orthodox religion has done about as much for forgiveness as Lance Armstrong did for professional cycling's reputation for doping. That's why it's vital that we re-examine the concept. You don't need to worry. I'm not about to suggest that you throw away all your worldly possessions and become a diehard follower of Jeez (and it's absolutely okay if you are). What I will do is invite you to put your disbelief on hold for a moment while I help redefine your understanding of forgiveness, because once properly understood and applied, it has the potential to create huge change in your life.

Forgiveness has been given lots of definitions. Oprah Winfrey once said, "Forgiveness is giving up hope that the past could have been any different," and I think she's spot on. Forgiveness isn't about changing what happened. It's about changing how you feel about what happened. Acceptance is key. For our purposes, forgiveness means letting the past go so you can stop recreating it and can finally live your life in the present. Sometimes it takes many years to forgive. It is a process that we have to show up to again and again. But when it happens, it is undeniable.

A Nightmare on Edna Street

When I was eight years old, our lovely oldie-worldly neighbour Auntie Edie (who incidentally wasn't my actual auntie but who used to make the worst pea soup on the planet) died all of a sudden, meaning that in the summer of 1977 we got two new neighbours: Edna and Marty. Edna was an imposing woman with a strong Austrian accent. She used to wear cardigans two sizes too small that scarcely fit over her huge breasts, and her skirt would always be hitched up at the back because of her enormous rear end. By contrast, Edna's husband, Marty, was insignificant in comparison. He was a tiny timeworn Jewish man, who wore a kippah on his head and shuffled around the planet like a wary nocturnal animal.

Soon after Edna and Marty moved in, we all became good friends and could often be found wandering into each other's homes for a chinwag. Dad became Edna's personal handyman and spent a lot of his spare time doing odd jobs around her house. Meanwhile, Mum would be out lending a hand with the shopping. During this time, I grew fond of Edna, who had become a kind of second mother to me. She was always available for hugs and I spent many an evening sitting on her knee, drawing pictures. She used to babysit for us occasionally so Mum and Dad could have an evening together and on the nights that she looked after me, she would read stories in her strong Austrian accent and make me laugh.

Nevertheless, there were some things that didn't quite add up about Edna. For example, she told us that she'd lost her children in a concentration camp in WWII, and showed me and my sis the lash marks on her back from where she'd been flogged. One time, however, whilst Dad was doing an odd job for her, he saw a photo album open on her bed displaying photos of her at the marriage ceremony of a German officer. Something didn't fit with those two stories—her presence at a German officer's wedding, but also her experience of persecution. Perhaps all was not what it seemed with Edna and Marty.

My bedroom at that time was no bigger than a shoebox, so small in fact that it had to have a sliding door. Edna took up half the room just by being in it. Sometimes she would babysit while Mum and Dad went for a night out. When she used to tuck me in, she would cover my whole body with kisses, leaving me feeling completely smothered by her size and girth. I would feel completely trapped, unable to breathe, and claustrophobic. In those moments, I couldn't utter a syllable of protest, not even a whisper. I was cornered like a frightened animal, unable to make a sound. I felt like I was being smothered to death. I couldn't speak about it to anyone, especially not to Mum and Dad, so I kept it all to myself and began to dread the nights when Edna would babysit.

The only way I could cope was to dissociate, cutting off from the experience psychologically and emotionally in order to protect myself and stay safe. That is all I know about what happened. I couldn't tell you if Edna did anything else to me. I simply don't know, and I cannot access that part of my memory that does. What I do know is that it felt wrong for this to be happening to me.

Then, one evening I heard screaming and shouting from Edna's house next door. I was scared stiff. Dad had been ill and unable to perform his usual odd jobs for her, and Mum had gone round to let her know. Moments after the yelling stopped, both my parents returned and warned me to stay away from her. I was confused: Edna was our friend, and now I was being told that I couldn't see or speak to her again. In an instant, our friendship was over.

From here on in, this story reads a bit like a weird B-rate horror film. Overnight, Edna went mad. The warm, kind, caring woman I had grown to adore was gone. In her place was a cruel, unrestrained monster; a crazy woman that would stop at nothing to terrify our family. Broken glass would get mysteriously scattered in the gutter where my dad parked his car. She repeatedly screamed abuse and hurled threats at the top of her voice, pounding the walls in the dead of night. And woe betide any football (or cat) that found itself in her garden; its fate would be sealed.

One winter, some of the kids in the area threw snowballs at Edna's back window. She shrieked loudly in the garden and amidst the din my name was mentioned. She yelled out that if she ever got her hands on me, she'd break my neck. I was totally petrified. Dad demanded to know why I'd been throwing snowballs at her window and struck me. I remember crying afterwards that I'd been hit by my dad for something I didn't do. Not only that, but a deranged woman was hunting me, hell-bent on breaking my neck. I actually thought that she wanted to kill me. I began to fear for my safety, often hiding in my bedroom. In the meantime, Mum's health began to deteriorate. She was on the verge of a nervous breakdown. That definitely meant that I couldn't speak up. Mum's health was the centre of attention; my feelings and experience faded into the background.

Over the next few years, I experienced secret panic attacks all the time, even after we moved away from Kelsall Avenue to our new house on Cedar Street in March 1978 when I was ten or eleven years old. At around fourteen years old I turned to alcohol, often drinking to numb the inner pain and anxiety I lived with daily. I fixed my funny man mask firmly in place. At seventeen, I discovered bodybuilding and set about creating a gladiator-like physique. It became my armour, a second skin protecting me from being vulnerable to hurt. And eventually, as I explained earlier, the Hulk emerged.

It was only in my early twenties that I realised that I had suffered both sexual and psychological abuse at the hands of Edna.

Even though I never saw her again for many years, a vital part of my heart had been left behind in the box room at the old house. I was quite severely scarred by what had happened, but I wouldn't understand the full impact of it until many years later when I met my first partner, Jane, who I wrote about in chapter six.

A Tale of Forgiveness

During a visit to my hometown in 1997, Jane and I drove around, revisiting some of my favourite childhood haunts—not for the first time. It was Boxing Day and the streets were near empty. Suddenly she asked me to stop the car and pointed out that we had just passed my old house on Kelsall Avenue, suggesting that we go back and take a look at it.

I started to shake and sweat, my body going into fight or flight mode. I didn't know how I could ever go back to this place. With Jane's encouragement, I made the decision to turn the car round and drive back up the hill, in search of the old house with the yellow door. As we approached the house I realised that I had one last thing to complete: to visit Edna.

I found myself a few minutes later standing at her front door, not knowing whether she lived there anymore or even whether she was alive or not. I took a deep breath, knocked loudly and waited for an answer. An old lady appeared at the window peering through the curtains. My stomach churned and twisted into a lead knot: I was sure it was Edna. I could tell from her eyes. The seconds felt like hours as I waited to see whether she would open the door.

Eventually, the door creaked open, just enough to see part of her face. I could barely see her through the narrow crack in the door, but the second I heard her frenzied shouting about intruders from behind the door in her unmistakable Austrian accent, I knew for certain it was her. Some things never change. The door quickly slammed shut in my face and she called the police.

I was about to give up and walk away, yet I knew I had to face her. I turned around and knocked again. Once again, the door opened slightly. This time, I told her my name. A silence followed. From behind the door, she mumbled about how difficult her life had been since my parents had "taken me away" and said that no one wanted to be her friend. I felt sad to see Edna this way—she seemed so pathetic—and encouraged her to open the door, but she refused, ordered that I prove my identity to her and then retreated inside to her living room.

I fumbled around for an old bus pass with my name and photograph on it, and moved over to the front window. Slowly, she moved back the lace curtain and finally, after 20 years without contact, we were both standing face to face with only a skinny sheet of glass separating us. I stood perfectly still and stared into her eyes. Tears trickled down her cheeks and I recognised in a single moment of connection that she was not really a monster after all, but a frightened little girl trapped in a grown woman's body. There was no Marty anymore. There was just her, and she was lonely, alone and scared. I saw her through new eyes.

I will always treasure the memory of that moment, and the expression of peace and relief on Edna's face. Soon afterwards, the police arrived, demanding an explanation as to why I was there. I replied, "Just visiting an old friend to wish her a merry Christmas."

This might read like a bit of a Hollywood story, but that encounter could only happen because of the years of deep and often scary inner work I had done. I hadn't planned to see Edna; it was my partner who had wanted to see the street I had lived on again. I hadn't even been there in over a decade, although truthfully I had often revisited my old box room in my mind. Each time I had re-entered the blackness of that all consuming experience, I was presented with yet another opportunity to find and reacquaint myself with that scared little boy that I had disregarded when I swore my allegiance to the ego and buried the pain. When I finally plucked up the courage to visit Edna in person all those years later I was scared stiff but knew it was a crucial step.

A Shift in Perception

That day marked a turning point. Sometimes I still get triggered and remember the feelings of suffocation and terror I experienced as a boy, but there was something new there after that final meeting, something different. I no longer felt like Edna's victim. Anger would come, but it would also go again as I remembered how it felt to stand on that doorstep, face to face with my childhood abuser, seeing her as a vulnerable, frightened old lady. I reconnected to the lost boy in me and realised that while I had been wounded, I was not permanently damaged. Scars of the psyche can heal.

The shift in perception I experienced that day brought down the outwardly impossible wall of fear standing between Edna and myself. As I stood there I realised, not just intellectually, but with every cell of my being that while she was absolutely responsible for her behaviour towards me, she was not responsible for the ongoing pain I had endured in the years that followed. The realisation dawned on me that despite all she had done, I too had played a part in the ongoing suffering I experienced. It was ultimately up to me to choose to let it go. No one else on the entire planet could take that step for me—not even her. No one else is in charge of my inner world: I am.

Nevertheless, establishing that Edna wasn't responsible for my pain doesn't mean that I excused her behaviour or denied my pain. As an adult in that situation, she had a duty of care towards me as a young boy which she failed to meet, and the knock on effect of her choices had crushed my spirit, confidence and trust in women for many years. I experienced a great deal of psychological and emotional distress about what had happened.

But in choosing to witness the scene of the crime through adult eyes, I started to appreciate the situation from a wider, more rounded perspective. I realised that most of the suffering I experienced was because of the beliefs I made up about myself rather than the act itself. I was a boy, and I wasn't the cause of the situation.

By now it should be clear what my point is—that we are *all* called to forgive. Forgiveness requires looking back at the situations and people that wounded you, and who you have wounded, and daring to see them differently, taking absolute responsibility for your part in it and for the beliefs that you internalised as a result of those events. This includes redefining your understanding of and relationship to masculinity. The trauma and hurt we experienced as boys—including the messages we internalised about who we need to be as men—may have wounded us, but we have tended those wounds over the years, investing far more energy in keeping them alive than anyone else.

As an adult, I can't change what took place back in that box room any more than I can prevent the sun from rising and setting, but by allowing myself to revisit the scene of the crime, the day came when I was able to raise my head and let the hurt boy look straight into Edna's eyes. That moment was the catalyst that helped bring about a powerful change of mind because I recognised with cast-iron certainty that irrespective of life's trials, beyond all suffering, who I am remains unbroken.

Forgiveness Isn't Easy—it's Critical

Forgiving another human being for how they have hurt you is one of the most warrior-like things a man can do. Becoming truly free of the wounds and grievances of childhood is hard. It's harder than running an ultra-marathon, harder than being pummelled in a boxing ring, harder than rocket science. We men are accustomed to pain but we have been taught little about how to truly forgive and let go. In fact, we've often been taught the opposite, that a real man bears a grudge and fights to the death. This is the most gut-wrenching, challenging work you will ever do. If you want to know what you're really made of, dare to face and be willing to forgive your past. Then you'll find out what being a 'real man' is all about.

Until you consciously change your mind, nothing changes. You alone are 100% responsible for your thoughts and you are 100% free to choose what you think and believe. If you carry on blaming everyone and everything for why your life looks the way it does, you will not see that you are exactly where you are today as a result of tens of thousands of choices that *you* have made—including the choice to be part of omertà. And yet it is in acknowledging this that you will be set free.

As hard as it is, the truth is that forgiveness is available to everyone, anywhere, anytime, anyplace. It's a kick ass tool that is vital for making the sprint from fear to love. It is the answer to attack of any kind. It requires a little willingness on your part to lay down your armour, and the determination to let yourself and others off the hook. Forgiveness opens up a space between your automatic victim thoughts and the new paradigm that is waiting for you to step into it. Once you change your perspective, life takes on a whole new outlook as all the worldly dramas turn out to be insignificant in contrast with the magnificence of the overall picture.

Someone wise once said that, "It doesn't matter how long you have forgotten the truth for, only how soon you remember it." And right now, we're going to put that into practice.

Exercise

1. Think about someone who wounded or hurt you when you were a boy — a parent, teacher, friend or family member, for example. *My example would be Edna, who abused and bullied me and my family.*

2. What shitty mistaken belief (SMB) did you make up as a result of what happened? *In the situation with Edna, I believed I was guilty and that it was my fault.*

3. What did you believe about the other person? *I believed Edna was a monster. I believed that women can't be trusted.*

4. Say out loud, "These are beliefs I have invented and they are not true. I am determined to remember the truth." You might feel a bit stupid saying this out loud, but it can't be any more stupid than attacking yourself all day long.

5. Ask yourself if the belief(s) from step 2 are true. For example, I would ask myself, "Is it absolutely true that as a child, I was bad and that the abuse was my fault?" The answer is always "NO."

6. Flip the SMB about yourself into a Big I Am — a simple statement of the highest truth about you. Always frame a

Big I Am as a positive statement in the present tense. Find the words you've been waiting your whole life to hear. *For example, I transformed the SMBs, "I am guilty" and "It was my fault" into "I am innocent" and "I was just a child."*

7. Write down the Big I Am and repeat the words out loud. Let the new belief land inside you. Try to feel it in your bones. Then tear up the paper with the SMB on it, and throw the paper away as a symbol of letting it go.

8. Now that you've forgiven yourself, you're in a position to forgive the other person. Forgiveness does not excuse the other person's behaviour, but it does ask you to see the bigger picture. ACIM states that any behaviour that doesn't extend love is a call for it. So if this is the case, what is the highest truth about the other person? What would have to be happening in someone's world to make them behave this way? Walk a mile in their shoes. *For example, the truth about Edna is that she was doing the very best she could.* If you're struggling, use the word 'maybe' to explore other possibilities. *So, maybe Edna was overwhelmed or scared. Maybe the abuse was her way of trying to be close to me. Maybe she tormented our family because she felt abandoned.*

9. Notice how you feel. Personally, I often feel peaceful after practising forgiveness. Now go about your day and look for evidence of the Big I Am. Make a conscious choice to be the change you wish to see in the world.

Don't be conned into thinking that it ends here. Staying one step ahead of the ego requires daily vigilance and practice—and people will continue to piss you off in the present. Any time that happens, use this exercise. Seeing other people's behaviour as a call for love (no matter how fucked up it looks) takes awareness and real willingness to see things differently. The truth is that compassion is the only appropriate response to a call for love. Sometimes you have to deal with your own fear-based, defensive reactions first. That's okay. You're allowed to be human. But if you make an unwavering commitment to living as a man who consistently breaks omertà, you will be called to a more accountable way of life. You are called to be a leader. You are asked to be a warrior of the heart, a man who is bigger than the petty tit-for-tat mentality the ego thrives on. Once you have identified the pain and call for love in how another person shows up, you have a responsibility to help them, because your interests and your brother's are no different.

Every time you change your mind about self and other, you activate a potent force that has the power to change the world by changing how you perceive the world. Once you accept that the Big I Ams state the real truth about you, you will come to know an unshakeable clarity and sense of inner peace and freedom that surpasses anything the ego's world can offer. You will experience a whole new mode of thinking, perceiving and behaving, and you will feel ablaze as this force moves through you and out into the world. You will come to enjoy your own company more than you ever thought possible—and you will be able to be with other people, letting them love you without getting pissed off, needing to shut down or feeling uncomfortable, claustrophobic or freezing up, loving them in the middle of their struggle. You've been away for a long time my friend. It's good to have you back. Welcome home.

PART THREE

THE NEW MAN

"When I am silent, I have thunder hidden inside."

- Rumi

Introduction

"Think not that happiness is ever found by following a road away from it. This makes no sense, and cannot be the way. To achieve a goal you must proceed in its direction, not away from it."
—A Course in Miracles

In this third and final part of the book I want to offer you a simple set of tools to help you walk the path of the new man. You have repeatedly broken the vow of male silence, decided to take responsibility and you have done some vital work to build a strong, new foundation. My intention now is to make sure you do everything you possibly can to stay true to the path of the inner warrior and keep moving forward. This requires building new habits because if you keep doing what you've always done, you'll continue to get what you've always got. Part three of this book will ensure that you are facing the right direction and will get you back on track if you come undone. Like I have mentioned at various times throughout this book, the ego is a terminator—it never stops. Your goal now is to stay one step ahead of it at all times and deliberately redefine what being a man means to you. This requires courage, willingness and discipline, especially during those times when you feel sucked back into the vortex of omertà.

As Morpheus said to Neo in *The Matrix*, "Sooner or later you're going to realise just as I did that there's a difference between knowing the path and walking the path. I can only show you the door. You're the one that has to walk through it."

CHAPTER 20

CONSCIOUS SOLITUDE

"I need to be alone. I need to ponder my shame and my despair in seclusion; I need the sunshine and the paving stones of the streets without companions, without conversation, face to face with myself, with only the music of my heart for company."
—Henry Miller

We live in a world that thrives on busyness and distraction, we're fed the lie that our freedom is somehow tied up in our worldly goings on. "The busier, the better!" we say through gritted teeth. We equate being busy with success when in truth it is anything but. Busyness is what Eckhart Tolle describes as "the collective disease of humanity." Since when did crazy busy become normal? Human beings have mutated into human doings and as a result have disconnected from the natural pulse life. As Socrates states, "Beware the barrenness of a busy life."

We are desperately in need of solitude. Unfortunately, it is about as common nowadays as VHS videos. Most of us are bombarded with stimulation and demands for our attention from the moment we wake up to the time we fall asleep, world weary and exhausted. If it's not the news, it's our news feeds and newsletters filling up our tiny, portable screens and heads full of other people's agendas. Most of us are probably more addicted to the constant drip feed of information overload than we care to admit. In the UK, the problem is so severe that a law was passed in 2016 doubling the number of points you can get on your driving licence if you're caught holding your phone—six points and a £200 fine. In Australia the fine for driving and holding your phone is $400.

Sam Keen writes in *Fire In The Belly* that a man must "take time to be with himself, to discover his desires, his rhythms his tastes, his gifts, his hopes, and wounds," to "listen to the dictates of his own heart." In order to accomplish this, we must consciously choose to strip our lives back to the bare bones and practise conscious solitude. This might seem contradictory given that we are talking about breaking a vow of silence, but choosing to engage in conscious solitude is actually one of the most important things you could engage in as a man committed to this work. It is vital that you carve out sacred space—no excuses.

Beware Unconscious Isolation

Let's talk for a moment about the difference between unconscious isolation and conscious solitude. Even though they may look very similar on the outside—a man spending time by himself, perhaps in the shed, perhaps out on a long walk, perhaps on a weekend fishing trip—the truth is that they are polar opposites of each other. Unconscious isolation is fear led; conscious solitude is heart led. Unconscious isolation is all about contraction and pulling away; conscious solitude is more about expansion and leaning in. Unconscious isolation depletes; conscious solitude nourishes. Time spent in genuine solitude isn't unconscious; it brings you into closer contact with yourself and your life. What matters is the intention behind your choice to be alone.

When a man unconsciously isolates himself, he tends to indulge his escape routes as a way of binding his anxiety. This only reinforces his sense of isolation, and the world reflects that back to him. When a man consciously retreats into solitude, however, he chooses to shut out the noise of the world so that he can really hear himself. A man who does this will not try to numb or block out his pain with escape routes. Instead, he will really commit to being with himself.

Conscious solitude is an essential part of connecting with your inner warrior and to breaking free from the shackles of omertà. The world, set up to reinforce the vow of male silence, will do almost anything to keep you from saying yes to it. Say yes anyway.

Leave Me Alone

I believe we have a natural pull towards solitude, which starts in childhood. Some of us might want more or less alone time, depending on how introverted or extroverted we are, but being alone is a universal part of the human experience.

My first memory of choosing conscious solitude happened when I was aged eight or nine. I had just shed my bicycle stabilisers in the local nursery playground, and Dad was there cheering me on. Losing my stabilisers could only mean one thing: freedom! Mum banned me from riding my bike on the road which I begrudgingly agreed to, but this didn't stop me formulating a backup plan. I would take my adventures into the back alleys. Every weekend I would rise with the blackbirds, eat a big bowl of cornflakes, (sometimes two bowls, because that's what Dad did), put on my scruffs, and head off down the alleys on my shiny red bike with the fat white tyres (which incidentally was a hand-me-down from my big sister). The mere thought of riding alone through the back alleys made me buzz with excitement. In those moments I was alone yet alive.

Solitude is just as vital in adulthood as it is in childhood, although we tend to go against our natural instincts more as grown-ups, perhaps not giving ourselves what we need. I wrote earlier that when Dad died I sought comfort in solitude. I felt the call to weight train outdoors in the back garden using battered dumbbells, an old stone bench with the earth beneath my feet. During these workouts I felt something stir inside of me that was primal and powerful. Every workout gave me an opportunity to re-focus my mind and breathe deeply, strengthening my connection with the world around me and the world within me. I observed the rhythm of the seasons; the warmth of the sun on my skin, the pouring rain, and the decaying leaves falling all around me; the endless surge of life and death in which we are all a part. As I said goodbye to my dad, I said hello to myself.

There are lots of different things you can do that will help you practise conscious solitude. My dad used to fix things up in his shed; he would say that it was his way of straightening things out. I can't say for sure whether his urge to go down to the shed was isolation or solitude; the most important thing to pay attention to is the intention behind your choices. As Thoreau famously said,

"I went to the woods," (or in my dad's case, the shed) "because I wished to live deliberately, to front only the essential facts of life, and see if I could not learn what it had to teach, and not, when I came to die, discover that I had not lived."

These times of conscious solitude have the ability to awaken your soul, allowing something intensely profound to emerge. You will discover an ancient knowingness that has never really left you, a memory of who you really are.

Exercise

Your task is simple my friend: go and find conscious solitude. Even five minutes will do. Go. Do it now.

CHAPTER 21

NOW

*"The decision to make the present moment
your friend is the end of ego."*
—Eckhart Tolle

We live in a past-future society, crammed full of distractions and diversions that serve to inhibit us from being here now. But it wasn't always this way. During school hols when I was a boy, I would leap out of bed at the crack of dawn and head out of the door to meet my pals. Every day was seen through fresh eyes. We had the uncanny knack of being in the now. There was nothing else. We played footy, built dens, and climbed trees like our lives depended on it. We were courageous, unapologetic and free, and in our own wild and wacky way we carved out a little piece of heaven in our own backyards.

When we became adults, however, things changed. I lost touch with my mates and watched as all the grown-ups around me lost touch with the present moment and started to become almost completely preoccupied with thoughts of the past or the future. As Eric Harrison says in the great little book *The 5-Minute Meditator*, "We carry the disappointments of past years, and project our worries decades into the future. We go through the day with our minds elsewhere. It makes you wonder 'was it a mistake to grow up at all?'"

In 2015, I joined a new gym for the first time in a few years and I was shocked to discover just how distracted modern bodybuilders are during workouts. Rather than using the workout as an opportunity to be present, these Charles Atlas wannabes are constantly checking their mobile phones, updating their Instagram feeds with enhanced selfies of their bulging biceps, and sending texts. The one thing they're not is *present*. Bodybuilding legend Arnie said during an interview that texting during workouts is Mickey Mouse stuff. I agree with him. It takes discipline to be present, just as it takes discipline to train properly. I think the gym is just one example of how distracted and unfocused we have become.

Sometimes I wonder how the heck we lost our way as adults, becoming so obsessed with updating our followers and staying 'connected' to people we may never even meet that we are willing to firstly expose the innermost details of our lives and secondly, to voluntarily opt out of the present moment.

The Present Is Painful

I'm not saying technology is fully to blame for why we are so unable to be present to our lives. Like everything else, it's not the thing but how we use it that is the issue, and in the case of technology, the incessant, obsessive way we lose ourselves in it is a dodgy cover up for a deeper issue: the nagging presence of our SMBs and our absolute determination to avoid being with ourselves. In a great video online called "Louis C.K. hates cell phones," the comedian describes how he hates cell phones because of how much they distract us from simply being with ourselves. He talks about how we experience a sense of "forever empty sadness" when we simply sit in the present moment. Stillness allows what's bubbling under the surface to emerge. What better way to run away from the pain your SMBs generate than to trash the simplicity of the present moment? The irony of course is that by attempting to run away from your pain, you create more of it. As you know well by now, defences reinforce what they defend against.

Seek and Do Not Find

To the ego, the present moment is the enemy. In the present there is no past, and without the past the ego doesn't have a leg to stand on. The present moment is guiltless. It is a blank slate. Life exists in the present moment without any of the shit, guilt, shame or weight of expectation generated in the past. The ego however deals solely in past and future and will only ever use the present moment as a means to an end, as an opportunity to momentarily acknowledge its worldly victories, offering you a fleeting moment of respite and a brief glint of triumph before plunging you back into the endless focus on the past and future. In a world steeped in toxic masculinity and omertà, we men are desperately in need of these empty victories so that we can prove how strong and manly we are, which makes us susceptible to treating the present moment simply as a means to an end.

It might look like you're being responsible and mature by constantly obsessing about the past and the future, but the truth is you are nothing more than a plaything in the ego's game of seek and do not find. As the saying goes, one foot in the past, one in the future, and you shit all over the present. The ego tells us over and over, "If you want to be happy, you first have to solve this problem"—and its problems are endless. They are also all out there in the world: *How will I pay the rent next month? My girlfriend's always nagging at me. Look at what those bastard politicians have done now!* Notice how sneakily the ego wraps up the concern with the past and future to make it look like it's really concerned with the present moment.

Remember, any answer offered by the ego isn't an answer at all, because the ego prefers the problem and has no intention of solving it. *A Course in Miracles* states, "The ego's primary dictate is seek but do *not* find." Therefore, the ego's solution will always lead you back to the problem. We buy into this line of thinking and convince ourselves over and over that by moving the external furniture around, we can finally solve the problem. Just look at the news or politics to see this at work. The last place we ever think of going is within. If you actually discovered the real answer to all your apparent problems is inside you and in the present moment, and that you don't actually need anything other than this moment, the ego would be out of a job.

You're Not Really Here

In the aforementioned book *The 5-Minute Meditator*, Harrison says, "We tend to operate on automatic pilot. We can scramble through the day not sensing or feeling anything clearly. What is worse, we can be too distracted to realise it. Some days, we're just not here at all."

Do you really want to be on your deathbed, looking back on your life and realising that you were never really present for any of it? When you were at work, you were thinking about sex.

When you were having sex, you were plagued by self-doubt and insecurity. When you were giving your kid a bath, you were on your phone checking your emails. When you were going to bed, you were thinking about tomorrow. Is this really how you want to live? Personally, I want to look back on my life and say that regardless of what happened, I was there for it.

If you're happy and content with this way of (not) living, you might as well skip to the next chapter right now because the rest of what I'm going to say will make no sense to you. But if your answer to the previous question is "No" and you recognise the true nature of the problem, the next question to address is this: how do we get back to the present moment?

How to Become Present

Luckily, the answer is simple, even though the ego doesn't want it to be (the ego loves complexity, in case you hadn't noticed). Good old-fashioned awareness coupled with commitment and presence is the key. The more aware and determined *you* become, the weaker the ego becomes. Your task now is, in the words of Mr T in the A-Team, to "quit yo jibber-jabber" and land, however clunkily, in the present moment. Simply put, to be here *now*.

Start by bringing your attention to simple everyday tasks. Pay attention when you get dressed, when you make a cup of tea, when you drive, when you sit at your desk. Children do this naturally because they haven't developed the motor skills yet to do things unconsciously, and old people do it too because they've lost the motor skills needed to do things we take for granted like turning on the taps or tying shoelaces. When you bring awareness to all the things you normally do on autopilot, you stop stressing so much about past and future and the task itself becomes a sacred stepping stone to the present moment. On the outside your life might not look that different, but the on the inside the quality of your thinking and attention will be.

A word of warning, however: don't waste your time trying to be present 24/7. You will fail miserably and might end up in the nut house! Instead, dedicate a few quality seconds here and there during the day to becoming conscious of whatever it is you are doing and allow that moment to grow. Method acting expert Lee Strasberg once said, "A single grain of real coffee is worth a ton of watered down." Go for the single grain. For example, in my experience even one conscious breath can work wonders for the monkey mind, bringing the ego's reign to an abrupt end.

Short bursts of being present have the potential to transform your relationship with life. Once you become present to your life, your life becomes present to you. As soon as you make friends with the present, seemingly ordinary things become extraordinary. It might only last for a few seconds but in that few seconds you have caught sight of something exquisite—the truth of who you really are, the Big I Am—and you are a changed man.

In *A New Earth*, Eckhart Tolle says, "The decision to make the present moment into your friend is the end of the ego. The ego can never be in alignment with the present moment, which is to say aligned with life, since its very nature is to ignore, resist or devalue the now. Time is what the ego lives on."

The ego won't want you to understand this and believe me, it will try every trick in the book to stop you from understanding and applying it. Do it anyway. The truth is always simpler than you think.

Exercise

The following is a simple, effective way of being in the present moment. For the purpose of this exercise I want you to choose a simple everyday task like brushing your teeth, or washing the car, or cooking a meal. Your job is to practise being fully present while you do this. To turn your attention away from thought by focusing on the senses—sight, smell, sound, taste or touch. It's really that simple. It doesn't really matter what you choose just as long as you do it thoroughly.

I'm not going to tell fibs here fellas: there are times when having to be here in the now is a little bastard. Perhaps you have lost your job, are in the middle of heartbreak or loss, or are facing great adversity. The present moment is the last place you may want to be because then you'll have to feel. Even during these times, it is still easier than living half a life.

I'll let Eckhart Tolle (who has pretty much hogged this chapter) have the final say on this matter: "Whatever the present moment contains, accept it as if you had chosen it. Always work with it, not against it. Make it your friend and ally, not your enemy. This will miraculously transform your whole life."

CHAPTER 22

RITES OF PASSAGE

"There's nobody to guide [boys] through the process of becoming a man... to explain to them the meaning of manhood. And that's a recipe for disaster."
—Barack Obama

Back in 2013, not long after I had said yes to the assignment of writing this book, Ell and I took a walk through a cobbled shopping and restaurant area called the Lanes in Brighton, a cosmopolitan English city a few miles from where we live. The next piece of the book turned out to be among the very first we wrote for *Odd Man Out*, and unfortunately, nothing has really changed in the last few years.

Boys Will Be Boys

Picture the scene: it's a rainy Saturday evening, 6:45pm, in the middle of August. Ell and I are walking towards a coffee shop when we encounter a group of guys outside a pub, rowdy and cocky, their arrogance on full display like male peacocks displaying their manly feathers with bravado and pride. One of them walks into the road and holds his arm out, stopping an approaching car. He saunters drunkenly round to the driver and leans into the window suggestively, mimicking a prostitute. His face is poorly made up in a pastiche of a drag queen, with arched black eyebrows, heavy eyeliner and lashes.

This strange, slightly grotesque man is, believe it or not, in the middle of celebrating his transition from being an unmarried man to a married one. He is the stag, and this is his stag party. In the UK, stag parties (and hen nights for the ladies) are big business. A whole weekend is often set aside to drink, and the overt aim is to get the stag as obliterated as possible without him passing out.

The stag is one of the most majestic animals on the planet, but wearing ladies' lingerie over a shirt and jeans as part of a bizarre, omertà-fuelled ritual to mark the transition from bachelor to husband is hardly majestic. During the evening, the stag will be forced to drink profuse amounts of alcohol, to do press ups on the concrete pavement and go to a strip club. His body will be pushed to the limits of what it can endure in terms of alcohol.

All this is going on while families wander past and diners tuck into burgers and chips. They unconsciously accept what they see as being completely normal—it's just what happens on a stag weekend after all. Onlookers tut in mock disapproval, ("Boys will be boys"), but we're so used to this patriarchy-driven, twisted rite of passage that we conveniently turn a blind eye to the damage it's doing.

For the men involved in the stag party, it is almost as if they are saying to their friend, the husband-to-be, "Let's get you ready for marriage by exorcising all your demons out of you. This is your last chance to fulfil all your primal urges and desires, because after this mate, you're fucked." There is a huge amount of lying involved on stag weekends. What happens on a stag weekend stays on a stag weekend, and everyone knows it.

The pressure on the stag to 'perform' is immense. He would rather be publicly shamed by his friends through taking up the ridiculous challenges presented to him than be shamed on an even deeper level for not doing it. He willingly makes a spectacle of himself because it guarantees that he will fit in and be accepted. The stag weekend represents what omertà has done to men's inbuilt capacity and need for meaningful rites of passage. This moment in a man's life has so much potential for men to connect and voice their fears and hopes about what it means to become a husband yet it has become an empty rite of passage in the way that fast food meals have replaced quality family dinner time.

The men in this scene will likely sit in the role of both stag and stag party attendee at different times in their lives. The stag Ell and I saw that summer will just as readily take up his position as chief rabble-rouser on one of his friend's stag weekends, and will subject his friends to the same rituals and humiliations that he experienced, making sure that the senseless cycle continues.

A man in the twenty-first century is very fortunate if he has friends who are emotionally literate and can offer the space to hear and respond with support and love to his fears. When it comes to these huge turning points in a man's life, in the western world, omertà runs riot.

Dare to Do it Differently

The stag weekend is just one of the empty rites of passage that men are subjected to in our society. Take the briefest of looks at history and you will find brutal rites of passage for males almost too uncomfortable to contemplate: from cutting off the skin of a young boy's penis, to suspending men from poles with hooks through their nipples, to years of university hazing which have even resulted in young men dying.

The essence of a rite of passage is that it's supposed to be a ceremony or event which marks an important stage in someone's life, the transition from childhood to adulthood, or the marking of a marriage or death. Getting your first car, or your first pay slip, or asking someone out on a date for the first time are all significant moments—and in our society, we have a strong tendency to acknowledge and celebrate each one with alcohol. We don't dare to do anything more significant or deeper than that, afraid of what we'll be called, afraid of what we'll feel and afraid of being rejected or shamed. Maybe we don't even know how else to celebrate these moments.

There is a distinct difference between a rite of passage that is meaningless and one that is meaningful: meaningless rites of passage are hollow attempts at connection. They tend to involve hurting, humiliating and inebriating the person involved. Our world today is so wrapped up in omertà that we've lost sight of how to have meaningful rites of passage.[6] We no longer really know how to experience solid, authentic connection. As I have reiterated over and over, we're so afraid of being labelled as a pussy or a sissy or a wimp or as gay that we don't dare to encourage, affirm and empower other men. This just keeps the cycle of omertà going round and round, with one generation after another picking up the broken baton. I really didn't like what I saw that evening with Ell, and I'm so glad that I never did that before my wedding day.

---

[6] Although projects like Mankind Project and A Band of Brothers, among others, are doing amazing work to change this. See the list of recommended organisations at the back of the book for more information.

If we are ever going to expect our boys to become wholehearted men, we have to stop glorifying the stag weekend and dare to do it differently.

We have bought into the lie that by subjecting a man to humiliating tests of bravado and 'manhood,' we are making a man of him. We try to convince ourselves that it's just a bit of harmless fun, but it's not. The truth is that *every* time we shame a man, we wound him and we reinforce the collective wound. Throughout this book, I have shown over and over again that all the bravado and bullshit is covering up the deep pain we feel inside, pain that we don't know how to talk about or feel. It seems safer and easier to shame or torture ourselves and other men than it is to venture into such uncomfortable territory but the cost is huge.

We men need to learn the difference between the meaningless and the meaningful. We have to be brave enough to say no to that which is damaging us, even if it means experiencing temporary or permanent exclusion from our social group. We have to dare to love, affirm and support other men, not just succumb to the pack mentality and ply each other with alcohol. A man's true power lies in him being brave enough to say no to omertà and autonomous enough to make up his own mind about who he is and how he chooses to live his life. A true leader is a man who is unafraid to challenge all the meaningless bullshit in our society. Will you answer the call?

CHAPTER 23

MEANINGFUL RITUALS

"It's no easy business to be simple."
—Mason Currey

Rites of passage take place at significant moments throughout a man's life, whereas rituals are those daily, weekly, monthly or perhaps yearly practices or habits that we turn to again and again in our lives. A boy becomes a man only once in his life, but a ritual is practised repeatedly.

Most of us already engage in rituals every day; we just call it our routine. The difference is that we tend to go about our routine on autopilot, but a ritual really asks us to be present. True ritual is a sacred practice. It adds something meaningful to your day. Let's take a closer look at the morning ritual.

The Morning Ritual

Self-help diva Louise Hay says how you start your day is how you live your day so it makes sense to set up your stall bright and early before the ego gets in there and starts to direct the show. The last thing the ego wants you to do is start the day on positive note because that would put it out of a job, so it will go to great lengths to distract you from what's really important. Then, when your day starts to fall apart, it will tell you that the world is doing it to you, when really *you* are the one doing it to you.

I encourage you to get into the habit of starting your day from a place of strength. Make a conscious, disciplined effort to feed your mind positive thoughts early in the day, because that's how you rewire your brain and realign yourself with the inner warrior. Think of it as conscious brainwashing. The ego has its own version of brainwashing too, only its version is unconscious. Remember, the mind is incredibly powerful and because it never sleeps you have to get into the habit of practicing mindfulness at every opportunity. Otherwise the ego will happily step in and trip you up.

You might want to do some research on the many benefits of a morning routine. However, don't let research distract you or be an excuse for procrastinating. Starting your day differently might just change your life.

Exercise

To start with, I want you to get into the practice of getting up out of bed bright and early. There's an old adage that says early to bed, early to rise, makes a man healthy wealthy and wise. I choose to start the day between 5:30-6:00am with a cup of steaming green tea and a bowl of oats.

Secondly, bin the bloody newspaper and read something inspiring instead. I read *A Course in Miracles* and more recently *A Course of Love*, but you are free to choose whatever you like provided it's soulful and takes you closer to where you want to go. It might be a bit awkward at first. I'm challenging you to unlearn a lazy, undisciplined way of living and to replace it with a disciplined approach instead. Introducing meaningful rituals into your life will accelerate your growth. Think of it as high intensity training for the mind.

Make a decision and start tomorrow. In 90 days' time, you'll be glad that you did.

CHAPTER 24

STILLNESS

"To be still is to be conscious without thought. You are never more essentially, more deeply yourself than when you are still. When you are still, you are who you were before you temporarily assumed this physical and mental form called a person."
—Eckhart Tolle

When it comes to stillness, everyone knows they should do it but very few people actually do. As part of my morning ritual, I spend a few minutes in stillness and silence every day. I would be lying if I said it was easy, but I do it anyway. Now it's your turn.

Exercise

1. Find a quiet space where you won't be disturbed.
2. Set a timer for 10 minutes
3. Sit upright in a chair or on a cushion and commit to keeping perfectly still for the duration of the exercise.
4. Pay attention to your breathing.
5. Rest for a few seconds in the gap at the end of the out breath and quietly repeat a Big I Am. For example: I am peaceful.

6. Whenever you find your mind wandering (and it will) name the thought (e.g. car/work/money) and come back to the breath.
7. Keep going until you hear the timer buzz.
8. Repeat every day for the rest of your life.

You know how slippery the ego is. Most of you reading this won't do it. That's fine: it's your life, not mine. But if you're one of the few who is ready to do something different and you want to stay on track, make sure you remind yourself daily why stillness and silence are so important on your journey of breaking the vow of male silence. They are the keys that allow you to access your real power as a man.

CHAPTER 25

TRUE BROTHERHOOD

"Now this is the law of the jungle, as old and as true as the sky,
And the wolf that shall keep it may prosper,
but the wolf that shall break it must die.

As the creeper that girdles the tree trunk,
the law runneth forward and back;
For the strength of the pack is the wolf,
and the strength of the wolf is the pack."
—Rudyard Kipling

Ram Dass once stated that we are all just walking each other home. We cannot break the vow of male silence alone. As much as we've been sold the lie of the "rugged individual," the truth is that relationship is the central part of the fabric of our lives. Given that loneliness is a direct consequence of omertà, I cannot stress enough the importance of connection and companionship on the journey. Walking this path alone is no longer an option. It is time to talk about true brotherhood.

Empty Brotherhood

Under the vow of male silence, brotherhood frequently masquerades as camaraderie full of mockery and backslapping. Omertà-based brotherhood is raw and tribal in places, but it's ultimately damaging, hinting at connection but not allowing men to truly make contact with each other.

This pseudo-connection between men is permitted in sport, on the battlefield or when under the influence of alcohol. This is one of the only times when men in our culture are allowed to experience a rare sense of solidarity and intimacy with each other, which is, as I wrote in the chapter on rituals, probably why the most significant events in a man's life, such as his stag party or wedding day, are alcohol-fuelled. We have become so estranged from our own gender that any attempts at closeness, if they happen in the sober light of day, feel foreign and often even carry with them a secret fear of sexualising the relationship. This narrow, fear-based perception limits what is possible in male friendship.

I love the friendship depicted between Gavin and Smithy in the British comedy sitcom, *Gavin and Stacey*. It is comical and full of playful banter, but as well as the usual guy stuff like attempting to taste every beer in the world, the sitcom also shows the brotherly (and for Smithy, very emotionally attached) side to their friendship. Gav and Smithy are a daily part of each other's lives, sharing pints, hugs and tears. They have an elaborate greeting ritual, which even Gav's parents and Smithy's sister know. I think the friendship between Smithy and Gavin is part of what made the sitcom so popular. They display an intimacy that I think is both relatable yet rare between men.

I know how difficult it can be to develop intimate male friendships. To be honest I can count my closest male friends on one hand, especially those whom I confide in, but honestly, it's hard to stay connected. If I don't contact my mates, rarely will they contact me (although they might say the same in reverse if you were to ask them). Sometimes, I lose complete contact with my male friends for months at a time. I know I'm not alone in this; it seems hard in general for us men to stay in touch. Perhaps the message that we have to go it alone is so deeply ingrained in us that it's a battle in itself to go beyond it.

To be honest, I'm a bit envious of watching my wife interact with her friends. There's an ease, a playfulness and a spontaneity about it. It seems so effortless for them to connect. Ell will just announce, "I'm just going to catch up with Liz," "I've just been on the phone with Lian" or "I'm hanging out with Hannah for the day." The sense I get when Elloa and her friends talk is that they don't constantly feel like they have to be on guard around each other. With men however it feels the opposite; a little bit guarded, clunky and forced. One of my mates for example is a master at deflecting the conversation straight back to me anytime I ask him how he is, like the question is a hot potato he can't wait to get rid of.

I still have days when it feels unnatural to break omertà in my male friendships even though I've been working at it for a number of years. Given what we were taught as boys and later as men, it is not exactly typical to sit with another bloke and to ask "How are you?" Even if a man does open up, it is difficult for him to allow himself to really take the space and be vulnerable; even as he's sharing, a man will feel the pull to open up and shut down at the same time. The fear of being seen as weak is huge amongst men, as we've explored in detail throughout this book, and it hangs over every conversation. The temptation to keep things light is strong.

Although it might seem easier to revert back to stereotypical ways of communicating, as we know, the cost of doing so is huge. For example, in Grayson Perry's Channel Four documentary *All Man*, a group of young men in their twenties were filmed having a discussion about one of their best friends who had committed suicide. These guys were supposedly very close yet none of them knew just how much their friend was suffering. In no way is this criticism because it was apparent that these men cared very deeply about their friend who had died; if anything it just highlights how even when men appear to be close, there are blind spots that prevent us from truly knowing each other, taboo subjects that we feel bound not to bring up. Given that the male suicide rate is so high, however, we have to take radical action to try to change the culture. As hard as it is for men to come together, the need for us to do so is urgent.

True Brotherhood

True brotherhood is the only way we will overcome the loneliness the plagues us. Men crave a safe space with other men to get honest and fall apart, to grieve the lost boy with the support of other men, and to find the inner strength to embrace our full humanity. Thankfully, some amazing organisations such as A Band of Brothers in the UK and the Mankind Project worldwide are providing men with safe spaces to do this. True brotherhood makes space for a deep connection without disregarding the fact that we are men. This isn't about creating a breed of unmanly males. I promise you bro, you will not lose your masculinity by taking the risk to build a heart connection with other men. If anything, you will strengthen it. This is really about offering men the opportunity to acknowledge that we crave connection with our brothers and that as hard as it seems for a man to love other men, it's also what he really wants. When a man takes the risk to speak his truth, he will also be speaking what is true for many others. His voice sends out a powerful invitation to other men and creates a ripple effect of change.

At some point, we have to do our work in the company of other men. Taking the risk to reveal your pain to another brother is a non-negotiable part of the initiation out of the vow of male silence. We have already established that women love to talk and men don't. Give a man some space however, with no pressure to perform and genuine permission to tell the truth, and he will talk—perhaps reluctantly at first, but he will talk. Telling the raw, unfiltered truth in the presence of other men heals our loneliness and pain. It creates solidarity and unity unlike anything we've ever known. That is how the weak become strong, how boys ultimately become men. It takes enormous guts and courage to do this work and I have to say that having witnessed men break the vow again and again, it never fails to move me.

We men who have broken the vow of silence don't take any bullshit. We know that this is a life or death situation and because of that, there is a sense of urgency. We use our strength not to shut other men down but to challenge them to break the vow with us, dismantling the wall of fear that threatens to destroy them and calling them out on their ego bullshit. Once trust is established, a man will do what he needs to do. That is the gift that has come from the command to 'man up': we men are very good at tolerating discomfort and pushing through to the other side. Now, we can apply that skill for a meaningful purpose.

So now that we know what true brotherhood looks like, the real question is how do we create it and how do we get men to actively participate? This is a big question. I don't have all the answers but I do have some insights and suggestions.

Pack Guidelines: How to Break the Vow and Create True Brotherhood

When I walk my dog, we walk as a pack. It doesn't matter if there are only two of us walking. One plus one equals pack. I learned this from the dog trainer Cesar Millan. When it comes to bringing this work to other men, the same principle applies; breaking omertà in the company of other men is such a huge task that it's vital that we rethink the word pack. From now on, remember this: one plus one equals pack. Over time, the collective pack will grow in size and strength. As Rudyard Kipling wrote, "The strength of the pack is the wolf, and the strength of the wolf is the pack."

Building the pack will involve you finding other likeminded men who are willing to reinvent the orthodox pack mentality. First you need to find a pack mate. Approach this like you're trying to find a training buddy. You are on the lookout for someone who is as committed as you are to doing this work, someone who won't flake out or fall at the first hurdle, a man with the hunger and grit to go the distance.

Your goal is to form a friendship with a brother that includes regular, honest, vow-breaking conversations. You will initially form a pack of one plus one, which might eventually include extra men too. For now, one plus one is enough.

I suggest arranging a weekly or fortnightly check in. Schedule it in your diary with the same level of commitment that you would with your boss or board of directors. Don't let yourself or your brother off the hook. No flaking out, no excuses. You're here to break the vow of male silence and the ego is going to do everything in its power to make sure this doesn't happen. This is a time for vigilance, commitment and courage. In any single moment, you can choose to recommit to breaking the vow and to the pack. When you do, you become unstoppable.

Exercise

You're going to speak to your pack mate once a week for 20-30 minutes. Each man will take 10-15 minutes to talk, uninterrupted by the other person. The goal is simple: open up and tell the truth about what is happening for you as a man. You don't have to force it or fake it. The point is simply to use your voice and let yourself be heard. For many men this will be challenging because you probably aren't used to talking about yourself yet.

When you check in with your pack mate, use the following guidelines:

1. Set a timer for ten minutes. Decide who is speaking first. Press 'Start.'
2. Talk about your current struggle.
3. Go below the surface and talk about how you feel. You won't die.

4. This is not a networking exercise. In support groups like AA, people do not ask the usual boring questions we ask when getting to know someone like "What do you do?" because they're not relevant to that person's recovery. The same principle applies here.

5. Be very wary when talking about other people in your check in. This is a sneaky ego avoidance tactic.

6. If you get stuck or go blank use the following prompts:
   a) I'm feeling...
   b) What I want you to know is...
   c) What I don't want you to know is...
   d) I'm struggling with...

7. When you are the listener, you don't have to do anything apart from listen—but you do have to listen. Have respect for your brother and the courage it takes to break the vow.

8. At the end of the ten minutes, the listener simply says, "Thank you for breaking the vow of male silence." Don't give feedback and don't try to fix your pack mate. He is not broken.

9. When the timer stops, swap over.

10. Repeat every one to two weeks.

This exercise might seem trivial but it's not. You might be wondering how talking with another man for ten minutes can possibly make a difference to your life and the lives of others. Consider this: a boat travelling in a straight line across the ocean will arrive in a completely different destination even if it only changes its course by one single degree. It only takes a one-degree shift to break omertà. These short, honest conversations are that one-degree shift.

The rise of true brotherhood is the subtle shift from unconscious to conscious. Once a man has experienced the power of true brotherhood, he has an anchor and a new reference point. In realising that he is not alone in his pain, a great burden is lifted from his shoulders. When a man has committed to this way of life, there is no going back.

CHAPTER 26

LEGACY

"Carve your name on hearts, not tombstones. A legacy is etched into the minds of others and the stories they share about you."
—Shannon L. Alder

I firmly believe that every man's life leaves a legacy, that our lives send out a message to everyone around us. In every moment, you are either demonstrating fear or love, building an unconscious legacy or a conscious one. For many men, the question of a conscious legacy is one we consider too late, often when we're on our death beds. Have you ever considered the impact that your life—that your heart—is making on others? As you break the vow and deepen your commitment to this new way of life, I hope that you will reflect on the legacy you want to create from this point onwards.

If you are a dad in any form, or an uncle, brother, mentor, role model or friend (and I can guarantee that you are at least one of these), I hope the following story inspires you to pass on a powerful, loving legacy to the people in your life.

Silly Buggers

My dad could light up a room with stories of his two-wheeled adventures with his pals from the good old days. There was Arthur

Banks (the clever one), Jimmy Savage (the idiot), and Dad (the demon hill climber). Together, they were the A Team. One time he told me about how his handlebars got tangled up in Jimmy's during a daring descent and they both ended up going over a hedge. Another time the boys cycled to Scotland to watch a footy match between Glasgow and Celtic and then supposedly cycled back home after the game. That's a 400 mile round trip, which seems near impossible, but the story was fun nonetheless.

I noticed that each time he told these stories (he told each one many, many times), they seemed to get bigger and juicier (perhaps that explains the 400 mile round trip). Once he even told me that the A Team cycled the biggest mileage of anyone in the whole country. God knows how he would have got that information because neither Google nor Garmin existed at that time. It smelled a bit fishy.

One day, however, Dad told me about an epic bike journey over Salter Fell, an isolated Roman road in between the villages of Wray and Slaidburn in Lancashire, which he wanted to take me on—if only he could pinpoint its location on the map. One morning I came down for breakfast and he looked at me with a mischievous glint in his eye and said two words. "It's time." He didn't need to explain, because I knew exactly what he was talking about.

Salter Fell was the kind of terrain you'd normally attempt on a mountain bike with very chunky, very tough tyres. We didn't have mountain bikes—I don't think they existed back then either—but we did have the next best thing: hefty handmade steel road bikes, made by my dad. These we duly prepared while Mum made up a batch of cheese and cucumber sandwiches with a look of amused bewilderment on her face.

Preparing the bike was no simple feat, because Dad was a meticulous planner and liked to prepare for every eventuality. The canvas saddle bag was bursting with life. Everything from first aid kits to rain jackets to toolkits to suntan lotion to flares to parachutes was stuffed into a space designed to fit a waterproof jacket and an Allan key. Meanwhile, the bikes had been cleaned and polished almost like they were brass door handles that were due to undergo an inspection by Julius Caesar himself when we were out. Dad checked the gears, the brakes, the saddles, the pedals, the wheels, the spokes, the handlebar tape, the seat posts, the chain and the mudguards, and then went back and did it all over again, just to be sure.

We finally set off in search of the fabled Roman road, weighed down like two pack horses about to trudge across a desert. Initially, we cycled on tarmacked B roads, winding our way through the beautiful Ribble valley. There was an air of excitement about us. As we approached Slaidburn, I started to feel nervous because I knew we were getting close to our destination, even though Dad still hadn't quite figured out exactly where it was. After a fair bit of faffing around, Dad finally led us to an unforgiving, undulating mess in the middle of nowhere, stretching ahead for miles and miles. "Well, this is it lad." We hauled our bikes onto it. It looked like the road to hell.

Dad meanwhile looked like he was in heaven. He was proud, reliving a piece of his past that we were bringing back to life. He'd been talking about this moment so much, and finally it was a reality. He was probably also relieved that Mum wasn't there, because one look at the terrain and she would have had something to say. Within half a mile, we had hit an unrideable part of the road and for the first time he looked like he was having doubts. He laughed it off as he always did, while I learned the true meaning of bearing a cross. I felt like I was being persecuted under Pontius Pilate, my steel contraption causing my legs to buckle and my back to crack as I heaved it over this cursed, horrendous, muddy, pot-holed, shitty Roman road.

We struggled under a blazing hot sun that got hotter by the minute until we reached an old stone barn where we stopped for lunch. With cycling comes a ravenous hunger especially when you're a growing boy and these cheese and cucumber sarnies tasted like a meal fit for kings. Dad had somehow managed to fit a family sized flask of builder's tea into the saddlebag as well, which we supped to our hearts' content. We sat leaning against the cool brickwork, our bikes propped up alongside it, looking back at the rocky road we had just travelled. Dad glanced across at me and smiled. All you could hear was birdsong interspersed with moments of complete silence.

For a while, it was as if nothing could intrude on us and only love was present. He loved me, and I loved him, and there was an unbreakable bond between us. This was a rite of passage, our epic journey representing my passage from boyhood into manhood, and for those few precious moments, me and Dad sat next to each other as equals. I felt held that day, but this was as much for him as it was for me. It was as if he had permission to stop being an adult, and we were just two boys sharing an epic adventure. Dad always had this faraway look in his eyes, like he was searching for something precious, something sacred, and on that day it was like he had found it.

As we made our way wearily up the big hill towards home in darkness many hours later, Dad's encouragement rang in my ears. "Almost there lad." I followed his back wheel like my life depended on it until we reached our final destination: home. When we staggered through the door, Mum was waiting to greet us with a brew in hand and the proud, congratulatory words, "Silly buggers."

I flopped into bed exhausted but happy. This was the greatest day of my life, and I knew there would never be a day like it ever again. Regardless of what was to follow, me and my dad had shared a sacred moment that time would not undo. We had remembered each other on this day. It was pure, and honest, and powerful, a ritual that rooted us in truth and filled us with life and love. Even though my dad has been gone for a number of years now, when I go out cycling, I can still sometimes hear his encouraging voice in my head. "Almost there lad."

If you were to zoom in from space that day, you would have seen two black dots moving infinitesimally slowly across a vast, unforgiving, barren landscape. Zoom in even closer and you would have found two wounded hearts beating as one. Father and son in sync with themselves and each other. Yes, it was tough lugging our hefty steel bikes on our backs across that battered ancient roman road but this was our time, and we were heroes. Just for one day.

CHAPTER 27

REAL MEN...

"Somewhere between the mask of being nice but invisible, and the armor of being right but alone, is the face of a man being truly honest, truly certain and loving."
—Duane and Catherine O'Kane

Our society doesn't hold back when it comes to telling us what it means to be a 'real man.' As you continue to break the vow of male silence, you'll need to be vigilant about redefining what being a real man means to you. In this chapter, I want to offer you some simple truths to remind you of all that is real—especially when you feel the weight of omertà bearing down on you. Forget the macho bullshit: this is what it means to be a real man.

Real men feel.
Real men reach out for help.
Real men trust.
Real men open up.
Real men are sometimes vulnerable.
Real men cry unapologetically.
Real men honour the lost boy.

Real men dare to love other men.

Real men choose integrity over herd mentality.

Real men know it's okay to fail.

Real men embrace their masculinity and their femininity.

Real men respect themselves, other men and women.

Real men say sorry when it is called for.

Real men refuse to man up, shut up or put up.

Real men express their right to be fully human.

Real men know their worth is non-negotiable.

Real men break the vow of male silence. Again. And again. And again.

Afterword:
Odd Man Out Origins

Normally, an author would put the section about how their book came about at the start, but I made a decision to leave it until the end because I knew the significance of the material contained in the previous pages. If I had said what I am about to say in the beginning, you might not have read this book.

This may sound nuts but the reason I knew that I was going to write *Odd Man Out* is that a voice spoke to me whilst I was sitting quietly—it was my voice but somehow different if that makes any sense. There were no mystical harps or angelic choirs, there was no parting of the clouds, but there was a reassuring sense of certainty about it. All I know is I didn't make it up. Anyway, the voice told me that I was going to write a life-changing book on relationships.

'Oh my God! This has to be a mistake!' I thought.

Perhaps I had misinterpreted the message or it could be there was a fault on the intergalactic hotline. *'Okay, I've written a few blog posts in my time,'* I thought, *'but that hardly qualifies me to write a book on relationships. Maybe the message was meant for someone better suited to writing a book on relationships like that Harville Hendrix bloke; after all, he's pretty clued up on teaching people how to stop killing their partners.'*

I decided to tell Ell just to see how she would react. To be honest I was expecting her to burst out laughing. So when she smiled and suggested that we prepare the new computer that my friend had given me to be used solely for the purposes of writing the book, I almost soiled my underwear.

Personally, I didn't really know what to make of it at the time but I do know that I had heard The Voice before, just hours after my dad had been diagnosed with lung cancer. On that occasion the voice spoke to me during the early hours of the morning and said that I would be giving a party for my dad to celebrate his life before he died. I remember telling Ell what I had been guided to do and she just smiled and nodded in the same way she later did when I was told that I would be writing a book.

At first, some people had been disgusted by the idea of having a party for Pops, saying that it was in bad taste, but I decided to trust the voice anyway and organised the party. It reminded me a bit of Ray Kinsella in the film *Field of Dreams* when he hears a voice whisper, "Build it and he will come." I encouraged Dad to invite the people that he really wanted to be there. Mum got involved organising the buffet, and my pal Kate suggested that I make a scrapbook of his life, and give it him on the day.

When the day of the party finally arrived Dad was sick in hospital and we were uncertain whether he would be able to attend, but we all agreed that the show must go on either way. Eventually, the doctor decided to let him go to the party just as long as we brought him back to hospital the following morning. When I gave him the scrapbook he looked at me and wept, and said it was the most beautiful thing he had ever received.

The party itself was wonderfully life affirming. People jived to rock 'n' roll. Old friends queued to speak with him, joking, laughing and crying as they shared stories about the good old days. I even surprised him and sang three of his favourite Sinatra songs. During the songs his face lit up like a young boy and his eyes welled up. He tapped his foot on the floor and quietly sang along. As the evening unfolded the message of the party became crystal clear—to allow my dad to experience love as fact.

Five weeks later he was gone.

That's why I decided to trust in the voice and write this book.

Initially, I had presumed that the book would be about my relationship with my wife (surely there was enough material for an epic tome on relationships there!), but shortly after starting the book I became increasingly confused and irritable. Something was wrong but I couldn't quite put my finger on it.

Around that time my Uncle Eddie died. Uncle Eddie was like a second dad to me. His passing was painful, so it only seemed fitting that I make the trip up north to attend his funeral. But it was only during the long journey back after the funeral, over miles and miles of monotonous motorway, that the title and purpose of the book finally made itself known. My mission should I choose to accept it was to break the vow of male silence for myself so that others could do the same. The assignment was non-negotiable.

When I first agreed to write *Odd Man Out*, I imagined myself channelling thoughts at the speed of light, each sentence flowing effortlessly into the next, the book completed and published in a matter of weeks. I was mistaken in thinking that. Instead, I felt like a train that had left the tracks. Some days I sat staring at a blank screen, a victim of my own sense of inertia; other days I would experience moments of utter genius. I wrote furiously in fits and starts, everywhere from libraries to noisy cafes. Writing this book was by far the hardest thing I have ever done. Some days I actually thought I was going crazy.

Meanwhile, Ell fought and wrestled with her involvement in the project. She fiercely resisted this assignment at different points over the four and a bit years that it took to write the book, knowing how much commitment it would ask of her, often moaning that she never asked to be part of this and sometimes picking fights with me (don't worry; she's not upset this is in the book—she actually wrote these words, along with many others in the book, which is why we put her name on the cover). But no matter how intense Ell's temper tantrums, I never once lost sight of her. I always trusted that she had an important part to play. Over time, and especially as the book neared completion, something happened for both of us. We realised that this was an urgently important topic and Ell's passion for it soared. She started to work furiously on the book edit, often prioritising it over running her own business. As we meticulously worked through each chapter, Ell would often exclaim excitedly that genius had visited.

The book took over four years to write, and it was only some 36 months into the project (when I first wrote the first draft of the afterword) that I began to get why I was asked to write the book. You see, *Odd Man Out* was always meant for me first. I had to make the journey myself and break the vow of male silence in multiple ways in my own life. That's the real gist of this. The voice came at a time when I had hit a low point my life. I was probably suffering from depression. At the start I resisted writing, because I was under the strange notion that I had to have it all together before I could write the book. I wrestled daily with the belief that I wasn't suitably qualified, that I didn't know an apostrophe from an exclamation mark, scared stiff that people would judge and mock me, call me uneducated and stupid (now the book's finished, I'm still a bit worried about that). To be honest, my only credentials were my life experience; then I figured Jesus wasn't really qualified to turn water into wine but he did it anyway. I chose to say fuck it to fear and keep moving forward.

As terrified as I initially was of owning the message of this book, I am often the confident, chatty, friendly guy who rubs people up the wrong way with my outspokenness and intensity. As different as these characteristics seem they are actually two sides of the same illusory coin. I crave others' acceptance, a need rooted in the belief that I am not worth accepting. Secretly, I still believed in what I concluded as a 6-year-old boy; that I am the odd man out. Thank God it's not true.

Every day I experienced fear in some shape or form: a tiny twinge in my heart, a strange feeling that this might be the last breath that I ever took. Often, I felt buried alive, consumed by anxiety, worried that I might die before the book was finished. Whenever I was suddenly jolted out of sleep, and found myself perched on the edge of the bed weeping, my heart bursting out of my chest, I came face to face with an extremely dark part of my own mind that would go to any lengths to stop me from finishing the book. Every time it tried to influence me I just kept going, and this became the fuel that encouraged me to encourage you throughout the book to do the same. Like

I mentioned earlier, everything written in *Odd Man Out* was meant for me first. But experience tells me that even though we all have our own unique worldly curriculum, the universal curriculum is the same for everyone—to remember the truth about who we are and to choose peace instead of war, love instead of fear.

As this book goes to print, the world is beginning to talk about men, masculinity, male depression and suicide. I don't know if the timing would have been right for this book four years ago, but I do know that however much we humans appear to prefer light entertainment and ogling tits and abs on social media, the world is crying out for this conversation and this movement—and this book.

By reading and answering the questions in this book you have started again on the path of the inner warrior. This new beginning has a quiet certainty about it and if you keep going, it will bring about the conditions that will transform you into the warrior that you were always destined to become.

The true definition of a warrior is a man who is willing to hunt the self. This is not a competition. Nobody will be keeping score. There won't be any gold medals. Yet each time you lay down your sword, break the vow of male silence and let yourself feel, you will catch a glimpse of the truth and you will experience freedom both inside and out. You will rediscover what it means to be a real man. You will find yourself living in a world where conflict is no longer an option, and love, peace and true brotherhood are your only real choices. You will awaken to the realisation that your brothers' interests are no different from your own.

And as you break the vow of male silence over and over again, you will come to know the truth:

> *That you, brother, are a good man.*
> *Important.*
> *Safe.*
> *Valuable.*
> *Enough.*
> *Whole.*
> *Loved.*
> *Free.*
> *Your heart matters.*
> *Your worth is non-negotiable.*
> *You are a gift to this world.*
> *You are exactly who you're supposed to be.*

I will close with a quote from Marianne Williamson: "We must be about the business of our Source which is love and love only. Anything loving that we do or think contributes to the healing of humanity. Any turning away from love literally holds back the planet. We are perched on the brink of a miraculous transition from the ways of fear to the ways of love."

The revolution has begun. Break the vow. Spread the word.

Love,
Nige (and Ell)

Appendix I:
The Science of Beliefs

For a long time, the following words were part of chapter three. However, it all felt a bit clunky and out of sync with the rest of the chapter, but since I had done my homework and learned all about beliefs and how they're formed, I thought it would be helpful to keep this info in the book for anyone who was interested. This is probably the least academic summary of belief formation you'll ever read, but I promise you, it took hours of reading and research.

Neural Pathways

Beliefs themselves are invisible, but when a belief forms, there are scientifically observable changes that take place in the brain: an actual physical connection in the form of a neural pathway is created, and with it, a feeling of certainty about what this event means. Even though the conclusion about what the event means is negative (*I am bad, I am a failure, I am weak* and so on), the brain hates not knowing, so there is a strange sense of relief about having reached a conclusion. The certainty piece is really important: to the brain, uncertainty equals danger. Therefore the desire for the illusion of safety that certainty provides stops us from questioning the beliefs later in life, regardless of how much misery they cause us. The threat to our sense of safety is so intense that most people would rather settle for being wrong but certain rather than having to deal with the ambiguity of not knowing. Being able to tolerate uncertainty is really the hallmark of a true adult. Saying "I don't know" doesn't mean you're weak; in fact, it's the opposite. It takes enormous strength to be able to do so, especially in a culture like ours where omertà reigns supreme.

Once a belief and a corresponding new neural pathway have been formed, repetition is what makes them stick. I didn't just think I was the odd man out once; I turned it over and over in my mind, and each time I did, it gained more of a foothold. The brain has to make sense of each upset, each event our brains interpret, each day at school, each interaction with Dad, Mum and friends, and so on. As the brain repeatedly comes to the same conclusion, the neural pathway will strengthen and the belief will intensify. The more ingrained a neural pathway becomes, the harder it is to forge a strong alternative.

Filtering Out Reality

Once a belief has been formed, your brain then starts to filter out any information that doesn't quite fit with your version of events. This is known as confirmation bias. Confirmation bias is the function of the brain that looks for patterns and information to support a particular viewpoint, providing proof that the meaning the brain is interpreting is 'true.' You know confirmation bias is in place when something happens and you find yourself muttering, "I knew it." Confirmation bias also prevents the brain from having to cope with too much cognitive dissonance, which is the mental stress the brain experiences from having to hold two or more contradictory beliefs or ideas.

Confirmation bias also ensures that you stop noticing evidence that doesn't fit the patterns the brain has identified, since the brain can only process so much information at once and needs to eliminate anything irrelevant in order to work efficiently. Any information that creates too much complexity or confusion is a prime candidate for elimination, which means that evidence that contradicts one of these core negative beliefs about yourself is likely to be filtered out, or if you do notice it, it will make sense cognitively but won't really land inside you. If for example you believe you are inadequate, you'll see evidence of that everywhere (the way someone looks at you, their tone of voice, their body language, and so on) while the ample evidence that shows that you are actually more than okay will pass you by.

Eeyore Syndrome

As well as confirmation bias, the human brain is also wired to be on the lookout for negativity. We are, in fact, five times more likely to notice something negative than something positive. Presumably this is a hand-me-down from our ancestors, guaranteeing that we wouldn't get eaten alive by wild predators. This nifty little trick of the brain is called negativity bias and it is bad news for you (because it sets you up for a hard time) but great news for omertà, which runs on fear and is strengthened by ideas such as conflict, scarcity, competition and survival of the fittest—all of which go hand in hand with negativity bias. Remember Eeyore in *Winnie the Pooh*, the donkey who walks around with a raincloud permanently over his head? He is negativity bias personified.

When you add negativity bias together with confirmation bias, it looks something like this:

The human brain's built in meaning-making nature +
Confirmation bias (looking for evidence to 'confirm' the truth) +
Negativity bias (noticing negativity over positivity)
= Shitty Mistaken Beliefs (SMBs) about self, other and the world

Eventually we become creatures of habit, thinking and believing the same thing over and over again even if it's negative. Add omertà into the mix and you get a lethal cocktail: a generation of boys who grow into men that are plagued by damaging, mistaken beliefs about themselves, living in a society that prohibits them from talking about it—because, as we all know, 'real men' are supposed to shut up, put up and man up.

Appendix II:
Bottom Line Behaviour Contract

If you have a history of violence, writing a new contract in which you lay out your code of conduct for yourself can be powerful. It doesn't have to be long to be effective. See the following example:

Contract with Myself

I declare that from this day forth, I commit to the following code of conduct:

- ❏ I will not hit, push or be physically forceful to another human being, no matter how much they provoke me.
- ❏ I will not allow anger or rage to become out of control and neither will I repress them. I will do my utmost to develop the skills to diminish and express anger safely.
- ❏ I will do no harm to myself or others when angry.
- ❏ I will not use anger as a weapon to intimidate others.
- ❏ I will take 100% responsibility for my behaviour and will make full amends for any mistakes in my conduct.

☐ I will always resort to self-defence before offence if I am being physically threatened in any way. Whenever possible, I will exit the situation. This does not make me a pussy. It makes me more of a man.

Signed: _____

Date: _____

Appendix III:
Questions to Ask Your Dad

The following list of questions can help start a deeper conversation with your father (or uncle, or brother, or friend) than you're used to having. Because this kind of conversation goes deep, you might also find that it is hard. Often, actually getting the conversation started is the hardest part, so ease in. It may take an hour or even a number of conversations for a man to get comfortable enough to open up. It might take months or years—maybe even decades. Bear in mind that you're doing brave work here to attempt to evolve your family system and change the way you conduct relationships with other men. Every tiny shift is worth celebrating.

1. What are some of your earliest memories as a boy?
2. What are some of your favourite memories of your mother and father?
3. And some of your least favourite memories?
4. What was your relationship like with your father?
5. What about with your mother?
6. What was the emotional climate in your family?
7. How did you feel special in your family?
8. Which parent where you closest to?

9. Which siblings did you feel closest to? Who did you feel most distant from?

10. (If your dad was an only child) How was it for you being an only child?

11. Did you have any recurring childhood nightmares or fears?

12. What do you see as particular strengths in your family life?

13. How did your family of origin deal with conflict?

14. What was your first experience of loss? How did you deal with it?

15. What was your first memory of death? Sex? Money?

16. How did your family deal with death? Sex? Money?

17. Were there any taboo subjects in your family?

18. What did you enjoy doing as a boy?

19. Who were your friends?

20. What was life like for you growing up?

21. Tell me about a major/defining event in your childhood?

22. Tell me about school.

23. Did you have any dreams for your future?

24. How do you really feel about your childhood?

25. Who was your first love?

26. What does being a man mean to you?

27. What are your values?

28. Who are your heroes and why?

29. What was life like before I was born?

30. When and how did you meet Mum/your current partner/ your first love?

31. What did you like about her/him?

32. How did you feel when Mum was pregnant with me?

33. How did you feel when I was born?

34. How did you feel when you found out I was a boy?

35. When I was a child, what did you want to teach me about being a man? What do you think you did teach me?

36. What were some of the significant turning points in your life?

37. Who are the significant people in your life?

38. What goals did you establish for yourself in your life? How close have you come to accomplishing them?

39. What goals do you have now?

40. What was your biggest challenge as a partner in marriage?

41. What was your biggest challenge as a parent?

42. What are your views on money?

43. What's your relationship to anger?

44. Was religion or faith important to your family?

45. What beliefs are important to you?

46. What qualities do you appreciate most in your parents and siblings?

47. What are some of your most important discoveries as a parent?

48. How do you make decisions? Who do you talk to about them?

49. How do you deal with conflict with parents, partner and children?

50. Whose death in the family has affected you most?

51. Do you have any regrets?

52. What are your greatest accomplishments?

53. How would you describe yourself as a man?

Advice and tips

- Adopt an attitude of high intention, low attachment—stay open to hearing whatever your dad (or brother, uncle, granddad or friend) is willing to share with you. Remember that anytime a man breaks omertà, he is pushing against generations of conditioning. Any time a man is vulnerable is to be celebrated.
- Stay curious. Listen more than you speak.
- Keep it friendly and relaxed; this isn't the Spanish Inquisition.
- Don't be attached to a certain outcome. Open heart, empty mind.
- Remember that whatever he shares, it isn't personal to you. I repeat, it isn't personal—even if it feels very, very personal! Your dad, if he chooses to open up, is inviting you into his world. This is a wonderful opportunity to get to know him.
- Your task is to get to know your dad as a three-dimensional human being rather than as the two-dimensional character you think you've been in relationship with all these years.
- Create some psychological distance from him if it helps—imagine you're interviewing someone for a project.
- Give yourself space after the conversation to absorb all that he shared. Consider confiding in your partner or a close friend. Give yourself permission to feel whatever the conversation stirs up for you afterwards.

Recommended Watching

The following were all featured in the book and will support your understanding of the vow of male silence, and what it takes to break it.

The Mask You Live In, 2014 (Netflix)

The Power of Vulnerability (2010) and *Listening to Shame* (2012), two TED talks by shame researcher Brené Brown

All Man (2016), three-part documentary series for Channel 4 made by Grayson Perry

Dead Poets Society, 1989

Fight Club, 1999

Hulk, 2003

The Manchurian Candidate, 2004

Seven Pounds, 2008

Rebel Without A Cause, 1955

Field of Dreams, 1989

The Wizard of Oz, 1939

This Is England, 2006

A Christmas Carol, 1970 (the Albert Finney version)

Control, 2007

American History X, 1999

The Karate Kid, 1984

The Kid, 2000

A Monster Calls, 2016

Batman: The Dark Knight Rises, 2012

The Incredible Shrinking Man, 1957

Good Will Hunting, 1997

The X-Men movies, 2000-2014

Recommended Listening

The following shows are doing amazing work in the men's movement and I have been a guest on both.

The Nathan Seaward Show: https://nathanseaward.com/blog/ Nathan's vision is to end male suicide in New Zealand.

Real Men Feel: https://realmenfeel.org Andy Grant and Appio Hunter allow and encourage men to express all of their emotions.

Recommended Organisations

The following organisations are doing amazing work with men.

A Band of Brothers: A UK charity established by men that seeks to change the world one man at a time. ABoB works with disaffected young men, building community and enacting positive social change. https://abandofbrothers.org.uk/

Mankind Project: A non-profit global men's community for the 21st century which provides training and education including peer-facilitated men's groups to "support men in leading lives of integrity, authenticity and service." https://mankindproject.org/

The Campaign Against Living Miserably (CALM): A UK non-profit dedicated to preventing male suicide, which is the single biggest killer of men under the age of 45. https://thecalmzone.net

Heads Together in the UK is doing great work to raise awareness of mental health issues while de-stigmatising them, especially for men. www.headstogether.org.uk

Clearmind International Institute: A Canadian organisation that runs life-changing experiential workshops and programs. Once you've done the foundational workshop, The Awakening, you are eligible to take their powerful Men and Miracles workshop. https://clearmind.com

If you are struggling with anxiety, depression, intense emotions or feel under pressure, remember that it's not 'unmanly' to seek additional support. Contact your doctor or GP at your local Health Centre. Consider writing down a list of what you want to talk about and telling someone you trust about the appointment.

In the UK:
BACP: British Association of Counsellors and Psychotherapists
NCP: National Council of Psychotherapists

The Samaritans: www.samaritans.org Call 116 123 (UK and ROI) or 1800 273-TALK (USA), or call your country's emergency services.

References and Recommended Reading

PART ONE: THE FALL OF MAN

Chapter 1: The Vow of Male Silence

Ministry of Justice statistics for 2012: https://www.gov.uk/government/uploads/system/uploads/attachment_data/file/220090/criminal-justice-stats-sept-2012.pdf

Ministry of Justice 2015 statistics: https://www.gov.uk/government/statistics/women-and-the-criminal-justice-system-statistics-2015

Overview of crime statistics: https://www.gov.uk/government/statistics/an-overview-of-sexual-offending-in-england-and-wales

UK suicide statistics: https://www.ons.gov.uk/peoplepopulationandcommunity/birthsdeathsandmarriages/deaths/bulletins/suicidesintheunitedkingdom/2015registrations

USA suicide statistics: https://afsp.org/about-suicide/suicide-statistics/

Campaign Against Living Miserably suicide statistics: https://www.thecalmzone.net/about-calm/suicide-research-stats/

Christophe Bassons' exclusion from the Tour de France peloton: https://www.theguardian.com/sport/2012/oct/13/christophe-bassons-not-bitter-lance-armstrong

Racing Through the Dark: The Rise and Fall of David Millar, David Millar, 2012, Orion

Shadows on the Road: Life at the Heart of the Peloton, from US Postal to Team Sky, Michael Barry, 2015, Faber and Faber

Chapter 2: The Masks of Masculinity

Marvel movies gross takings: https://www.zacks.com/stock/news/229350/youll-never-guess-how-much-money-the-marvel-universe-has-grossed

The Mask You Live In, 2014, Netflix

Daring Greatly: How the Courage to Be Vulnerable Transforms the Way We Live, Love, Parent, and Lead, Brené Brown, 2015, Penguin Life

Rebel Without a Cause, 1955

In Defense of Feminine Men, Lux Alptraum, 2016, Fusion: http://fusion.net/in-defense-of-feminine-men-1793862306

Billy Elliot, 2000

Chapter 3: Beliefs

Geneen Roth quote sourced from *Women, Food and God: An Unexpected Path to Almost Everything*, 2010, Simon and Schuster UK

A Course in Miracles, 2007, Foundation For Inner Peace

For abuse statistics, see Gold, Wolan Sullivan & Lewis, 2011 cited in: https://www.childwelfare.gov/pubpdfs/long_term_consequences.pdf

Multi-generational transmission of trauma: Special Interest Area Group on Intergenerational Transmission of Trauma and Resiliency, for example, or look up multigenerational epigenetics.

Orphanages study: http://www.huffingtonpost.com/maia-szalavitz/how-orphanages-kill-babie_b_549608.html

Confirmation bias: https://www.sciencedaily.com/terms/confirmation_bias.htm

Negativity bias: https://www.psychologytoday.com/articles/200306/our-brains-negative-bias

Awaken the Giant Within, Anthony Robbins, 1992, Simon and Schuster

Chapter 4: Guilt and Shame

Duane and Catherine O'Kane, founders of Clearmind International Institute: https://clearmind.com

Seven Pounds, 2008

The Power of Vulnerability (2010) and *Listening to Shame* (2012), two TED talks by shame researcher Brené Brown, 2015, Penguin Life (in particular, we recommend reading the section on how men and women experience shame differently, p. 83-101)

Healing the Shame that Binds You, John Bradshaw, 2006, Health Communications

Crawling, Linkin' Park, 2000: https://www.youtube.com/watch?v=Gd9OhYroLN0

A Christmas Carol, Charles Dickens

Laurel and Hardy

A Course in Miracles, 2007, Foundation For Inner Peace

Chapter 5: Attack

Fight Club, the 1999 film based on the novel by Chuck Palahniuk

Barbara Stanny quote sourced from *Overcoming Underearning: A Five-Step Plan to a Richer Life,* 2005, Harper Business

The War of Art: Break Through the Blocks and Win Your Creative Battles, Steven Pressfield, 2002, Black Irish Entertainment

Chapter 6: Hulk

The Incredible Hulk TV Series, 1978: https://en.wikipedia.org/wiki/The_Incredible_Hulk_(1978_TV_series)

Chapter 7: War

Fire In The Belly: On Being a Man, Sam Keen, 1991, Bantam Books

US Army Recruitment numbers: https://www.usatoday.com/story/news/politics/2016/09/27/army-hits-target-recruits/90941076/

Spending on the military, worldwide and in the US: http://www.telegraph.co.uk/business/2016/12/12/1570000000000-much-world-spent-arms-year/

Nuclear weapons: http://www.ploughshares.org/world-nuclear-stock pile-report and https://www.armscontrol.org/factsheets/Nuclear weaponswhohaswhat

Britain selling arms to Saudi Arabia: https://www.theguardian.com/world/2016/feb/13/eu-criticises-british-arms-sales-saudi-arabia and https://secure.avaaz.org/campaign/en/no_more_saudi_arms_deals_loc/?pv=146

This is Belonging: https://www.army.mod.uk/belong/belonging and http://bellacaledonia.org.uk/2017/01/22/this-is-belonging/

The Manchurian Candidate, 2004

Veteran suicide statistics: http://afsp.org/wp-content/uploads/2016/06/2016-National-Facts-Figures.pdf

The PALS Battalion: http://www.iwm.org.uk/history/the-pals-battalions-of-the-first-world-war

UK Armed Forces Recruitment statistics: https://www.gov.uk/government/statistics/uk-armed-forces-monthly-service-personnel-statistics-2016

Sources for information on World War II: *Veterans: The Last Survivors of the Great War,* Richard Van Emden, 2005, Leo Cooper

PALS Battalions: http://www.bbc.co.uk/schools/0/ww1/25237879, http://www.pals.org.uk/sheffield/ and http://www.iwm.org.uk/history/the-pals-battalions-of-the-first-world-war

Shellshock: http://www.bbc.co.uk/history/worldwars/wwone/shellshock_01.shtml

Chapter 8: Ego Run Riot

A New Earth, Eckhart Tolle, 2005, Penguin

The Way of the Heart, 2014, Heartfelt Publishing

Illuminata: A Return to Prayer, 1995, Riverhead Books

Read the Ted Bundy interview here: https://lifesitenews.com/news/serial-killer-ted-bundys-warnings-about-pornography-re-aired-on-20th-annive

Information on human trafficking: www.equalitynow.org/traffickingFAQ

The Mask You Live In, 2015, Netflix

Look up 'arousal addiction' and see for example Noah Church's website, https://addictedtointernetporn.com and https://protectyoungminds. org/2017/03/23/porn-addiction/simplified/ or https://elitedaily.com/ dating/gentlemen/porn-can-kill-arousal-response/

On how the US military utilises video games and the differences between killing in the virtual world compared to the real world: http://theconversation.com/how-the-us-military-is-using-violent-chaotic-beautiful-video-games-to-train-soldiers-73826

On the cumulative effects of playing violent video games: http://researchnews.osu.edu/archive/violgametime.htm

Statistics on exposure to violence in the media: *The Mask You Live In,* 2015, Netflix

Gentile and Anderson's 2005 research on how violent video games prime aggressive thoughts: http://drdouglas.org/drdpdfs/Gentile_Stone_2005.pdf

The study showing increased P300 amplitudes in the brain: http://scanlab.missouri.edu/docs/pub/pre2010/bart_bush_sest_jesp2006.pdf

Awaken the Giant Within, Anthony Robbins, 1992, Simon and Schuster

To learn more about porn addiction visit https://addictedtointernetporn.com

Value of the video games market: https://newzoo.com/insights/articles/ the-global-games-market-will-reach-108-9-billion-in-2017-with-mobile-taking-42/

Sales statistics for the *Call of Duty* franchise: https://www.statista.com/ statistics/321374/global-all-time-unit-sales-cal-of-duty-games

Additional video games statistics: *The Mask You Live In,* 2015, Netflix

Spending in the games industry: http://essentialfacts.theesa.com/ Essential-Facts-2016.pdf

Chapter 9: Depression

I Don't Want to Talk About It: Overcoming the Secret Legacy of Male Depression, Terrence Real, 1997, Tantor Media Inc

Women's and men's communication: See for example Deborah Tannen, 1990, Dale Spender, 1980, Robin Lakoff, 1975 for seminal studies on the differences between the two.

Poll regarding depression on the Men's Health Forum: menshealthforum. org.uk

Reasons to Stay Alive, Matt Haig, 2015, Canongate Books

CALM, The Campaign Against Living Miserably: https://www. thecalmzone.net

The Incredible Shrinking Man, 1957

Daring Greatly, as before

This article provides a great rundown of how depression can manifest in men: https://www.rcpsych.ac.uk/healthadvice/problemsdisorders/ depressionmen.aspx

Symptoms of depression adapted from https://www.thecalmzone. net/help/get-help/depression/ and https://www.thecalmzone.net/help/ get-help/depression/

Chapter 10: Suicide

The Journey Home: "The Obstacles to Peace" in A Course in Miracles, Kenneth Wapnick, 2000, Foundation for "A Course in Miracles"

World Health Organisation Suicide Statistics: http://apps.who.int/gho/ data/node.main.MHSUICIDE?lang=en

Male UK suicide statistics: https://www.ons.gov.uk/peoplepopulation andcommunity/birthsdeathsandmarriages/deaths/bulletins/suicides intheunitedkingdom/2015-02-19

The Dead Poets Society, 1989

The Good Men Project, https://goodmenproject.com

All Man, Grayson Perry and Channel 4, 2016, Channel 4

The Mask You Live In, as before

CALM, the Campaign Against Living Miserably, as before

Chapter 11: Dark Night of the Soul

The Dark Knight Rises, 2012

The Thirst for Wholeness: Attachment, Addiction and the Spiritual Path, Christina Grof, 1993, HarperCollins

The End of Days, Nige Atkinson

PART TWO: THE RISE OF MAN

Chapter 12: Taking Responsibility

Under Saturn's Shadow: The Wounding and Healing of Men, James Hollis, 1994, Inner City Books

Crazy Good: A Book of Choices, Steve Chandler, 2015, Maurice Bassett

A New Earth, as before

It's All About the Bike: The Pursuit of Happiness on Two Wheels, 2011, Penguin

Chapter 13: Escape Routes

Daring Greatly, as before

A New Earth, as before

Humans watched 5,246 centuries of porn in 2016: http://www.pornhub.com/insights/2016-year-in-review

2016 mobile phone statistics: https://deviceatlas.com/blog/16-mobile-market-statistics-you-should-know-2016

How porn affects adolescents: https://www.psychologytoday.com/blog/sex-lies-trauma/201107/effects-porn-adolescent-boys

Chapter 14: Beyond Anger

Healing the Shame that Binds You, as before

Alexander Milov, Burning Man installation: http://www.boredpanda.com/burning-man-festival-adults-babies-love-aleksandr-milov-ukraine/

Gill Schwartz's article in Men's Health: http://www.menshealth.com/guy-wisdom/show-anger-or-stay-calm

Rebecca Linder Hintz quote sourced from *Healing Your Family History,* 2006, Hay House

Rising Strong, Brené Brown, 2015, Vermilion

Chapter 15: Grieving The Lost Boy

Daniel Prokop's quote sourced here: http://www.goodreads.com/quotes/319794-we-live-in-an-adolescent-society-neverland-where-never-growing

Healing the Shame That Binds You, as before

Good Will Hunting, 1997

Tom Golden quoted from here: https://journeysthrugrief.wordpress.com/2013/02/04/growing-through-grief-warren/amp/

A Year to Live, Stephen Levine, 1997, Crown Publications

Danny, the Champion of the World, Roald Dahl, 2007, Puffin

Chapter 16: Real Men Cry

Crying research: Bekker and Vingerhoets, 1999; 2001; Vingerhoets and Schiers, 2000, https://pure.uvt.nl/ws/files/428251/marrieb/PDF

Lauren Bylsma, Ph.D's research into crying: http://www.apa.org/monitor/2014/02/cry.aspx

The Prosperity Game: The Wealthy Way of Mind, Heart and Spirit, Steve Nobel, 2006, Findhorn Press

On emotional tears vs. irritant tears: https://www.thenakedscientists.com/articles/questions/do-emotional-or-pain-induced-tears-differ

See also: https://www.academia.edu/457235/When_is_crying_cathartic_An_international_study

Chapter 17: Your Dad, Forgiveness and You

Manhood: An Action Plan for Men's Lives, Steven Biddulph, 1995, Finch Publishing Australia

Danny, Champion of the World, as before

Chapter 18: What About Mum?

Under Saturn's Shadow, as before

Chapter 19: The Decision to Remember

No references

PART THREE: THE NEW MAN

Introduction

The Matrix, 1999

Chapter 20: Conscious Solitude

A New Earth, as before

Australia driving and texting: https://www.rsc.wa.gov.au/Road-Rules/Browse/Mobile-Phones

UK driving and texting: https://www.gov.uk/using-mobile-phones-when-driving-the-law

Chapter 21: Now

The 5-Minute Meditator: Quick Meditations to Calm Your Body and Your Mind, Eric Harrison, 2003, Piatkus

Louis C.K. Hates Cell Phones: https://www.youtube.com/watch?v=5HbYScltf1c

Chapter 22: Rites of Passage

Projects like Mankind Project and A Band of Brothers, among others, are doing amazing work to change the lack of support for boys transitioning into manhood.

Chapter 23: Rituals

A Course in Miracles, as before

A Course of Love, 2014, Take Heart Publications

Chapter 24: Stillness

A New Earth, as before

Chapter 25: True Brotherhood

Gavin and Stacey, 2007-2010, BBC Three

All Man, as before

A Band of Brothers, https://abandofbrothers.org.uk/

Mankind Project, https://mankindproject.org/

Chapter 26: Legacy

No references

Chapter 27: Real Men

Ten Responses to the Phrase 'Man Up': https://www.youtube.com/watch?v=QFoBaTkPgco

Afterword: Odd Man Out Origins

Field of Dreams, 1989

Marianne Williamson quote sourced from *Everyday Grace*, 2002, Hay House

Acknowledgements

Writing a book can be a very lonely experience but as I reflect on the process as it nears completion, I realise how many people have been involved, offering their support, energy, expertise and love.

Thank you to you, the reader, for buying and reading this book and for breaking the vow of male silence. A special thank you to the women for passing this book on to the men in your life. I salute you all.

I'm deeply grateful to my family for everything that you are and do. This book would not have been possible without you. I love you.

I am grateful to my beloved wife and mighty companion Elloa Atkinson, who not only helped co-write this book, but also edited it and brought it to life. It was Ell who first encouraged me to write this book, who taught me the influence and potency of the written word, and the significance of getting my truth out on paper over and over again. It was Ell who gave me the courage to believe in something bigger than myself, who helped me become a vessel for this book, and helped me to water the *Odd Man Out* seed day after day. Ell took the words that were etched across my heart and shaped them into something understandable and powerful. Her perseverance helped that tiny seed grow into a great oak, and for that I am truly grateful. I love you.

To all the trailblazers leading the way with men's work: Grayson Perry, James Hollis, Terrence Real, Robert Bly, Sam Keen and Steven Biddulph, amongst others. Thank you for paving the way. Thank you also to the amazing men and women who have helped carry the message of *Odd Man Out* into the world, including David Ryan, Nathan Seaward, Andy Grant, Roxanne Hobbs, Bruce Lee Krager, Robyn Starr and all the other people who have been cheering us on.

Thank you to Duane O'Kane for creating the work that cracked me open all those years ago, helping me understand that it's perfectly okay for a man to feel. Thank you also to Catherine O'Kane and all the gifted teachers at Clearmind International Institute for all that you give.

To my oldest bezzie Kate for offering to share a locker with me on my first day at school and for standing by me ever since. You will always be family to me. Love you more than impossible.

Thanks to my mentor and friend Paul Goudsmit, who has never once lost sight of me; and to you and Jane Tipping, thank you for both being crazy enough to travel hundreds of miles just to have a cup of tea and a biscuit.

To the late Brian Alner, thank you for hearing the first draft in its rawest form. I have fond memories of the laughter and the tears we shared during those early morning readings across the kitchen table.

A Course in Miracles is like an old friend to me and has helped change the way I perceive myself, others and the world. *A Course Of Love* has fast become another staple companion on my journey. I am grateful for both.

Thank you to Molly the Westie for showing me how to be present, and for her dogged commitment to the pack.

Dave Richards, thank you for always believing in my ability to be a pioneer. To Brooke Meservy, thank you for being the first person to water the seed.

To the first readers of the book, thank you. Don Fulmer, David Leander Hastings, Ian Patrick, Mike Kimliko, Liz Frances Hobbs, Michelle Wildman, Robert Kuang, Lian Blue and Julia Fehrenbacher: your input was invaluable.

Thank you illustrative artist Georgia Flowers for bringing my vision of the self-pointing gun used in chapter five to life. Your attention to detail and talent with black ink are phenomenal. It was a real honour to work with such a gifted artist.

Thank you to photographer Michelle Wildman for capturing the perfect blend of intensity and vulnerability that sums up what breaking the vow of male silence is all about. Thanks also to Debby at the Bloomsbury Clinic in Steyning and Kevin Harris for helping me look the part for the shoot.

Thank you to our typesetter and cover designer Rochelle Mensidor for making this book visually impactful.

Thank you Ty Francis and Jon Riley for your generosity in offering to create a powerful trailer for the book so that the message could spread far and wide.

Thank you CP for your support, expertise and help in building the *Odd Man Out* website.

To all the amazing people who contributed financially, helping us get this book out into the world, we owe you huge thanks and the biggest hug ever. TW for starting us off and showing us we could dare to believe that people would want to support this project.

To Marie Simpson, Kimmy Scarpine, Liz Frances Hobbs, Pete Ingledew, Sandy Newman, Mike Kimliko, Don Fulmer, Matt Gunn, Fiona Everest-Dine, Helene Santamera, Steve Yates, Dave Richards, David Ryan, Ali Cowley, Hannah Massarella, Amy Aldridge and Sharon Archer, your generosity and vision made this possible.

To the publisher and agent who said no to publishing this book. This prompted us to take a risk and publish *Odd Man Out* the way we always intended it to be—undiluted, gritty and heartfelt.

And finally, I know this is a bit cheeky, but I'd like to thank Oprah Winfrey and the other thought leaders in advance for their ongoing support in bringing the message of *Odd Man Out* to millions of people worldwide.

About the Authors

Nige Atkinson, author of *Odd Man Out*, is a champion natural bodybuilder, workshop facilitator and teacher who has been described as the voice for a new man. He is passionate, insightful, funny and unafraid to challenge the status quo. Nige firmly believes that every man is whole and has the right to express his full humanity.

Elloa Atkinson has extensive coaching, therapeutic facilitation and teaching under her belt. Co-author and editor of *Odd Man Out*, Elloa is fascinated by what it means to be fully alive, how to heal from shame, and the art of vulnerable yet emotionally responsible relationships.

Nige and Elloa offer 1:1 and couples coaching, speaking engagements and workshop facilitation. They are passionate, funny, eloquent and engaging speakers and teachers.

Nige and Elloa live in Sussex in the UK with their West Highland White Terrier, Molly Miracle.

Join the Movement

For more information about the Odd Man Out movement, go to https://breakthevow.com

Contact Nige: nige@breakthevow.com
Contact Elloa: elloa@breakthevow.com

Join the movement on social media:
www.facebook.com/breakthevow
www.instagram.com/odd_man_out_book

23155470R00190

Printed in Great Britain
by Amazon